Praise for the Olive series

'Drinkwater has a sharp eye for character, and the people who populate *The Olive Route* will not disappoint her fans'
Independent on Sunday

'Drinkwater is a rare writer who tackles other people brilliantly . . . Vibrant, intoxicating and heart-warming'
Sunday Express

'A storyteller of great economy and deftness and one who, in telling tales, captures the Midi effectively. There are few better portraits of the different worlds – farmers and water-diviners, crooks and Euro-trash, Algerians and wearying officialdom – that intersect to create the Côte d'Azur' *Daily Telegraph*

'The new leader of the pack' *The Times*

'Charming and well written. As the olives ripen to a luscious, dark-purply black, the reader is drawn into the peculiarities and joys of Provençal life' *Daily Mail*

'A spellbinding memoir and a must for anyone who dreams of moving to a kinder climate and starting a new life' *Choice*

'A lot of its attraction for me stems from the honesty of the writing, the attention to detail, the intensity of the writer's relationship with the land . . . Above all you feel like you're observing a very intimate moment in someone else's life . . .'
Waterstones

By Carol Drinkwater

Best known for her role as Helen Herriot in BBC Television's *All Creatures Great and Small* (for which she was awarded The Variety Club Television Personality of the Year Award), Carol Drinkwater has enjoyed a long and distinguished career as both an actress and writer.

During her acting career, she has worked in film, television and theatre. Her credits include working with Laurence Olivier at the National Theatre, Stanley Kubrick on *A Clockwork Orange* and Max Von Sydow, whom she played opposite in the film *Father*, for which she won the Critics Circle Award for Best Film Actress.

Carol Drinkwater has written novels for both adults and children, including *Abundance of Rain*, *Akin to Love* and *Mapping the Heart*. Her bestselling children's novel, *The Haunted School*, has sold more than 170,000 copies and was made into a film and television series which won the Chicago Film Festival Gold Award for children's films. She is also the author of the bestselling memoirs *The Olive Farm*, *The Olive Season*, *The Olive Harvest*, *The Olive Route*, *The Olive Tree* and *Return to the Olive Farm*. Visit her website at www.caroldrinkwater.com

THE
OLIVE
HARVEST

*A Memoir of Love, Old Trees
and Olive Oil*

Carol Drinkwater

PHOENIX

A PHOENIX PAPERBACK

First published in Great Britain in 2004
by Weidenfeld & Nicolson
This paperback edition published in 2005
by Orion Books Ltd,
Reissued 2011
by Phoenix,
an imprint of Orion Books Ltd,
Orion House, 5 Upper St Martin's Lane,
London WC2H 9EA

An Hachette UK company

7 9 10 8 6

Copyright © Carol Drinkwater 2004

A CIP catalogue record for this book
is available from the British Library.

ISBN 978-0-7538-2936-3

Typeset at The Spartan Press Ltd,
Lymington, Hants

Printed and bound in Great Britain by
Clays Ltd, St Ives plc

The Orion Publishing Group's policy is to use papers that
are natural, renewable and recyclable products and
made from wood grown in sustainable forests. The logging
and manufacturing processes are expected to conform to
the environmental regulations of the country of origin.

www.orionbooks.co.uk

Contents

You are gone. The river is high at my door.
Cicadas are mute on dew-laden boughs.
This is a moment when thoughts enter deep.
I stand alone for a long while.
. . . The North Star is nearer to me now than spring,
And couriers from your southland never arrive –
Yet I doubt my dream on the far horizon
That you have found another friend.

Li Shang-yin, *Thoughts in the Cold*

*Je ne puis pas regarder une feuille d'arbre
sans être écrasé par l'univers.*
I cannot look at a leaf on a tree
without being bowled over by the universe.

Victor Hugo

Acknowledgements

Firstly, I would like to acknowledge all those who are involved in the distribution and sales of my books; without you I would be lost in the dark.

Special thanks to Jonathan Lloyd at Curtis Brown for handling my affairs; to my copy editor, Caroline North; to friends in other houses who continue to look out for my books and to Denny Drinkwater for enormous support.

My special thanks to everyone at Orion and Weidenfeld & Nicolson for welcoming me so warmly aboard, particularly Malcolm Edwards for opening the door and my editor, Alan Samson, for his poetry.

For Michel

I love the gypsy soul in you and the joys
and sorrows of your changing face.

A Dry Welcome

A puzzling silence is the welcome that awaits us. Only the familiar screech of cicadas cracks through the early summer stillness on our Mediterranean hillside. In fact, so mute is the reception from our olive farm, so scruffy its terraces, that the place gives off a melancholy air. It appears abandoned, not tranquil.

'Good heavens, I hope nothing awful has happened to Monsieur Quashia.'

'He was in good spirits when I telephoned yesterday morning to say we were on our way. He talked of a surprise.'

Michel and I are climbing the driveway on foot, looking from left to right, baffled by what we are discovering. We pause to inspect the veteran as well as the young olive trees, most of which are sadly lacking fruit, as we saunter up to the parking area, to the threshold of our romantic home. Arriving in front of the garage, our suitcases ditched at our feet, still clad in our city clothes, hot, sticky and bemused, we linger, taking stock. Everywhere is shuttered and locked up.

'I hardly recognise it as Appassionata. It's as though we're strangers here.' That quickening excitement of arrival, of expectation, of being back home, has been replaced by dismay.

'Come on, Carol, it's not that bad.'

I spin around in a circle. The bougainvillaeas are in

livid blossom and have snaked their way around the villa's creamy, weathered balustrades and are now coiling in heavy magenta plaits up the electricity lines towards the roof; the swimming pool has turned slimy green, while browning rose petals and dead geranium heads lie scattered in puddles on the terracotta terrace.

'It is bit of a mess, that's true,' murmurs Michel.

'What's all that up there?' I am pointing midway up the grounds, to beneath the first stands of pine trees. There, alongside our woodshed and my modest fruit garden, are several substantial hummocks of rusty red earth, spires of stacked stones and three hefty boulders.

'I can't really tell from here. The vegetation is so dense,' sighs Michel. 'Have you got your keys handy?'

'They're in my case. And where have all these materials come from? Quashia wouldn't have ordered them.'

Surrounding us and our two cars, both unwashed and splotched with sticky patches of resin, is a veritable cargo of treated pine beams and what must amount to something in the region of five hundred locally baked, cambered Provençal roof tiles. 'And where are the dogs? They are always here to greet us.' I scan the slopes hopefully, eyes piercing our ten unkempt acres in search of three rough-and-tumble mutts bounding towards us, or one lone Arab busy at his chores, but I cannot see a soul, not a whisper of life. 'And Monsieur Q. gave you no inkling?'

'He said there was a surprise.'

'Well, he can't have been referring to the condition of the land. It hasn't looked this grotty since we bought the place. It must be something to do with all this masonry equipment!'

'Let's take a look up the hill,' says Michel, moving on ahead, leaving me to clip-clop an unsteady path after him. My low-heeled sandals are hardly suited to the loose stones and the sharp verticality.

It is mid-June. The weather during our absence has been unseasonably hot and Quashia has been complaining about the lack of rainfall since late April. The fields of spring wild flowers are long over and what remains, what has grown up in their place, is bone-dry, scratchy and pallid. The greensward is made up of knee-high, dehydrated grasses. Within it, I spot a bristly purple-blue flower that I recognise as viper's bugloss. I point it out to Michel who frowns, continuing his ascent. I believe it was once thought to be a remedy for snake-bite. This is the first time I have run into it because our grounds are usually kept neatly shorn to counter the risk of fires that accompany this climate's long dry summers.

'This is dangerous,' I mutter.

'Quashia and I will have to cut it back as soon as possible.'

I am puffing, out of breath, out of the habit of scaling our steep, pebbled hill, particularly in open-toed shoes and a skirt, and I feel saddened and confused by the disorderliness we have returned to. Michel, long-legged and lean, is striding purposefully ahead. He says nothing more, but his silence tells me that he also is frustrated. We come to rest alongside the upper cherry tree whose fruits this year would have been devoured by the flocks of thieving magpies who nest here. We have both been away from the south on extended career assignments and have not been around to harvest the crop.

'Strange there's no sign of Quashia.'

In the distance, from one of the neighbouring medi-aeval villages perched high above the coast, I hear the keening of a works siren and I glance at my watch. It is midday. Time for lunch.

'He's probably gone off somewhere for a bite to eat.'

And then suddenly, from beyond the curvature of the hillside, we hear a cry: '*Monsieur 'dame!*' It is Monsieur Q., waving and smiling, wading through the hip-high grass to reach us. In spite of the heat he is wearing his black lambskin hat and dark ankle-length trousers. He never shows up in shorts or without a long-sleeved shirt, no matter what the weather. Behind him, through the thick undergrowth, I make out a pair of upright tails: Lucky, our Alsatian, and Bassett, the little black and white hunting dog, are following in his wake.

'He must be boiling in that battered old hat. Where's Ella?' I mutter. Ella, our golden retriever, is past retirement age, fat and arthritic these days and I worry that while we are away there will be a message from Quashia or Gérard, our vet, informing us that she has been taken ill, or worse.

'She's probably dozing in the stables and didn't hear us arrive.'

Yes, on top of everything else, the poor old girl is going deaf. Lucky and Bassett have spotted us and are bounding on ahead of their companion, a chorus of howls and dribbling affability.

Monsieur Quashia speeds up his pace as he draws near. He is laughing, delighted to find us here. Our loyal Arab gardener and the pivotal cog of this modest olive farm has obviously been doing his rounds, completing a reconnoitre of the land. It is essential that our fencing is inspected regularly for signs of illicit entry by the wild boars who gnaw through it, dig up the earth, buckle the walls and tear at the branches of all our newly planted trees, particularly the apples. The trunks of our two hundred young olives have been encased with wire netting to protect them against rabbits who chomp away at the bark; this needs occasional reparation. A further requirement is to visit our basin at the hill's summit to gauge the water level and guard against stagnancy. The hundreds of metres of piping that transport water up the land's gradient must also be kept under close observation in case a length perishes, springs a leak and dribbles away our most precious commodity. All these tasks take time and require attention on a twice-weekly basis.

'*Bonjour! Bonjour!*'

He pulls out a creased, purple checked handkerchief and mops his tattooed brow before kissing the two of us twice on both cheeks. Hearty handshakes and back-slappings are exchanged with Michel, a twinkling, ageing, appreciative eye is turned on me, and then he begins to set forth about 'the project in progress'. Profuse apologies that he has not found time to cut back the land as yet but he is digging foundations, he announces proudly.

'But for what, Monsieur Quashia?' I beg.

To create a toolshed extension to our woodshed,

which he built for us a few years back. 'Just a few structural changes and improvements I have been attacking during your far-too-long absence.' He winks and shrugs with theatrical modesty. 'Oh, but it's good to have you both home!'

'What are the dimensions of the extension?' enquires Michel uncertainly.

'It will go as far as . . .' our obliging Arab is goose-stepping in his dusty brogues along the terrace in question, '. . . *cinq, six, sept,*' counting aloud – each of his strides is loosely, very loosely, measuring out a metre – until he arrives at the eastern extreme of our land, where he stops, turns and faces us again, beaming. 'Here. *Vingt*! Plenty of space! It's what you've been dreaming of, eh, Carol?' he grins proudly, hollering back at me.

'Well, I . . . but twenty metres plus the fourteen already in service, Monsieur Quashia, seems a little long for a shed.'

'*Pas du tout*. Not at all.'

I have been banging on for some time now about clearing out the garage, which has never housed the cars and currently serves as a desperately overcrowded and ill-organised work room. I have been hoping that, when we can afford it, we can transform the front half of it, plus the two horse stables adjoining it (where the dogs sleep and the dusty washing machine lives), into two light and airy guest bedrooms with en-suite shower rooms and, next door, a tiled, L-shaped laundry room.

'I wanted to surprise you!'

'Well, you certainly have,' smiles Michel politely.

6

Tired of listening to my idle speeches and grand schemes that rarely get off the ground, Quashia has, in our absence, taken matters into his own hands and ordered the requisite materials from the builders' merchants where we keep an account. His reasoning is that the first stage of my project necessitates creating alternative storage space for our numerous gardening utensils and ever-escalating collection of farm gadgets and machines. This argument is perfectly logical, but it will involve us in unforeseen expenses. I glance at Michel, who does not return my look; he is surveying the scene with furrowed brow. Quashia has never taken such an initiative before, certainly not on decisions of structural or financial consequence.

Michel and I are both stressed, edgy from a surfeit of time spent apart, living independent city lives, and are a little unsure of how best to handle the situation. At least that is my reaction and what I detect from my husband's expression.

Aside from all this, I had been lovingly planting up and tending this particular patch, which is located a couple of terraces up behind the house, below the pine forest and Michel's amazingly fertile little palm grove, as a mixed-fruit orchard. Looking at it now, the plot resembles nothing more than a heavily tramped-over building site. Solid blocks of rock, recently quarried from the limestone mountainside on which our farm has been constructed – Quashia must have hired an electric drill from the builders' yard for this stage of the proceedings – have been hewn into manageable slabs, piled into two triangular towers and left. Later, they will be used to construct what, when accurately measured, proves to be a 24-metre retaining wall to his shed extension. He has broken up half-a-dozen rough-wood pallets used by the builders' merchants to deliver tiles (and which, contractually, are supposed to be returned) and nailed them back together, transforming them into crude but rather natty hand-made trestles. Unfortunately, he has left them stacked over several of my recently potted bougainvillaea cuttings. Freshly dug earth has been chucked everywhere – its final resting place to be decided by Michel and me later, he explains – leaving holes and shallow trenches. The upheaval is causing sections of the farm's original, free-standing stone walls to be displaced. Two wheelbarrows, rusted and contorted with age, seamed with dried mortar, stand empty and idle; several tons of blond Biot sand have been shovelled into three hillocks alongside further hillocks of the coarser, grainier sand *normal*; all lined up on corrugated-iron sheets in readiness for mixing with the dozens of bags of cement currently stabled next to our chopped wood in the area of shed already in use. The sand must have been there for some time because there are native ground-pines (which though they smell like pine are in fact of the mint family), growing up through it.

Michel walks the length of the site. I look about me and sigh. I dread to calculate the total cost of the bills Quashia has run up.

Fortunately, my young fruit trees – two peach, one pear, a nectarine, three apricots, one stupendously robust, self-seeded almond, my beloved pomegranate (the Phoenicians transported these bushy trees from west Asia to Carthage. Mine has travelled a far shorter and, no doubt, less hazardous journey. Still, I was obliged to uproot it and rehouse it a respectable distance from our lower olive grove by order of one of the many agricultural inspectors who have visited us) – are all holding their own, thriving even, some with clusters of unripened fruit on offer, in the midst of this nightmare building scene.

'I even found out the name of the wood merchants we used last time and organised the delivery of the beams,' grins Quashia triumphantly. He lifts his arm and points an oil-stained finger towards the lengths of wood lying about in the *parking*, and my heart softens. I am saddened to observe a slight tremor in his hand. The wrinkles on his dark-skinned face have deepened and he has grown a gut. Several years back he stopped smoking during Ramadan, a moral obligation of his Islamic faith, and afterwards he announced to me: 'If I can stop for Ramadan, then I can kick the filthy habit altogether.' I was pleased and promised to support him in any way I could. He had been a sixty-a-day man and I knew it might prove challenging, but I misjudged him. He beat the addiction, just as Michel had several years earlier, and never said another word about it. Still, in spite of his rigorous physical activities, he has an indisputable belly on him now, and he is looking older.

'Yes, we noticed the beams when we arrived.' How could I be angry with this man? I love Monsieur Q. His life is dedicated to this farm. How could we fault him for his initiative? Nevertheless, there were plenty of other projects I would have preferred he had launched into ahead of this one. There's no money for my dreamed-of additional bedrooms, not now or in the foreseeable future. Nor have we commissioned architectural drawings or submitted the endless forms and documents required for planning permission. We would have lived with the higgledy-piggledy clutter in the garage for the time being and concentrated on more pressing matters such as drilling for a subterranean spring-water source, which has been on our to-do-list for way too long. Single-handed, this shed development will take Quashia the entire summer to accomplish and employing extra manpower to assist him cannot be an option for us right now.

'Why don't you let me cope with this?' says Michel to me in English.

'Yes, of course.'

Michel hands me his keys. I take my leave, descend to the house and circle to the main door while the men above are locked in a discussion about masonry matters, costings, the unkempt state of the land and Lord knows what else.

As a rule, Michel and I would deal with these small problems together. It is unlike him to send me away.

Inside, I am greeted by imprisoned heat. I slip off my sandals and splay my tired feet against the cool, ungiving *tommette*-tiled floors, and I pad from room to room, throwing open the slatted shutters and French windows, letting in sharp sunlight which instantly floods the tall-ceilinged spaces, and the lovely old house seems to sigh and expand like a woman discarding her corset. '*Bienvenue*,' I hear it softly whisper. I breathe in trapped fragrances of dried lavender in bowls, eucalyptus leaves fallen from a vase on top of the television set, whiffs of lingering cologne and humidity, while I attempt to allay my uncertain mood by rediscovering *home*.

In comparison with the galloping growth in the garden, the interior of the house feels pleasingly calm and surprisingly neat, aside from legions of mummified insect husks decomposing on the bookshelves and chairs. The house needs airing, of course, and there are cobwebs hanging like miniature hammocks from the corners of a couple of ceilings, but the plants have been watered and much has been cared for. Serenity.

Peering through the open glass doors, beyond an outdoor living area with its begrimed teak furniture, I am faced with a bank of bougainvillaea so tall and perpendicular it looks as though it has been electrified; punky pink shoots screening the sea from view. So much pruning and tidying up to do!

Back inside, our pine dining table, which we purchased at an auction on the Left Bank in Paris, is strewn with books and files. Mine. I was the last at the farm and departed in a mad dash for the airport, leaving myself no time to return my papers to the shelves in my den. Amongst the piles, I discover a stack of letters curled with heat, awaiting our return, and I decide to get stuck into them. Circulars, journals, fortnightly notifications of upcoming diary dates from the olive farmers' union and a depressingly thick wad of bills.

I find a communication from the local council informing us that if our land is not cleared '*sous quinzaine*', within fourteen days, and maintained 'in accordance with the Code Forestier articles L322–3 and 14, and the prefectoral *numéro* 96–00261', we will be liable to a considerable fine. The letter goes on to point out that the condition of our land does not meet with any of these requirements. I am crestfallen. There is no other holding in the neighbourhood that keeps their terrain as pristine and fire-risk free as we do, but, for once, we have no grounds for debate. Quashia has left the terraces to their own devices. I glance at the date at the top of the correspondence. It is already more than a month old. You can bet your life as I dig deeper through the envelopes there will be a follow-up letter with an order to pay. And there it is, stipulating settlement within seven days. A staggering 1,500 francs is the demanded penalty. Michel will have to attend to this one. He handles the bureaucracy. He is a past master at sweet-talking all those *fonctionnaires*. I washed my hands of all that a while ago. I lack the patience for it.

I toss the final demand aside and make for the kitchen, deciding to mention it later. Through the window I see Michel coming down the slopes. He is deep in thought, head bowed. He looks tired, strained, in need of a haircut and city-pale. I noticed it last night when I arrived in Paris from London and he met me off the Eurostar. We haven't seen each other in over six weeks and I thought he would be upbeat, over-joyed by our reunion, but he was distant and pre-occupied and has remained so since. I hear him enter the house through the wide-open French windows in our bedroom. 'We are soon to become the proprietors of a thirty-eight-metre, curving garden shed,' he calls, pulling off his linen jacket and tossing it on to our bed. He turns the corner – there are few doors in this open-plan space – and bumps into me, a little awkwardly, in the spacious *salon* with its original brick fireplace, on my way through to the dining room, where I am returning to the letters.

'I am brewing coffee. Want a cup?'

'It's not straight.'

'What isn't?'

'The wall. He hasn't aligned it accurately. I will have to keep an eye on it. I can't think what possessed him to begin it.'

'Well, he did warn you on the phone that we have very few olives this year, so he obviously decided to get on with something else.'

'Barely a crateload on the lower slopes.' This is Michel's gloomy but accurate appraisal of our olive situation on this sunny morning back at the farm. 'I asked him about the swimming pool and he said the chap hasn't been by to clean it for several weeks.'

'I'll call the company.'

'The wild boar have broken two more walls below the old vineyard. Quashia's repaired the fence twice.'

'I hope he didn't request a gun again?'

'Yes, he did, and he mentioned the bees, reiterating just how much he had been looking forward to our own honey.'

Quashia loves honey and frequently asks one or other of us to bring home a few jars from our travels. He hates the choices on sale in the supermarkets, claiming they are 'boiled'.

'Well, as the hives never arrived, let alone the bees,

it was pretty obvious there wasn't going to be honey. Did you stress that we want no guns here?'

'It might be our last resort.'

'Michel, we agreed. No guns.' I sigh. 'You promised.'

My mind is also on the olive yield, or rather the unexpected lack of one. This will be the first year since we bought our farm, a little over a dozen years ago, that the mature trees have not produced fruit. It is not a question of a poor-quality crop: the groves are practically bare. Why? I decide that I must call René, our olive guru, later. He may be able to furnish us with an answer even though he is no longer directly responsible for our olive production and doesn't oversee our harvests any more. Because he was so rarely available to lend us a hand during the season of gathering and pressing yet continued to insist upon two-thirds of the rewards for himself, I made the decision a while back to ease us out of that rather too costly financial relationship. I allocated the lighter manual tasks to Quashia and myself. We heave and ho with them while Michel deals with bureaucracy and business affairs and, when he's home, Michel and Quashia attack the more gruelling labour together.

We could manage without René, I reasoned, but now, in spite of several years of truckloads of fruit and first-class oil, I fear I have made a hash of it. Might I, out of ignorance, have caused long-term damage to the trees by pruning them incorrectly or neglecting to feed them sufficient quantities of organic horse manure at a crucial moment? I have no answers to these nagging doubts. I am baffled by this year's shortfall. Yet I know these trees to be hardy; they are survivors par excellence. When we acquired the farm they were entombed beneath a jungle of creepers, snaking ivy and overgrown *maquis*. We hadn't the slightest notion of what was there – or that we were purchasing not only a house but an ancestral way of life – but, in spite of countless years of neglect and a stranglehold of gorse and climbers, when we cleared back the land and discovered the craggy trees they were bursting with health, growing vigorously, and lacked only drastic pruning and tender care; sixty-four gnarled and weathered, silver-grey *oliviers*, each one close to 400 years old. So, what has gone wrong?

I can usually hope to find René at home in the evenings for no matter how elusive he proves to be during the day, he always returns to eat a late dinner with his octogenarian and, sadly, housebound wife. René, our canny seventy-nine-year-old Provençal olive expert who generally arrives bearing bountiful gifts and leaves having attempted to fleece me over some deal or other. Just the same, I am extremely fond of him, particularly now that I am honing my own brand of Provençal cunning. These days, he makes me an offer, I counter it with another, we raise our glasses, settle on terms that suit us both and then toast one another appreciatively. When I reach him on the phone later and he learns that we are back he is delighted and suggests dropping by 'bright and early' the very next day. 'And I will bring you some exceptional tomatoes,' he offers enthusiastically.

'No, thank you. We have plenty.'

'Oh, you have some?'

'Plenty!'

'But mine are splendid, you'll see.'

'So are ours. Please, René, don't bring tomatoes.'

He giggles. 'Ah, I thought I could offload some of them on you. See you tomorrow, then.'

The following morning, after a hurried breakfast and a struggle to get Michel's decades-old blue Mercedes running – the batteries in both our cars were flat and the windows on his were caulked with dried, crumbly moss – Michel sets off for the *mairie*. He is determined to persuade the forestry department at the town hall to cancel the fine or at least minimise the penalty with assurances that the herbage will be docked before the week is out. From there he is intending to pay a visit to the builders' yard to establish the precise sum Quashia has run up on our account. Afterwards, he'll make a swift stop at the garden centre, pick up a roll of nylon thread to feed the strimming machines, be back for lunch and then begin the cropping.

I have spent my morning washing suitcase-loads of clothes and hanging them out to dry on the line running between one of the cherry trees and a eucalyptus. Already they are bleached by the sun and fading to limp rags in the noonday heat. I am in the garden folding the laundry into a basket, puzzling over what might be troubling Michel, when I hear René's silver Renault chugging up our drive.

'*Diable*, you won't have easy access to your *oliviers* with all this growth. I have never seen the farm so untidy,' is his greeting to me as he clambers from his car and circles to open up the rear, which is cluttered with chainsaws, cans of oil, corked bottles brimming with an assortment of home-made wines transported for safekeeping in plastic milk crates, a store of pesticides, rubber tubing and baskets crammed with allotment-grown produce, all of prize-winning proportions.

'I know you said you have one or two but they won't be as fine as these so I brought you some tomatoes just the same,' he calls. His words are muffled because his head is buried in the boot.

'Tomatoes, did you say, René? We don't need them! By the look of things, they'll be the only harvest we reap this year.' I point to the vegetable garden, two terraces beneath me as I descend to the *parking*, laundry basket clutched against my hip. All the lettuces have bolted – some stand more than a foot high – but our criss-cross caned tomatoes are plentiful and lustrous. 'I think we'll be facing our perennial glut. I wish I could say the same for the olives.'

We greet one another with the customary *bisous* on the cheeks.

'Is it hot enough for you?' he puffs. His cheeks are shiny and red as beetroots, but his face is drawn and he has lost weight. There is a rheuminess and strain in what were always fiercely blue, calibrating eyes. Sometimes, because he has always looked so much younger than his years, I forget that this remarkably active man will soon be celebrating his eightieth birthday.

'So, you have no olive crop?' he quizzes, barely disguising his triumph, which I choose to ignore.

'Could it be the persistence of this warm, dry weather that has killed off all the drupes?'

'No moisture in the soil for the roots, you mean?' He shakes his head. 'No, their root systems are far too well established; they've been burrowing for centuries. All my other farms are flourishing.' He is frowning, glancing here and there, and toddles off to the edge of one of the terraces to peer closer. 'You haven't treated these trees, have you?' René's answer to every farming crisis or difficulty is to spray every hectare with gallons of pesticides. It is an ongoing argument between us and one that I believe can never be resolved.

'Why would we treat the trees if there's no fruit? The problem is not that the olives have been attacked by a fly or worm and rotted. Quashia assures us the trees flowered but the blossoms didn't produce any olives.'

'You must treat the trees whether they bear fruit or not. It's just the same. All your young ones, too. You should be treating those as well. I tell you what, I still have a litre or two of insecticide left. You pay for the hire of the machinery and I'll throw in the product for nothing. Alas, I'll have to charge for my hours because I can't work for nothing. I won't include the time spent collecting and returning the spraying machine, only the stretch it'll take to treat the trees for you. It'll be *une demi-journée*.'

I smile silently. René is cunningly opening up negotiations.

In the early days, I would have read this offer as my silver-haired colleague doing us a huge favour, helping out the novice olive farmers. Today, I can better interpret what is behind his words and I would lay bets that, any day now, René is due to treat the olive trees on one or other of the farms where he serves as olive master. It is also possible that the absent proprietor will have already paid him for the insecticide he is offering to 'throw in'. All he needs is a spraying machine to treat someone else's trees. Instead of forking out for it himself (a cost of approximately £100 a day), he is cleverly attempting to organise us to pay for it. Our requirement will be a *demi-journée*, half a day. The other half, he'll drive the machine elsewhere and make use of it there. Because he no longer rakes off any profit from selling our oil, he finds other ways to earn from me.

'What do you say, Carol?' He is walking back towards me.

René augments his two pensions by *petit* cash arrangements. From each farm he claims his two-thirds of the virgin olive oil produced by that estate. This he sells on and pockets the revenue. In return for this rather substantial personal allocation he oversees the pruning, treating and harvesting of the olive trees, which does involve him in hard work as well as certain expenses, I do not dispute that, but he usually manages to wangle a deal whereby someone else foots every bill.

'I can telephone the depot right now from my mobile – see, I got myself one! But what a darned nuisance they are when you're up a tree! I can order the machine for the day after tomorrow, if that suits you. What do you think? Here, if you don't need tomatoes, have some marrows and a couple of cucumbers.'

Fleshy veggies direct from the earth as well as luscious, round-bellied fruits that beg to be eaten are pressed into my hands and laid across my swan-white laundry while his eyes bore into mine.

'Mmm, what do you say, Carol?'

Paying for the hours he works for us is one thing; paying another farm's expenses is quite another matter.

'No, thanks, René,' I counter. 'As the trees are not bearing olives this year, I intend to give them a year off. Ourselves, too. As you can see there is more than enough work to keep us occupied throughout the summer so I have made the decision not to treat the trees.'

He shrugs, but looks grave. He can tell by my tone that this is not up for negotiation. 'Suit yourself, Carol, but you are making a mistake and you will regret it. Keep those anyway,' he nods at my armfuls of goodies, glances towards the rich blue sky and squints. Sweat runs in rivulets from his forehead, into his eyes and down his cheeks.

'*Diable*, it's hot. Any chance of a little refreshment?'

'Of course. Let's go into the shade.' I lead him towards the summer kitchen where a few bottles of rosé are kept chilled in the fridge and he makes himself comfortable at the small table beneath the magnolia tree. Lucky, who is dozing at the foot of the trunk, out of the heat, rises and staggers half-heartedly to greet him.

When we are settled and René has accepted that there are no deals to be won today, I confess to him as a friend that I am bewildered and not a little disturbed by the dearth of fruit. 'After we bought this farm, once we had eventually cut back the land and uncovered our Herculean trees, in spite of all the years of neglect they had suffered – years during which they were not treated with any pesticides whatsoever,' I emphasise, 'they were still producing first-class fruit, and in abundance too. Is it possible that this lack of productivity has a deeper significance? Might the trees have been, how shall I put it, overgrazed? Or have we messed up the germinating process? Upset the cycle?'

René swigs his wine and chortles and his round face creases with wrinkles. 'Are you worrying that your stubbornness and ignorance might have terminally damaged these centuries-old groves?'

'Ignorance! Well, I would not have . . .'

'You think your inexperience might have weakened the trees' prospects, is that it? That due to mismanagement on your part, they are exhausted, worn out, or, worse, are dying?'

I shrug, embarrassed, suddenly aware how illogical my doubts must sound. I am also hurt that he is being so unkind about my farming methods and is laying the blame so roundly at my door.

'Patience and faith, Carol. It will all come round again. Believe me, the trees are more resilient than you are. Haven't I ever told you the story of 1956? A legendary tale.' He knows full well that he has recounted the saga to me on several occasions. Every aged farmer from the Midi and all along the Mediterranean still recalls it and will relate at the drop of a hat and with pantomimic relish their horror story of the devastating winter of 1956. It has been passed on from one generation to the next and has gained story-book status. And I first heard it from René.

'Yes, you have.'

'Well, you haven't learned the lesson from it so I shall recount it again.' He reaches for the bottle, fills up his glass, coughs and prepares his narration. René is never more content than when he finds an opportunity to enjoy *un petit verre* in the dappled shade with an enraptured audience across the table from him, and I am usually happy to oblige.

'In January of that crippling year of 1956 the days were mild and sunny,' he begins. 'A bumper olive harvest had been accomplished and the people of the *terroir*, the soil, were preparing for their annual olive *fêtes*. The mood was light-hearted and it was as though spring had arrived early. The olive trees all along the south of France and the northern coast of Spain began to bud early, promising for the following autumn yet another auspicious yield. And then suddenly, without warning, at the beginning of February, catastrophe struck!' He pauses to sip his wine, enjoying a *bon* moment of suspense. 'The temperatures plummeted, bottoming out at below minus seven centigrade. Minus seven. *Diable*, can you credit it? No man in living memory has seen worse. The ground froze; the olive trees froze and, it is reported, many of their trunks exploded. Baf! Baf!'

'But why did they explode, René? I have never quite understood.'

He waves away my question impatiently. He has never elucidated on why such a phenomenon should have happened. Perhaps he does not know. When I first heard the story I doubted the verity of combusting tree trunks but I have since read that it is a fact of that winter.

'More than half the olive trees in Provence were destroyed by that frost, which lasted almost three weeks. It was an agricultural disaster. Not only the Provençaux farmers but the people of the south, *la France méridionale*, still judge it to be the worst olive calamity since record-keeping began in 1739. Six million trees were damaged and one million perished. Trees that had been growing on those farms for centuries. Imagine the distress. The northern Mediterranean olive industry was in crisis. "We are ruined," predicted the majority. "Are we living in Siberia or Provence?" Despair set in. Some found comfort in a surfeit of pastis, while others, one or two, turned their hunting rifles against themselves. They were the pessimists of the bunch, the non-believers.'

Here, René refills his glass. His face is growing more flushed. He looks merry.

'When the weather improved, the *oléiculteurs* who remained, those who were not drunk or bankrupt or buried ten feet under in the village cemetery, set to work. They dug up and tore out the old roots, burned them, tilled their lands and began to replant the fields and hillsides with vines or sunflowers or whatever crops would survive in their particular district. "Finish with olives! Good riddance!" they cried vehemently. But a handful of the wiser and, some would claim, wilier farmers weighed up the situation, took stock and, against all odds, these stoics decided to fight back. *"L'olivier est l'arbre de l'éternité,"* they declared with deadpan conviction. "You can flirt with other crops, but you'll see, the olive tree is the eternal tree."

'Their sanguinity, their naïve credo amused certain of their serge-clad neighbours seated in the village squares sipping their *apéros* in the shade beneath the plane trees, playing pétanque, giggling about their fellow countrymen behind their backs. "By this time next year, old so-and-so will be on his knees, you'll see, and we'll be able to buy his farm for a sou." Those were the avaricious dreams whispered between them.

'But, elsewhere, in the peaceful harbour and silence of their groves, the handfuls of obstinates were busy at work. They were sawing back their wasted trunks sheer to the ground and when they had finished, they wiped their brows and they waited. They did nothing while their neighbours continued to mock and gossip.

'Over the following seasons those weathered faces paced their groves; they inspected and tidied their grounds tendentiously. And within the year their determination was rewarded. Slowly, small delicate shoots began pushing through; pale, feathery growth encircling the deadwood remains of the wizened stumps. These *oléiculteurs* chose the hardiest shoot from each of their trees, staked them, cared for them and remained patient. And day by day the trees grew and flourished. Within six years, maybe eight, the farmers began gathering their crops and selling them for astronomically high prices. *Mais, oui*, Carol. And not for nothing were these agriculturalists to be seen driving through the country lanes in their new Citroën vans, triumphant smiles breaking across their leathered faces, for they had accurately calculated that

French table olives and olive oil would be at a premium for decades to come. They could name their price and, being canny Provençaux merchants of the land, they swiftly did so and were rewarded with healthy bank accounts. You see, there were far fewer olive farmers, fewer harvests and their returns were all the greater.

'Now, almost fifty years on, there are olive-farming families who will proudly take you on a tour of their groves striped with half-a-century-young, fruit-producing trees. And they will hail those *oliviers* as the perfect example of the resilience, the immortality of the olive tree. "*Eh, voilà*, the tree of eternity," they exclaim. Quite a morality tale, eh, Carol?'

What I enjoy most about hearing René relate this story is noting the embellishments he slips in between one performance and the next. He has never before given such emphasis to the financial aspects. The first time, I don't believe he even alluded to the gains the farmers hoped to pocket if they stuck with their beloved olive trees and succeeded in re-establishing their farms. I say nothing. He exhales as though puffed from exertion and empties the remains of the rosé bottle into his glass.

'*Santé*.' He lifts his drink and clinks it against mine. 'The olive is the tree of tenacity, endurance and faith.' He seems exceptionally pleased with himself. 'So you see, Carol, in spite of the mistakes you have been making, you and your nincompoop city ideas about farming, with industry and faith and a sprinkling of much-needed common sense' – he emphasises these last words – 'you will be able to repair the damage.

This is not an irreparable situation. I will help you, but you must listen to me and follow my advice.'

'René, I don't doubt that the groves are hardier than I may have suggested. Of course, I am worried and disappointed by this year's results, but I am not in despair, and I certainly do not intend to shoot myself! What's more, there are others all around the Mediterranean basin who strive to achieve their "nincompoop" ideas and succeed in producing first-class organic oil.'

'Not in Provence. Carol, we have flies, worms, maladies here that we need to protect against. No, my very best advice to you is to spray the trees, young and old alike, immediately. Do it before the week is out. You can count on my assistance. I'll give you the juice for nothing.'

These are René's final words on the subject.

But, still, I stubbornly refuse his offer.

Once upon a time I might have accused Michel of bagging for himself the least strenuous fraction of the farm's responsibilities, the paperwork, but that was in the days before I became acquainted with French agricultural bureaucracy. Now I am not so sure. He returns from the town hall a while after René has departed, looking stressed and in an uncommunicative frame of mind. I had hoped to run René's thoughts by him and receive his support – 'Yes, *chérie*, you are making the right decision. You are not being stubborn' – but when I see the expression on his face I decide to leave it until later.

'How did it go?'

'They cancelled the fine. Did you get through to the pool company?'

'There's no reply and no answer machine. I'll try again later.'

'Here.' On his way through to his office he hands me the mail he has collected from our letterbox at the foot of the drive. I call after him, 'Well done for the fine!' but he has disappeared.

Michel rarely if ever loses his temper. He expresses his displeasure by retreating into silence. If possible he will disappear off on his own and remain unforthcoming until he has shrugged off whatever is bothering him and he is ready to talk. I have learned not to intrude on this private time of his. So I accept the small batch of letters and set about the preparation of lunch. As I begin to lay the garden table I notice that one of our letters is from the Chambre d'Agriculture. Ever hopeful that it could be feedback relating to our farm's AOC status – the coveted AOC, Appellation d'Origine Contrôlée, awarded for the finest-quality produce – I rip open the envelope, but no. Instead it contains our olive oil classification. A fellow arrived here some months ago and requested a bottle of our produce which he took away with him to have tested. This letter, stamped and signed by the Chambre d'Agriculture, is the result of those official testings. It includes evaluations on the quality, taste and acid content of one bottle of oil, pressed from last year's harvest. The oil we are using now.

As I unfold the page, I call to Michel to come and read it with me. He does not answer. I scan the results hungrily. Even before I have gleaned its entire contents my eyes are moist with glee. I hurry to find him, certain that it will make him smile too, and come upon him kneeling in the *parking*, head bent in concentration alongside Quashia, clutching strips of a discarded sheet, now in use as oil rags. The two strimming machines are laid out between the men on the hot asphalt. They are threading the nylon yarn into the spools and cleaning the spark plugs ready for a strenuous afternoon's work.

'One jolly piece of news to arrive with the mail you brought up is our very first *"commentaire organoleptique sur l'huile d'olive, ainsi que la mesure du taux d'acide oléique"*.' I read this first bit aloud and then, as I hand him the letter, I add, 'I think it will tickle you.'

Michel does not take it from me because his hands are smeared with grease. I hold on to it as he rises and leans in to read it and then bursts out laughing. 'Terrific!'

Quashia looks on queryingly. He cannot read French so there is no point in showing it to him. Instead, Michel reads it out to him, playing the humour to the hilt.

'The acid content in our oil is suitably low, zero-point-seven. This is excellent news, Monsieur Q. It confirms that we are farming oil that can bear the label "extra virgin".'

Oil requires an acid compound of 0.8 per cent or less to earn this ticket.

'Now, look here, what do you make of this, Quashia? The commentary on the official tasting is as follows: "The nose of the oil—"'

'Nose?'

'That refers to its aroma. The nose, using their words, is described as "a combination of ripe apple, smoked meat and cocoa" while the taste is "slightly sharp, with flavours of green banana and cold cuts of sausage and hams". Our oil has been pronounced, by these highly skilled agricultural control experts, to be "very long in the mouth".'

Quashia looks bemused. 'Long in the mouth?' he repeats.

'Let's put it another way: the oil's flavour lingers, it stays with you, which is also judged an important ingredient in quality control. All in all,' concludes Michel with a certain flourish, 'it would seem that we have deliciously high-quality if somewhat unusual-tasting oil! What do you say to that, Monsieur Q?'

Quashia lets out a shrieking, one-toothed hoot. These descriptions, which are colourful enough to our ears, are to him and his Arab way of looking at life totally absurd.

'Our oil has a nose and a long mouth,' he cackles. 'And it tastes like banana-flavoured sausages! Not for me, then!' Quashia loves to be amused. My play-acting frequently delights him, but I have rarely seen him so crippled with laughter and the sight of him rocking like an amused child makes Michel and me giggle all the more. We glance at one another and grin. Michel winks at me and it breaks the ice between us. I move in towards him and he wraps his arm about me, closing his grease-caked fingers into a fist around my bare shoulder, beneath my sleeveless

T-shirt, leaving his blackened print on my flesh as he squeezes me tight. I feel a deep sense of relief that all is well between us and that this is what it means to be *home*.

Out of the Firing Line

During our absence from the farm, Michel's name has been added to the mailing list of a weekly agricultural journal. We are not familiar with it and nor have we ordered it, but eight copies, packaged in clear plastic wrapping, await us. My first instinct is to chuck them in the wastepaper basket without a second glance but a coloured front-page spread about organic farming in the western Mediterranean catches my eye and I decide to flick through one or two of the issues. As it turns out, they make fascinating and useful reading, chock-a-block as they are with facts and dates relating to Alpes-Maritimes traditions, practices and customs. Twenty pages in each, written in a style which is casual and user-friendly on all matters of interest to those who enjoy nature or are involved in the cultivation or distribution of local produce.

I learn, for example, that the inland town of Opio, only a few kilometres from where we are, will be hosting a watermelon festival in early July and that Solliès-Pont, a village situated between Hyères and Toulon in the Var, benefits from a microclimate that is particularly conducive to the propagation of figs. It boasts an annual production of over 2,000 tonnes from a mere 233 hectares. In late August this humble commune celebrates its harvest of the 'violette de Solliès' during a three-day pageant. Elsewhere there is an annual bread festival. Baking is regarded as a time-honoured and noble artisan trade in France. The Fête du Pain de Saint-Martin-Vésubie is organised by an association dedicated exclusively to traditional French ways of living. It is a two-day event held over a week-end and culminates on the Sunday with the baking in the communal village oven of 400 kilos of giant loaves, which are then offered as prizes in the evening tom-bola! And there are a few fascinating titbits about olive farming. One article informs me that there remain approximately fifteen varieties of olive tree growing on our coastline that cannot be identified. Fifteen! All have been surviving on this southern lip of France since '*antérieur au gel*', which translates as 'before the frost', and refers to the harsh winter of 1956 René has so recently depicted. It is clear from the article that 1956 is seen as a turning-point in the modern history of French *oléiculture*.

The telephone breaks into my reading. Noticing the clock, I see that it is already half-past ten. As I idly reach for the receiver, the answer machine kicks in. I decide to leave it and make my way through to the kitchen. It is time to take replenishments of fresh water to the men up the hill.

Slipping from slapping flip-flops into my running shoes, I ascend the serpentine track, skipping and leap-ing from shade to shade beneath the towering pines to avoid the amplifying heat. The ground is springy underfoot from the pine needles. The small rucksack on my back carries my provisions for the workers: bottles of cool, but not chilled water – it is judged unwise down here to consume very cold liquids in melting temperatures – a flask of coffee for Michel and another of verbena tisane for Quashia, plus the encouragement of a treat: fresh dates and slabs of dark chocolate.

Both men are grateful for the excuse to take a break. We choose ourselves a patch where the vegetation has been cleared and we can perch beneath a prehistoric Judas tree. Its one remaining upper limb – the others have been pollarded – as thick as an old ship's mast, provides us with leafy cover.

It's a while since I have been up here. Relaxing back against the nobbly liver-brown trunk, eyes raised through a canopy of evergreens, I reacquaint myself with this sky, with its rods of thick potent light, its dense, enveloping emptiness and its infrangible blueness, as blue as a kingfisher. All is quiet save for the pouring of refreshments and chatter at my side. I drink deep of the hush of morning. The dry climate is settling in for the season, permeating plants and soil. The air, filtered through a bouquet of fragrances, burns into my nostrils: the oniony scent of lopped herbage, which always conjures up poignant memories, and the heady pungency of rosy garlic. It grows like a weed on our land. I turn about me and spy a wilting cluster of its felled, pallid-pink umbels. Reaching for one, I crush a length of stalk between my fingers, sniff its tart narcotic aroma and lick at the glistening viscosity where it has dripped a snail's trail across my palm.

'It's a pity I didn't know these were here. I could have collected them for our salads,' I murmur, but Michel is not listening. He is in amicable debate with Quashia; something to do with the shed.

Squatting on our haunches like a trio of monkeys, we munch the sticky dates, suck our coated fingers as if they were lollies and take stock of what is or isn't all around us. Quashia reminds us that the coast has seen no rain in several months.

'Dry as a biscuit. Might that be why we have so few olives this year?' I suspect that he is as quietly concerned as we are by the dearth.

'There are handfuls here and there,' I protest, remembering René's blatant accusations.

'Yes, but the majority are on the saplings,' chips in Michel. 'I made a tour earlier this morning. The size of their fruit is quite remarkable; they look set to provide us with exceptional future pressings.' We all agree. 'And the trees themselves are shooting up fast, no longer resembling shrublets. They are in excellent condition.'

'But the mature fellows are almost bare.'

'Should we attempt a *récolte* of any sort this year?' asks Michel. 'Or should we allow the groves a year off?'

'A sabbatical? Mmm, perhaps that is what they have chosen for themselves.'

'I doubt that we have sufficient to make even one trip to the mill, if we wish to maintain our classification as producers of single-estate pressed oil. And, with our AOC pending, I certainly don't want to have to send off another batch of papers to the various oil bodies informing them that we have changed our status!'

Our summers are usually dedicated to the tending of our autumn olive harvest, spraying when needs absolutely must to avoid the black *mouche*, the fly that bores its way into the base of the drupe, installs itself there and destroys the olive's ability to cling to the branch – we have tried fly traps but they haven't solved the problem – and other insects and fungi that can attack the groves when the heat is brutal. So there is always a watchful eye trained on the trees' well-being and precious fruit development, but if we decided to do nothing with our paltry harvest this year then our summer duties could be, if not negligible, then at least light.

It is not the season for pruning or planting. Watering, as always, will be the most arduous task. It is a time-consuming job because it must be done by hand; lugging brimming buckets, splashing and spilling, to and fro, scaling and descending. Not to mention heaving and dragging snake-like lengths of hosepipe from one corner of the land to another. When fastened together, they can measure up to a hundred metres. Pumped with water, they are unwieldy and heavy, but because Quashia has decided not to return to his family in Algeria for these mid-year months he will be around to manage this with us.

'We could try marinating the drupes we have and if they are edible and delicious we could present the farm as a producer of table olives instead of oil for this one season.'

'There's so few, even for that,' I sigh. 'And the cost of husbanding them all summer may prove prohibitive.'

'Then I must inform Marseille and Nice that we foresee no harvest.'

'But a barren olive farm will not be granted an AOC ticket.'

My male companions help themselves to more dates and glug water from their bottles and we fall silent, chewing over the dilemma.

'Mmm, what's that perfume?'

Etruscan honeysuckle is in blossom in amongst the wilderness that is our neighbour's plot. Its nectareous scent wafts our way.

'I wonder if the Hunter's trees are bearing fruit.'

We gaze sadly upon the rows of olive trees beyond our fence. They are being strangled within a thicket of twine, white flowering bindweed and woody confusion. It breaks my heart to see such neglect. We have been attempting to buy that parcel of ground for some time, to rescue those throttled immortals and, once the terrain were cleared, to plant another dozen or so *oliviers*, but the proprietor, who lives in a village close by, chooses to hold tight to his tenure. In spite of the incendiary dangers, which are profoundly worrying, he prefers to leave the land wild because he dedicates this expanse to hunting.

Cleverly hidden within the tangles of 10-metre high unruliness are his crooked huts, which he has cobbled together out of wonky old planks, cuts of plastic tablecloths, frayed curtains and dusty rags. These are where he hangs out in wait for his prey, predominantly birds and rabbits. I usually know when he's in situ because I see his ill-kept estate car parked on the grassy bank overlooking the valley across from our lane. He doesn't like me or, more accurately, I made myself his enemy.

In the early days of our life here, before we had any fences, he was in the habit of hunting on our land, too. The proof was that when we first began to hack our way through our own scrub we unearthed, in the thick underbrush, several of his hideouts. Inside, they were cluttered with old sardine tins, fag ends, a single boot or sock, stinking blankets, a crumbling bone or two, boxes of matches warped by age and humidity and buzzing flies. On several occasions during these illicit escapades of his I bumped into him, or the dogs alerted me to his presence and I would hare about the grounds until I found him, rifle slung over his shoulder, game bag hanging from his arm, cigarette glued to his lower lip, striding and stalking from one terrace to the next, scowling and spitting at our barking hounds as though they were the intruders. When I politely requested that he extinguish his cigarette because it was a fire risk, he scoffed, and when I insisted he leave our grounds immediately, warning him that he was trespassing on private property, he replied with an expression and in a tone that was, to say the least, uncivil.

I was incensed and, in response to his manners, I nailed up planks of wood everywhere which stated in bold white lettering, clumsily painted by me: 'CHASSE INTERDITE' – hunting forbidden.

Looking back, I see that I was rather overzealous in my stance because I fastened several of my white-painted, plywood messages to trunks of trees that, I later learned, belonged to his frontage, not ours. He'd tear them down, of course, and, days later, when I found them jettisoned in the *maquis*, I'd gather them up and bang them furiously back in place. I was resolute, on the warpath, but he paid not the slightest bit of attention to me, the mad, irritating *Anglaise* on the hill, and blithely went about his trapping affairs, whistling merrily whenever he caught sight of me.

'These locals have been hunting these hills for donkey's years,' Michel would warn me. 'It's part of their ancestral tradition and their kitchen. This is not fox-hunting. It is not merely a blood sport. They kill to eat. You won't stop them, and you don't have the right to, either.'

How those distant rifle shots used to drive me crazy!

'I will on our land,' I'd retort with sweeping arrogance. Michel and I were newly in love and he would not argue the point further. He indulged me, or perhaps he was blind to my blindnesses.

Even today, I stumble upon rusty blue and red cartridges scattered about our terraces. The dogs must scavenge them and bring them back, or they were dropped long ago, because this rural monsieur, nicknamed by us the Hunter on the Hill, doesn't trespass on our patch any more. At least, I'm reasonably convinced of it, though sometimes the cartridges appear to be disturbingly recent. These days I am in less furious opposition to his ways or, rather, I have made a pact with myself to let him be and, as long as he shoots nothing that draws breath on our territory, I avoid confrontation, though I remain opposed to the principle of hunting. Unfortunately, he continues to harbour a grudge. Michel contends I cooked our goose with him long ago and that even were I the last woman left in Provence he would burn his plot to the ground before he'd sell one square centimetre of olive trunk to us. So the Hunter on the Hill's trees battle on, neglected and unloved. Still, and here René's tale of '56 gives me heart, although they are in need of drastic pruning, they are surviving with olive-tree tenacity.

The men at my side rise, reaching for their protection glasses, which remind me of racers' goggles, ready to return to the land clearance. I gather up the remains of our makeshift picnic and blow a parting kiss to Michel as I begin my descent, still gazing at the irritating jungle beyond the fence. It looks like a tract of impenetrable rainforest.

Later in the afternoon, sequestered within the shuttered tranquillity of my den, arms aching and scratched from hacking at the overshot bougainvillaea on the upper verandah, I return to my perusal of the local magazines while listening to the reassuring hum of strimming machines high on the hill above me. I have a little plan hatching. I am toying with suggesting to Michel that we slip off for a day or two. My film-producer husband has recently completed delivery of a demanding, eight-part documentary series; he is mentally worn out, I can see that. A short break would do him the world of good. I am contracted to an independent LA-based company to adapt a Brazilian short story for the screen, but I do not have any pressing deadline so we could steal away, set aside time for us, which we haven't done in a while. I had hoped that we'd find leisure hours together here at the farm but returning to chaos and fruitlessness means there are unforeseen chores and complications to address and, once we get stuck into everything, we will be lucky to have any private life at all.

Better to dedicate a few days now. Attendance at one or two of the local harvests I have been reading about might be fun or we could find ourselves other early-summer *fêtes* or simply venture further afield to discover parts of Provence we have never explored before. I am eager to extend and deepen my impressions of these southern provinces, to enrich my knowledge of the original language, and Michel is usually up for a jaunt so why not, once the land has been cut back and before farming commitments engulf us?

I flick casually through pages until a feature catches my eye. Some way north of us in the southern Rhône region of Vaucluse sits the renowned village of Châteauneuf-du-Pape. Its name dates from the era of dual papacy and its reputation as a wine-growing district is the oldest and most revered in Provence, I read. Their earliest vineyards were planted in the fourteenth century on papal land. Today, thirteen different varieties of grape are cultivated on their hills, producing some of the most celebrated wines in the Rhône valley.

We might make a short tour to some of those esteemed wine domains to learn a thing or two about their farming techniques. Since all our well-laid plans to host beehives on our farm have fallen through, we have been discussing the possibility of restoring the small vineyard that flourished, in bygone years, on several acres of the southern section of the Appassionata estate, before we became the proprietors of what, these days, is a much-reduced holding.

A string of festivals marking the passage of the grape's development are on offer in Châteauneuf-du-Pape. The Fête de Saint Marc, the patron saint of wine-growers, *vignerons*, is held on his feast day, 25 April. Unfortunately, we are too late this year to raise a glass to Saint Mark. The next round of revels is the Fête de la Véraison. This takes place during the first weekend of August so doesn't fit any imminent escape schedule, but what an inspiring notion, to gather together to toast the ripening colours of a fruit! Later still, the Fête des Vendanges is the busiest and reputedly best of all their summer parties. This one is held in mid-September and honours the harvest kick-off. Still, although it is a spirited jamboree, it is not exclusive to Châteauneuf-du-Pape. Many of the wine-growing regions of France get out on the streets to cheer the prelude to grape-picking; the birth of that year's 'vintage'. I sigh and toss my magazine on to the table.

Reading about Châteauneuf-du-Pape has evoked doubts about our AOC and I ask myself, not for the first time, whether we will ever be granted this ticket of excellence for our olive oil. I think that deep down Michel and I are both beginning to lose faith in this elusive acknowledgement coming our way, though we have worked hard to meet the mandatory standards. An AOC for olive oil is a relatively new concept in France, little more than a decade old, and the olive industry along this coastal strip around Nice is only the fourth area in the country deemed to possess conditions conducive to the production of oil that warrants such an accreditation. Obviously the recency of the business will have created teething problems for the various offices of bureaucracy but, even so, I would never have dreamed that it would prove to be so darned long-winded.

The concept for such a quality control originated, interestingly, in Châteauneuf-du-Pape in 1923 when a local *vigneron*, Baron Le Roy, compiled a set of rules that laid the foundations for production of first-class wines from his region. This prompted the establishment of an Appellation d'Origine Contrôlée. Today, it is regarded as a French benchmark for top-quality comestible produce. Châteauneuf-du-Pape became a certified vintage in 1929 and over the years has become world-renowned for its full-bodied red wines, which lay claim to the highest alcohol content in France with a minimum strength of 12.5 per cent. A simple calculation shows me that it took six years from the birth of the Baron's idea for it to be implemented and, counting on fingers, I realise that our wait is soon to rival that span of time.

I am browsing again, greedily gleaning facts, darting about the columns in an attempt to find articles reporting events due to take place in mid- to late June: any day now. I turn to the penultimate page of one of these curiously informative little magazines and see that it is dedicated to *les petites annonces*, the personal columns. In the vague hope of finding us a vinekeeper or a replacement beekeeper for the one who never showed up to put his hives on our hill, I momentarily change tack and begin to scan these boxes. My eye is caught by a three-line message that could well be of great use to us in the establishment of our vineyard, if not, alas, with our long-sought-after bees. I flick to the front cover of the paper where the date reveals that this particular issue is five weeks old. Never mind. I pick up the phone and punch out the numbers recorded in the advert. The bell rings without response and I am on the point of replacing the handset when a wheezing, reedy voice barks, '*Allô*?' I am not immediately sure whether it is male or female.

'*Bonjour*. I read your advertisement—' I begin, picturing an elderly person, a man hobbling through leafy vineyards.

'Listen, if you're a car dealer . . .' He speaks with a thick Provençal twang, still trying to catch his breath. His remark confuses me.

'I'm not.'

'You're referring to vine cultivation, then! You have a foreign accent, madame, are you ringing from abroad? I receive many calls from California. I'm a wine variety expert, you see.'

'Yes, I realise that, monsieur. No, we live in the Alpes-Maritimes, just a few kilometres inland of Nice.'

'Ah, the eastern side of Provence. Roman vineyards. Splendid. A Bellet domaine?'

'Actually, we are not a vineyard at all.'

'Well, if you're not a wine producer and you're not trying to flog me another car, what do you want?'

His manner is disagreeable and I am tempted to put the phone down, but I press on.

'We are operating a small olive farm, but in earlier decades, long before we purchased the estate, there was a *vignoble* on several acres of the land. We

43

occasionally find a rogue vine, even after so many years, and these days we allow them to grow and have been pleasantly surprised when one or two have produced fruit. The grapes are always white and slightly sharp.'

'Have you identified the *cépage*, the variety of vine?'

'No, we haven't. To be honest, it only recently occurred to us to try. But, surely, monsieur, there must be one grape variety that thrives best on the soil and intense heat hereabouts, *non*? Our olive groves, for example, are all of the *cailletier* variety. I thought perhaps you could help us with this information and supply a few plants?'

I hear him harrumph. 'Wine production is a more complex business than olive farming, madame. Intelligent wine-growers mix their stock, using one principal choice. There are eighty-eight different *cépages* in Provence alone. What's your situation?'

'Our hill is south-west facing. Most of the land, including what was the vineyard is *en restanque* and we are keen to replant vines on those self-same inclines.' I choose *en restanque* because it is an old-fashioned Provençal term used to describe sloped land that has been ridged or terraced with drystone walls. I am attempting to create the right impression with this rather grumpy viticulturist. I would like him to perceive me as *du terroir*, of the soil, and not as a foreigner with 'nincompoop' notions, as René would have the world believe.

'Mmm. Your grounds are not chalky, not in that part of the world, being so close to the sea. How many hectares are you intending to plant up?'

His assessment is accurate. Our soil is limestone-based, but we have never ordered an expert analysis of the earth's properties. Perhaps we should have. I skip over this point. 'Approximately four acres. Our holding is not large. Still, our olive oil may receive AOC status so we cannot plant vines on the acreage dedicated to the olive groves. The Chambre d'Agriculture seems rather strict about this.'

Of the countless olive inspectors who have appraised, surveyed and pored over these grounds, I cannot recall one who has tested the soil. No doubt they know the region's attributes too well to bother.

'Four acres is feasible. You will have room for close to two thousand *pieds*.'

'Two thousand vines?' I am astounded by this information and suddenly picture the cost of what we might be embarking upon.

'Yes, we usually calculate four thousand plants per hectare. Are you considering grapes for eating as well as for wine?'

'Predominantly wine.' My response is a little less enthusiastic now. I am asking myself how many litres of wine we might produce from such a quantity, but I decide against enquiring.

'I'd better visit you and examine the terrain, which sounds as though it could be quite *caillouteux*.'

'*Caillouteux*?' I have to think quickly to remember what this word means. Stony! 'Yes, it is. Actually, it is mountain rock. Is that a problem?'

'No, it can be useful. It serves to store the heat for use at night and can aid water drainage. Châteauneuf-du-Pape, for example, is well known for its stony soil and benefits admirably from such ground. But I need to cast an eye over your site before I can correctly assess what varieties might be suitable.'

'I think we'd prefer to visit you at your nursery first. Where are you?'

'Not far from Arles. How are you fixed for next Tuesday, early afternoon?'

I see the excursion I am plotting for Michel and myself falling neatly into place and hurriedly jot down the details of this *vigneron*, who introduces himself as Guillaume Laplaige from Maillane. 'Frédéric Mistral territory,' he boasts. 'The Provençal poet. Heard of him?'

I assure him that I certainly have and that when my husband returns we will confirm the rendezvous. I replace the receiver feeling exceedingly pleased with myself. I hope Michel will agree to go. Fate seems to have taken a hand in offering us the perfect opportunity to mingle farm business with a delicious break.

Evening falls late. We are approaching the summer solstice; high sun, creeping hot days, which I will spend beneath the whirring fan in my den until, exhausted, I step gratefully out of doors to irrigate the terracotta pots around the swimming pool and the flowerbeds, where this evening I discover self-seeded white Naples garlic and electric-blue tassel hyacinths in amongst the roses and lavender. I ought to weed them out, but for tonight I leave them be. We need new watering cans, but not more plastic ones. The dogs have chewed the nozzles to old bones so the water fizzles and spits everywhere. Plants attended to, I settle back to bask in the cooler gloaming hour. It is well past eight o'clock when Michel and Quashia eventually descend the hill. Both men are sweating, sticky and masked from head to foot by strips of felled herbage. Quashia unburdens himself of his tools and bids us a friendly goodnight, refusing even a soft drink.

While Michel swims in the pool he cleaned this morning, I draw a cork and pour him a well-deserved glass of rosé. The wine tumbles into the glass as I listen to the motion of his body, arms plashing, feet kicking lazily through the clear blue water. I love this time of year. It seems joyous to me with its promise of sweetly mellow autumn offerings. I am seated now at our wooden table, legs outstretched across another chair, the canine trio at my feet, playing audience to the sinking rays of light, rich with a shot-red sunset, when my husband joins me, showered, hair damp, looking decidedly more relaxed. He takes a sip of wine and his long slender limbs spread reposefully. Satisfied, he declares himself, after his strenuous afternoon's work. 'There's a message on the machine from Madame B., asking me to call her. I wonder what she wants after all these years.'

'Really? Well, she can't have the farm back!' I josh, recalling our first encounter with the fierce and outstandingly wealthy woman from whom we purchased this postage stamp of paradise.

'I'll wait and give her a ring at the end of the week, when we've cleared the land. With these long days, it should be finished by Friday.'

'Terrific.' I show him the *annonce* and relate my

brief phone conversation with Guillaume Laplaige. 'What do you think?'

Michel's easy expression disappears in an instant. 'Where is he?'

'A few miles north of Arles. I know it's a two-hour drive, but—'

'You seem to have forgotten all the difficulties we had trying to find ourselves a beekeeper, and we still don't have one! People are reluctant to travel such distances.'

'Laplaige didn't seem to object when I gave him our address, and it's not as though he would be calling on a regular basis, unlike an apiarist. I suggested that in the first instance we see him. We could find a small hotel in Arles, stay overnight, or . . . I would love to discover the Camargue . . .'

Arles is the capital city of the Camargue, the south-west region of Provence.

'Think of it, Michel, those wide flat salty planes, white horses, cowboys, black bulls, pink flamingos . . . It must be France's answer to the Wild West, as well as home to the authentic heart of Provençal poetry. It strikes me as a region of high romance. Do let's go.'

'No, Carol. We don't have the resources to restore the vineyard, particularly since Quashia has embarked on that shed, and it will only put further pressure on our already overtaxed watering difficulties,' is Michel's answer and I cannot deny that I feel a pang of disappointment, but I say no more on the subject for the present. His exhaustion reveals itself in remoteness, and we spend much of the lovely evening preparing our supper as a team, sitting, eating, serving one another, always together, but in semi-silence. My envisaged jaunt has pushed him away again and I am puzzled as to why.

Elbows on the long wooden table, I gaze heavenwards, count stars, lose track of the billions of bleached blots in an ink-navy sky, wishing that I could read from afar the map that is unfolding before me, divine its configurations, while wondering what, aside from work burn-out, could be disturbing the man at my side. Should I try to encroach on his silence, to worm my way into his veiled world? Tonight it seems as dark and impenetrable to me as the heavens above.

Early the next morning we receive another call from Madame B. She is staying in Cannes and presses for a rendezvous. Michel invites her to lunch. She demurs, offering apologies; even a chauffeured journey inland is too taxing for her. If we would be so accommodating as to meet her at the coast she'll book a table at the Carlton for the following midday.

It sounds urgent. We ought to accept.

'A bit of a nuisance because we were getting on so well. Never mind. If Quashia doesn't mind working Saturday morning, we'll still have the land stripped before the week's out.'

And so we drive to the beach, for our *déjeuner* with the ex-proprietress of our residence. There we find her awaiting us at a waterside table laid for four, protected by a rectangular linen-white parasol skirting the shimmering Mediterranean. A teak boardwalk leads us to her: unnecessary to soil one's shoes in the sand.

Around us, the clink of glasses, the distant shout of children at play, the wash of well-mannered waves, the heady scent of headily priced colognes, gold jewellery brushing against silver-plated cutlery. Motor yachts scud and dock; clouds of sleek-haired, leggy females in the company of world-weary men in white slacks and tasselled loafers disembark on to the scrubbed, bleached jetty dotted with sunbeds and sharply pressed waiters. Here, the privileged and their playmates are about to lunch.

Our bulldog-spirited Madame B. is alone when we arrive, handsomely attired in a *framboise*-tinted, slub silk frock with matching three-quarter-length coat. We assume that Monsieur B., a frail man on the one occasion we met him, is on his way. She rises somewhat clumsily as we approach and I see from her fallen face how much she has aged. She holds out exquisitely manicured hands to Michel; chunky precious stones glint in the noon rays. He kisses her hand with the gallantry she claims and, although she barely acknowledges my presence, we politely exchange the two-cheeked *bisous*. A bottle of champagne arrives. It must have been pre-ordered; a vintage Dom Perignon. I pray to God she is not expecting us to pick up the bill. Menus are laid discreetly on the table but it is unlikely we will even glance their way. The lunch buffet on offer here is legendary and probably one of the most lavish I have ever eaten. The irony is that the majority around us will merely pick like birds at their plates; either their meal tickets depend on their desirable physiques or they are too decrepit to digest and so they shift food lackadaisically round their plates, hungering for better days when life offered more than expensively traded acts of sex and Havana cigars.

While the waiter pours the wine, the fourth of our party arrives: Yvette Pastor, Madame B.'s personal secretary and perennial travelling companion. A nervous woman who nods and twitches and shuffles in the shadow of her generous but omnipotent employer.

'Monsieur is not joining us?' ventures Michel, raising his flute to offer a toast to our hostess.

'Monsieur has passed away, monsieur.'

'Ah,' Michel replaces the glass.

'I wanted to inform you personally and I want to thank you for your enormous kindnesses to Robert and myself.'

We are both mystified by this statement. We bought a property from this woman, the smallest of several estates she and her deceased spouse owned on this Riviera coastline. Aside from a visit to their home in Brussels – the only occasion at which he was present – one other lunch with her in Paris at the George V Hotel, where she was residing, and two meetings at the *notaire*'s office to conclude the purchase of the farm and, later, the remainder of the land, we have had no intercourse with them.

During the meal – Yvette delivers Madame B.'s plate to her: servings of fish and *les crustacés* chosen from the buffet table, but our hostess swallows scarcely a mouthful – we are given an account of the final years of Monsieur's life; their last days together. Why she has chosen to unburden herself on us is really not clear. I fear that for all her fortunes she is a lonely creature, and her words begin to move me.

'He didn't care for money,' she discloses. 'He cared only for his plants and his gardens.'

I am distracted by a memory of the landscaped parkland beyond the floor-to-ceiling windows of their Brussels home, where a bevy of gardeners were at work on cedar topiary, herbaceous beds and perfectly velvet lawns, where water jetted from fountains of Italian stone and arranged in rows everywhere were marble statues of minor classical deities. I remember, too, how, at the time, she confided to us that she and he had been childhood sweethearts and that it was almost by accident, aside from her single-minded dedication, they had become so fabulously wealthy.

'I grew angry with him.' She is divulging now. 'I was frustrated because he resented donating the time our financial assets demanded. I am ashamed to admit it but somewhere along the road, I realise today, I stopped *seeing* the gentility of the man at my side. I judged his gardening pursuits as time-wasting, a frivolous hobby. Yet I knew he was a cultured man. Self-made, of course, like me. We began with nothing, but he was – how should I put it? – well, innately cultured. I should have allowed him his horticulture. It was his mode of expression, and if that was what our fortunes could buy him, then who was I to begrudge him his path to creativity?' She falls silent. Even the recreational noises encompassing us cannot intrude upon her loss. 'I failed him, monsieur.'

There is little we can say as comfort. I rattle off a platitude or two because I feel I must make a gesture, offer some token, and she accepts my efforts graciously and smiles. 'Your French has improved greatly, madame.'

And the lunch is terminated.

Sincere apologies, but she must get back to work. She has an important deal going through. How irritating the banks are, with their delays and their excuses, holding on to one's funds unnecessarily. Yvette skitters off to sign their account and we accompany Madame, mounting the steps from the beach to the esplanade. She and Michel stroll on ahead. I dawdle behind, appreciating the bay. She has purchased a duplex apartment here on the waterfront; the view is magnificent; she has works afoot, she is recounting. Michel suggests that she flies down for the film festival next year and he will escort her to a première. 'Oh, what fun,' she giggles. 'I have always wanted to climb that red carpet. *Merci beaucoup*. It has been enchanting to see you again, and your wife. She is becoming quite French, don't you think? *Au revoir!*' And off she struts across the palm-lined street, cowing traffic, determined, mobilised and businesslike, armed once more to face the march of money merchants. Hot on her heels comes Yvette, darting in and out of the hooting cars, flapping to keep abreast. And one would never guess the quiet torment our hostess is carrying in her heart. We dally awhile on the Croisette looking after her and then out to sea. Michel takes my hand. '*Un peu triste, eh?*'

'A little sad indeed.'

That evening, replete after a great lamb dinner, Michel caresses my shoulder and tells me that if I still fancy an excursion, he has reconsidered and is not averse to the idea. 'Only for two or three days, mind. There is too much to be attacking here. I have a business dinner on Saturday in Monte Carlo, but we could leave Sunday.'

'A business dinner on Saturday?'

'A producer is flying in from Australia with first-draft scripts of a series and we are meeting up with the Monaco-based financier. He and I are attempting to put the budget together.'

'Can't it wait till we return?'

'No, it's important. I have been working on this deal for a long time.'

'Anyone I know?'

He names two Australians, both of whom I have met on several occasions.

'You haven't mentioned this opportunity before.'

'Too important, I guess.'

'I see. Shall I confirm Tuesday's appointment with the viticulturist?'

'We can prepare the disused vineyard, by all means, but I don't want us to engage in any further financial commitments for the present. Let's see how my deal goes. If you are still keen to visit the Camargue, though, I would love to see it again. I haven't set foot there since I took the girls camping when they were eight.'

So the Camargue is our chosen destination, and it will involve no flying. We can travel by car, at our own pace, and immerse ourselves in our Provençal homeland, searching out its time-worn ways and culture.

The following morning, back at the coast, I decide to pop along to a local *librairie*, a stationery store and vendor of tourist manuals. There are few outlets in Cannes for the purchase of literature so I am not optimistic that I will find what I am looking for. I am after a two-volume Provençal dictionary compiled by Frédéric Mistral with assistance from several of his poet colleagues. To my surprise, the store is carrying a sizeable collection of the late man's works, each published bilingually. Mistral wrote in Provençal and then translated his work himself into French. Astoundingly, they also have the dictionaries in stock. I lift up one of the weighty tomes – this was a labour of twenty years – and open it. Alas for me, they translate only from his native tongue into French and not the other way around, and certainly not into English (no translation, as far as I am aware, has ever been made between the Provençal and English). Even so, I am delighted by the material on offer and decide to take the lot, though I seriously doubt I will ever master poetry-reading in Provençal. The two lady shopkeepers grow quite chirpy and throw in a pocket diary and several biros for good measure. I carry off my hoard triumphantly, determined to acquire a few rudimentary phrases from this region's native tongue to try out during our excursion.

In an upbeat frame of mind on this warm June morning, I make a circuitous detour to a favourite organic baker, which is situated off a busy transit street in the hills behind our farm. There, I choose an olive *fougasse* still warm from the oven for our lunch and a *baguette à l'ancienne*.

Exiting the baker's courtyard, I am obliged to wait in the lane for a break in the traffic. From the right, jay-walking, zigzag fashion, comes a lone bearded figure, thin and bent as a pipe-cleaner, with matted, shoulder-length hair, who halts directly in front of my car. I give him a minute but he shows no signs of budging so I lean my head out of the open window and cry, '*S'il vous plaît*,' but he doesn't register my plea. I lower the volume on the radio and call again. Still he remains by my bonnet, swaying perceptibly, clutching a plastic bag containing a bottle which he is swigging from. I notice his black, encrusted finger-nails, his hands red with open sores and scabs. An awareness of a presence behind him dawns, and he turns slowly. His face is also grazed, mauved with bruising. For a brief second he squints at me, frowning, and then staggers off, muttering. Something about his dead-fish eyes puzzles me; they strike a note of familiarity. Manuel, the gardener! I employed him once, years back, for a few hours – until he passed out drunk in the garden. I have not seen him since that day when René and I were obliged to bundle him into the boot of René's shooting brake and return him to the woodshed where he appeared to be living, an operation that was accomplished without him ever regaining consciousness. What a sorry figure he has become.

This hinterland route home takes me through lovely open parkland with reed-screened ponds and an observation tower for birds. In the distance, the amphitheatre of Alps. When we first moved here, all this nature together with its stately manor house was family-owned but, due to a default in inheritance tax payments, the acres were seized by the state and, subsequently, given over to the community for leisure activities. Ever since, it has been humming with the light-hearted vibe of trippers picnicking on the grass, joggers pounding the track, kite-flyers plunging and lifting, their wide-open arms battling with wind, and strollers with bounding, roisterous dogs. Curiously, though, not today. Today, the green is deserted and I am rather taken aback to see that its border has been blocked by dozens of monolithic boulders while the adjoining *parking* is cordoned off with tape as though it were a crime scene. No sign has been posted to offer an explanation.

I turn right from the park on to a crooked country lane that spirals south and eventually passes the only vineyard in the neighbourhood before circum-navigating the rear of our hill. I choose it because, in spite of how close we are to coastal urban living, these acres remain a green zone and a tapestry of nature's mysteries. Here is where I first encountered René so many years back and where I found our lovely, long-lost, much-mourned Belgian Alsatian, No-Name. It is also wild boar habitat. Traversing these lanes late at night, we encounter families of the pests feeding at the roadside. From here they mount the hill, cross our boundaries and infiltrate our grounds, where they damage everything in sight. Quashia and Michel are at odds with me because I will not agree to the purchase of a rifle to shoot the scavengers. Yet, stubborn as I am, I realise that at some point I may be forced to concede if we cannot find a more humane method of putting a halt to their nocturnal romps and gourmandising on our land.

Lost in wild boar deadlocks, I narrowly miss running over a bird I have mistaken for a curled leaf. I pull over to the lane's edge and reverse. Crouching by the upturned creature, I am uncertain whether it is dead or alive. Close up it looks as though rigor mortis has already set in, but then it blinks. It is stunned, not dead. It must have been walloped by a vehicle's headlight or mudguard and tossed in a whorl of speed out of the immediate passage of further traffic. One of its wings has been badly scuffed and hangs like frayed threads on the cuff of an old brown sleeve. Obviously, he is incapable of flight and, being grounded, is at the mercy of any number of predators. I cannot abandon him to such a fate and so I attempt to gather him up in the cup of my hands but the little fellow resists me with an unexpected flurry of frightened flappings. The touch or scent of me has alerted him to danger and, in spite of his wounds, he is determined not to be trapped and struggles with the force of a minuscule prize-fighter. Claws and beak scratch and peck me but there's no real damage done and I eventually manage to calm him with gentle strokes to his soft-furred belly and pinkish breast. He may be quiet but he is still afraid. I receive his fear through the pitter-patter of his tiny heart beating fast against the mound of my thumb. Shoving my bags of books and shopping to the floor, I settle him, fluttering and confused, on the passenger seat, to deliver him to a safe shelter.

I turn into our lane at a snail's pace, tracing the curvature of the bends, until I am halted by an approaching white van. Our *chemin* is not wide enough for two cars to pass. It sits high above a major road and, once upon a time, was probably a donkey track. One or other vehicle is forced to reverse, either back up to the lane's inlet or further down to a bay in front of one of our two neighbours' gates. The unspoken rule of thumb is whoever is closest to a clearing is the one who retreats. In this case, it is the van. I salute my thanks to the driver in anticipation and turn my attention to the bird who, out of terror, has excreted on the seat. I rummage for a rag; there is usually one on the passenger mat. When I look up the van has not budged. On the contrary, it has inched forward. I am worrying about the bird's wellbeing and now gesticulate with both hands, signalling to the man to back up. Meanwhile, I turn to ascertain the distance involved if I give way. It would mean renegotiating the bend backwards and I fear overshooting the track. I look back helplessly to the opposing car. It is now approaching, metres at a time, towards my stationary Mercedes. I hoot – what the blazes is he up to? – and thrust my gearstick into reverse, but the fellow suddenly shoots forward and narrowly avoids shaving my bonnet, forcing me to swing my old convertible to the right, sheer up against our neighbour's stone wall. Cedar branches hanging from on high snap and crack against my windscreen and plop on to the bonnet. Leaves and pine needles scratch and whisper on the surface of the soft top. The bird panics, flutters and attempts to fly. 'Sssh,' I coo, desperate to get past this rude imbecile who is drawing up alongside me and – now I see there are two men in the car – laughing heartily and malevolently. Teeth exposed like rabbits, hatted heads thrown back, I recognise the driver instantly. I had not identified him because I have not seen him in this vehicle before. It is the Hunter on the Hill.

'You are a selfish, inconsiderate lout!' I shout in English, but he gets my drift. He and his companion rock with derisive laughter again and skid off, leaving me to continue my hearse-like crawl to the bottom of the track, stewing over his manners and the braces of freshly shot blackbirds and thrushes or wretched rabbits he'll be transporting in that stinking game bag of his.

I leave my feathered companion in the car while I race to the summer kitchen – shooing our ever-desirous-of-affection hounds away from me – to fetch a *cocotte* dish, which I fill with a spoonful of diluted milk and a few breadcrumbs hurriedly torn from the baguette I have bought. I settle the bird in an empty shoebox grabbed from the garage – Quashia hoards crateloads of such 'useful' articles – cover it with a fly dome and place him, for safekeeping, in one of the stables where there is plenty of light. The door is bolted from the outside, thus securing him out of harm's way, beyond the reach of the three dogs who are currently patrolling the yard, jealously determined to find out what I am about and what unwelcome being is receiving attentions that are their God-given right.

Back upstairs in my den, I telephone the swimming pool company once more, but the number rings into a deserted office. I have better luck contacting M. Laplaige. I offer our apologies as I cancel our rendezvous, explaining that our proposed vine-planting is not looking feasible at this moment in time.

'Lost interest, eh?'

'No,' I argue. 'We intend to go ahead, but not immediately.'

He suggests that I take cuttings and send them to him, taking care to wrap them in clear plastic bags so that the leaves do not dry out in transit. He is confident that he will be able to identify the *cépages* used to create our farm's original vineyard. 'If the vines were planted up for rosé wine and the same variety of plant is still available, my husband and I would like to reinstate a rosé-producing vineyard.'

'The grape might well have been a grenache. It thrives along your Mediterranean shore and, consequently, has been cultivated for generations. I can furnish you with excellent quality *pieds*. Unfortunately, although I will almost certainly be able to recognise the varieties grown there, it will be impossible for me to confirm whether the original plants fruited white or black grapes. So I cannot say whether the farm produced rosé wine or not.'

'But what percentage, approximately, of each would we require for rosé, monsieur?'

I hear a long-distance sigh. 'Madame, you have not understood the principle of wine-making at all,' he tuts. 'While white grapes are used exclusively for white wine and red to create red, rosé is not a diluted hodge-podge of the two tints. It is not a red wine with a splash of white thrown in to lighten its shade.'

Even though this gentleman cannot see me, I feel myself blush. '*Ah, oui,*' I blather.

'Black grapes are used for rosé wine. It is a question of the balance and fermentation process.'

'*Excusez-moi, monsieur.*' I have been keen not to make a mistake similar to the one I made with our olive groves. Out of ignorance, I jumbled everything in together by purchasing six trees from a local garden centre – not an authorised nursery, to boot! – only to discover later that these were *tanche* and not the *cailletier*, the Olives of Nice variety, which grows everywhere else on our property. As a consequence the drupes gathered from those poor six trees must never, *never* be included in our harvests when our crateloads are pressed into oil, not if we remain hopeful of an AOC rating. No, we must adhere to the stringent quality-control rules which do not allow the chucking of every Tom, Dick and Harry olive variety into the same basket. When my mistake is spotted by the many experts who have inspected our ancient groves, which it invariably is, I am made to feel, well, in René's words, a 'nincompoop'. Now, I fear that M. Laplaige may be forming the same impression of me.

'Post the cuttings, madame, and we'll take it from there.'

And down goes the receiver.

Later, when I return to the stables, I discover my bird upside down and still as a stone, though breathing. He appears to have fallen while attempting an escape. Handicapped by a broken wing and exhaustion, he has not been able to right himself. Deciding that the cardboard walls are a prison to him, I discard my choice of container and replace it with a round wooden chopping board from the kitchen. This creates a solid and generous base and fits snugly beneath the fly mesh. Once the new house has been assembled the bird seems reasonably quiet and I leave him sitting with his torn wing outstretched like a shabby shopping bag.

Once again I bolt the stable doors because Bassett has taken up post outside and glares at me with black-eyed malevolence whenever I pass by.

'Have you given him a name?' asks Michel, when he comes down for lunch from the top of the hill.

I shake my head.

'Any idea what species he is?'

Looking at him closely, with his white-bibbed neck and cloudy eyes, we decide that this fragile few ounces of life could be some kind of warbler. I recount my discovery of him and of how the Hunter tried to drive me off the road. Michel looks at me in a kindly way but makes no comment. 'It would be nice if we christen the little fellow, don't you think?'

I consult my ornithological encyclopaedia. The rescued bird resembles the illustration given for an Orphean warbler. They frequent olive groves and scrubland.

By Thursday, the jungle on the terraces surrounding the old ruin has been thoroughly docked. The men have almost reached the summit now. So, armed with my secateurs and three small plastic bags, I cross the land behind the house to snip precious vine cuttings. Studying the plants more closely than I have in the past, I see that there do appear to be leaves of varying shapes and sizes propagating here. M. Laplaige's appraisal must be accurate; the vineyard, or what remains of it, was planted with mixed varieties. I try to see if I can decipher an order, or a dominant strand, but fail. So I decide to pluck at random. I take five or six cuttings from three terraces and slip them carefully into the plastic bags. Having achieved this, I return to the wall alongside the swimming pool where two very healthy vines sown by me are fruiting vigorously. In season these grapes make delicious eating, for breakfast in plain yoghurt or as a dessert with goat's cheese, but I have no idea if they are intended exclusively for the table or if they could contribute towards our house beverage. They are black, so it's promising for rosé! I snick foliage from both types, choosing soft green, budding shoots rather than the tougher-to-cut, woodier stems. What fun if we have inadvertently been nurturing plants that could provide us with wine as well as fruit and how splendid it would be if this old farm is still throwing up the vestiges of exceptional wine stock. Our unexpected olive-oil treasure was buried within groves abandoned on this forgotten hillside long ago, so why not wine too? I carefully package up my mini-harvest and drive it to the post office, dreaming of vintages and *grand crus* from this olive farm on the Côte d'Azur.

Our warbler is showing signs of recovery. The poor little fellow is still unable to get airborne – his attempted take-offs land him back on his breast or beak – but at least he is able to right himself again and his will to live is perceptibly more buoyant. Michel thinks that in a few days he will be fit enough to be released. We will continue to protect him until he is able to fend for himself and in our absence

Quashia will care for him. He loves all creatures and I find him first thing on Friday morning in the laundry room, mixing up a dish of bread and milk while chatting away to the bird in Arabic.

On Saturday evening, having showered and rested after the graft of land clearance and knowing that we are setting off bright and early the following morning, our loyal gardener returns. Walking the hill together before our departure is a ritual of his and Michel's, but today, because Michel has already left for Monaco, I invite myself to take his place.

We climb at a leisurely pace, accompanied by the frantic drilling of a woodpecker, pausing to admire the slowly setting sun and the sweet-smelling, freshly cut grounds. Pushing upwards on outstretched stalks out of the drystone walls are red and pink Valerian. Their bluish-green leaves clasp long waxy stems. In the early days when I was obsessed with hacking away at everything so that we could more easily classify what was growing or had been cultivated here, Michel stayed my secateurs, begging me to preserve the Valerians. 'See, how graceful they are.'

'They are weeds,' was my rebuttal. 'Their roots have infiltrated almost every one of the stone walls and destroyed them.'

'They are wild flowers, *chérie*. They are doing no harm. Why not leave them to express their beauty?' he'd quietly insist, and he was right. This evening, as Quashia and I stroll from place to place, bemoaning the lack of olives, the Valerians are in colourful blossom all around us and I take pleasure in them.

'Well done, Monsieur Q.,' I say.' The land is as it should be now. Thank you.'

But Quashia shakes his balding head and points to the level above the small palm grove. 'I haven't seen that before,' he states sullenly. An entire wall has fallen into rubbled piles. It is the wild boars not the flowers who are the terminators of the terraces.

A Late Homecoming

I wake and turn in the bed to discover that Michel is not at my side. Opening my eyes I try to think. Ah, yes, Monte Carlo. What time is it? Why hasn't he returned? If there were a problem I would have been informed; he would have telephoned. Almost synchronised with my developing thought, the phone begins to ring, echoing round the tall-ceilinged, open-plan rooms. My heart begins to race. I switch on the light. It is twenty-past one. I am almost too afraid to pick up the receiver.

'Hello?' My voice is thick with sleep and fear.

'Sorry to wake you, *chérie.*' I hear tension in his words.

'Are you all right?'

'The car has packed up. I have been trying for over an hour to get it started,' he sighs, 'and I haven't been able to raise a soul to come and look at it.'

I am so relieved to know that he is safe. 'Where are you?'

'Still in Monte Carlo. I could stay in a hotel tonight, take the first train back in the morning if I can't find an open garage, but it will delay our departure, or . . . could you bear to come and collect me?'

We arrange a rendezvous point outside one of the major hotels for half-past two. I hurry to get dressed and on the road. The night is clear as far as Beaulieu, where it begins to drizzle lightly. My motor speeds along without a hitch and I arrive in Monte Carlo ahead of the appointed hour. Michel is waiting by the lobby entrance looking exhausted but glad to see me.

'Thank you for doing this. Do you want me to drive?' he asks, climbing in.

'I am pleased it was nothing more serious,' I say, omitting to mention that I had woken with an unsettled feeling in the pit of my stomach.

The rain, such as it is, seems to be easing and, says Michel, assessing the heavens, probably won't continue. Still, it is late. He offers again to take the wheel but I shake my head. He looks beaten.

'How did it go?'

'Not as well as I'd hoped,' he mutters.

'In what way?' No response. I glance to my right. Michel is nodding off. All the better; he needs the rest. 'Sleep,' I whisper, stroking his knee. 'It will be easy to find the road.' After a dozen or so kilometres I will join the Aix-en-Provence autoroute which will give us a straight run all the way to Cannes. From there I will turn inland on to lanes that I could almost trace with my eyes closed; we will be tucked up in bed within the hour.

Leaving the principality is less direct. The roads are labyrinthine, a steep, corkscrew ascent into the mountain face, and tonight they are shiny with slick from the almost invisible rain. But the sky is clear and even the light downpour gauzing the windscreen does not opaque my vision. I can see constellations of stars and, to my left, where the moon's narcissus-lemon beam is hitting the satiny surface of the Mediterranean like a central spotlight, I have a bird's eye view of fantastically proportioned ocean-going cruisers crossing overnight to Corsica and beyond. Mmm. This time tomorrow we will be at the Camargue coast, discovering the fishing village of Saintes-Maries-de-la-Mer. On the path to romantic, authentic Provence; its uncorrupted heart. I can't wait.

I switch on the wipers and then the radio. It plays softly and we neither of us talk, enjoying a sleepy, companionable quietude. Michel is dozing. I am listening to the smoky jazz and silently trying to identify the pianist. We continue to climb, negotiating the bends, back and forth, looping and twisting, like a bat rising to its heavenly belfry. 'It's Brad Mehldau!' I cry without thinking. The man at my side stirs, shifting in his seat. 'Sorry,' I mouth. Dug out of the craggy rock face, way above us, are dwellings. One or two. A lone house here and there clinging to the vertiginous mountainside, lording over the Principality of Monaco and far across the sea to Africa. Stupendous must be the views they enjoy. An isolated luxury villa and then another, nestled into the cliffside, abuts our road. All are in darkness. The world, save us, is aslumber. I glance at the clock. It is a quarter to three. Beneath piano and drums I hear the engine's soft whine, a spring unfurling, as my coupé spirals on upwards, hugging these figure-of-eight, alpine curves.

Michel opens his eyes and because he is seated to the right of me he sees the approaching beam, reads its warning, before I do.

'Watch out,' he whispers softly, without panic, but it is too late.

Seconds later a small saloon appears, orbiting out of

control, and crashes with the force of a high-speed train full tilt into the left side of my engine. My face is slapped against the glass of the left-hand window. I feel rocking, ricocheting, bodywork buckling, and a sharp, instant stinging.

I lift my thumping head, trying to focus.

'What'z zappened?' I slur.

Through a mental fog, I try to recall. Approaching too fast, an automobile descending this perilous incline at breakneck speed.

Headlights.

'Watch out,' Michel's voice.

The car slams on its brakes and skids on the slippery surface. I hear the withering scream of wheels. A vehicle orbiting out of control. Slewing, turning circles, spinning like a top down this precipitous hillside. Its circumrotation appears to be in slow motion until it begins bearing down on us. Propelled across the narrow road, it spins faster and faster and crashes with the force of a high-speed train full tilt into the left side of my engine. I feel rocking, ricocheting, bodywork buckling, and then nothing but blackness.

I lift my thumping head, trying to focus.

The flesh beneath my left eye feels cauterised. Blood is trickling from where the skin has split open. I taste the saltiness of my own life juice.

Rivulets of liquid are coursing down the hillside and I hear howling. 'Michel!' I swing to my right, which sends my head whizzing, to find him collapsed forward like a rag doll, completely motionless.

'Oh, my God!' I release my seat belt – my hands are jittering to the point of clumsiness – and push open the door, shoving frenetically, repeatedly, beating at it with my shoulder and fists because the front of the car, bonnet and frame, has been concertinaed. Stepping out into the dampish night I am overcome with teeth-chattering indecision and panic. My head is swimming. The caterwauling is chilling. It has to be coming from the other vehicle. I must release Michel first. I stagger to the passenger door and wrench at it manically. It opens with ease, sending me flying backwards; here the bodywork is undamaged. Blood is pouring from his brow like a forgotten tap on to the knees of his grey trousers and the floor mat. The rearview mirror is in shards at his feet and claret-stained with his blood.

Should I try to drag him out? I don't know what to do.

I appear to be the only one who can move, who has released themself from the wreckage, so I somehow deduce that the onus of responsibility, of getting a rescue team to the scene, lies with me. I must act fast. My brain, though, is muddled. Decisions are not locking in. The radio is still playing, lyrical harmonious notes.

'Michel,' I am kneeling at his side. There is petrol running and bubbling all around me. 'Michel, please, can you hear me?' I am fighting hysteria. My heart is pumping so fast I think it will explode.

He nods imperceptibly. He has responded. Thank God!

'I'm going for assistance. We passed a villa.' I rise.

'Please don't die!' I yell, head thrown back, yowling at the moon. Hurtling in the direction we have travelled, sliding on liquid, I pound down the track. From somewhere distant a dog is barking. I am tugging on a substantial bell-pull outside imposing, black, wrought-iron gates. 'Help! Ambulance!'

A middle-aged woman in a cardigan and nightdress unlocks a solid door. 'My husband has called the emergency services. They're on their way. He's getting dressed. Do you want to come in?'

I shake my head, too breathless to speak, already retracing my steps. I can taste blood. My eye is weeping, closing up. I think I am going to vomit. I am reeling, staggering. When I arrive back at the car, Michel has lost consciousness, or . . . I don't allow myself to contemplate the alternative.

I am dancing with madness on the alpine path, skidding in floodlets of petrol, hopping to the other motor, where a young man is trapped at the steering wheel. 'Get me out of here,' he blubs, whimpering like a cur. I lean in to see what can be done and smell the fumes on his breath.

'Someone's coming,' I tell him.

A police car skids to a halt behind my Mercedes, which is skewed across the byway and has swung a full quarter-clock to the right.

'Please, my husband!' I cry. 'Come quick!' The two young policemen separate. One follows me while the other legs it to the drunken driver.

'Michel, Michel!' I am kneeling on the tarmac, soaked in stinking diesel, hands on his bloodied hands, limp in his lap. 'Can you hear me? Oh, God, can you hear me? The police are here and an ambulance is on its way.'

Michel lifts a finger weakly to his lips, requesting me to be calm and then, eyes closing, his head flops lightly forwards.

The policeman joins me at Michel's side. 'He's not dead, is he? My husband, he isn't dead, tell me he isn't!'

The policeman gazes on helplessly – he looks no more than a boy, he won't have a clue – then uncertainly brushes his fingers against Michel's freezing hand. 'I'm afraid I think he is, madame.'

Words cannot express the chaos spewing out of the pit of my stomach. 'Where the fuck is the ambulance?' I bawl, deranged, like a lunatic losing control of any faculties still operative. I stomp off several paces along the grass verge, hitting my fist against a boulder, attempting to get a grip on my emotions and the cold, cold terror that has me in its vice.

I run back. I wait. There is no visible change in Michel. I wheel about, looking up and down the hill. The world remains dead and indifferent. 'Why is the ambulance taking so long?' The young cadet has no idea. The other, more senior perhaps, is on a walkie-talkie.

A while later, it seems like for ever, a fire-brigade truck screeches up the hill. Out jump the emergency services. A stretcher is being organised. It seems that we, or rather, Michel is the priority. Thank God. A uniformed man in his twenties is at Michel's side. I rush to be there, nagging and skipping, getting in the way, sizzling like a rocket waiting to launch. 'Is he alive?' Shooting questions, leaving no space for the paramedic to do his job. 'Is he alive?' I beg repeatedly. I am ignored. The stretcher is delivered and laid out on the tarmac. Beacons have been positioned in both directions to prevent the approach and destruction of further vehicles. Michel is unclipped from his seat and lifted out. Soundless and floppy, like a puppet. His body is gently spread out on to the stretcher and a dark grey blanket unfurled over his lower half. A tube from some portable life-giving apparatus has been attached to him. The rear of the fire engine is open and in he goes, like a dish into the oven. I am instructed by the police cadet to follow.

'What about the car? Where shall I park it?' I ask moronically. It is a write-off and as if it matters.

'We'll deal with it. We'll see you at the hospital. Here, don't forget your handbag.'

I climb in and crouch at Michel's side. His eyes are closed. The blood still pouring from his forehead is drying in jewelled crusts on his face. I take his hand. Now I begin to weep. I feel as though we have been locked in a cave. The young stretcher-bearer who accompanies us confirms that Michel *'vit encore'*, is still living, but he has lost consciousness and a rather distressing amount of blood. The journey back into town to the hospital is bizarrely short. Certainly after all that climbing and waiting. A gurney arrives. Michel is wheeled into emergency and I am skittering along behind. Within the building's casualty wing he is rolled sharply to the right. Someone runs off in search of a doctor. I am trailing the cortège when a night sister steps forward, dyed-black hair scraped tight beneath a triangular cap, severe features, and blocks my path. 'I'm sorry, but you must wait here,' she informs me.

No way, is my response. I barge past her and as the swing door is about to close on a spacious, white isolation room where a handful of night staff are preparing to examine Michel, I slide in.

One of this team, a young nurse, hurries to my side. She attempts to harry me away but I won't move.

'Please wait outside, you will be seen shortly.'

'I am not concerned about me. I want to stay with him, my husband please.' She looks tired, uncertain.

'I won't leave,' I press.

She is about to protest when a shocking noise draws our attention to the table where Michel has been settled. His body has begun to rock and clatter. It is clacking like the music of castanets; gypsy castanets in a frenzied dance. His entire being is jumping inches into mid-air, nerves going haywire. A fish caught on a line, wriggling for freedom. The nurse rushes back to the bed. She and two other members of the emergency team attempt to calm or quieten him; they are holding him down by the ankles and wrists. His eyes are closed and I don't know what this threatens. I have been forgotten and so I draw close, watching from a vantage point by his lower end, at a few metres' distance.

One white figure inserts a needle into his arm. No easy feat given the violence of these spasms. The solution seems to act almost instantaneously. His body sinks like a released air cushion back into repose. One of the crew is speaking on an internal telephone attached to the far wall.

'Is he going to be all right?' I beg. Michel's clothes are being removed. His jacket, his tie, which one of the paramedics had already loosened, his shirt congealed with blood against his chest. I hear pale strands of his chest pelt being peeled from his skin as the white cotton is stripped away, but he is oblivious of all of this. Where are his shoes? I had not noticed that he is in blue-socked feet. I see a tiny hole at the apex of one of his toes and the outline of shoeprints on the soles of the socks. Something about his feet breaks my heart. The vulnerability of this. Unshod. And now naked from the waist up. He begins to tremble again. It grows more violent. The door opens. Two men have arrived. A gurney waits beyond. Michel is being taken elsewhere. Where? The first nurse, the stern sister who greeted me in Reception, is at the door again, instructing me to 'remove myself'. Michel's gyrations are growing more forceful and now he begins to moan. Deep chthonic or subaqueous groans. A lumbering beast trapped, wailing from an underground lair.

Is he conscious? I ask anyone. No, I am told. Another syringe is being inserted into his arm. He begins to drift into stillness, silence. Oblivion. A masked man is swabbing the open wound, frowning. It reminds me of a hole that Quashia might drill, irregular, not quite circular, but this hole has been bored into the curved dome of my husband's head.

The two men at the door hover expectantly. Where is he going? The word is given, a discreet nod, and they step forward, negotiating their trolley with habitual skill. Both swing doors are flung open and the patient is wheeled away. All activity within the room dies down. The emergency team exit. There are blood clouds where Michel was lying. One man is left cleaning up. He lifts his head, seeing me for the first time, puzzled by my presence, and then returns to the business of metal kidney dishes, dressings, needles, medicaments and Lord knows what else. I return outside to Reception, at a loss.

A nurse carrying a file, marching purposefully by, stops and asks 'Yes?'

I am confused. 'Yes what?'

'Have you registered at the desk?'

'I'm fine.'

Patently not. She grips me by the sleeve of my cardigan and leads me to a desk where a curly-haired, bespectacled woman in civvy wear, eyes cast deskwards, asks the same question, 'Yes?' without lifting her head. My guide has moved off, marching on through the medical night.

'Please be seated and someone will be with you shortly.'

'It's not me. It's my husband. I don't know where they have taken him or what will happen.'

'Sit over there, please, and you will be attended to before too long.' I shift in the general direction of the bench but in spite of an overwhelming fatigue that descends upon me I cannot be still. I am a ball threaded with elastic and attached to a bat. I whack back and forth, never in repose. The receptionist insists that I sit down. I have a raging headache. My eye has closed over and I cannot imagine what is happening to Michel. Is he being admitted, operated on?

Will I ever see him alive again? Why, why have they taken him away? I glance at my watch. It is half-past four. Break of day. I ought to be doing something constructive. Instead, I allow myself to give in to the weight of tiredness and settle heavily on to the bench. I close my eyes. My head falls forward. A voice is saying my name. I open my good eye. The left one is glued shut.

'Are you Mme Drinkwater?'

I nod wearily. How has the woman standing before me acquired this information?

'The doctor is waiting to see you now.'

'Later,' I insist. 'When my husband comes back.'

'Please follow me.'

I shake my head. The logic, if any exists in my resistance, is telling me that if I leave this spot I may never find Michel again. I must stand sentry, as it were, and await his safe return.

'You will require a scan.'

'I'm fine.'

This messenger, a nurse, raises her eyebrows, sighs heavily and disappears. Moments later the doctor is in front of me. I am staring at the arrival of his shoes. This is not the footwear of an English doctor or an employee of a British National Health hospital. This man is sporting elegant brown suede casuals and beige silk socks. I lift my head and see a ruggedly handsome individual, fifty-something with iron-grey wavy hair, a tanned complexion, gold-rimmed Cartier reading spectacles.

'Mme Drinkwater.' He has a kindly, composed manner; highly practised. A Latin man confident of his own lean masculinity. 'Your face has been quite severely cut. For your own sake and insurance purposes, I will need to examine you before I can sign you out of the hospital. I would like to recommend that we submit you for a scan. It is quite painless.' Although this tiny horn of land has its own dialect, everyone communicates in French or English here. This specialist, speaking to me with his thick Italian accent in my mother tongue, is no exception.

'Do you know what has happened to Michel?' I ask, visualising the hole in his sock.

'He is undergoing the same scan I have scheduled for you – just to confirm that there is no internal damage – and then we will stitch him up. It is a rather deep incision he has suffered to the skull.' The man smiles impassively. 'Now, madame, how about you?'

It must be the madness of the night, but even with one eye sealed shut, encrusted with blood, and a skull that feels as though there is an ear-splitting drum solo playing within it, I adamantly refuse to be examined. The doctor barely restrains visible impatience, grimaces tightly and moves on to other more accommodating cases.

Once I am left alone in the corridor, sleep takes hold.

The rattle of trolley wheels rumbling loosely over the tiles stirs me. It is Michel, embalmed in a starched gown. He looks like an elongated fish, *en croûte*, brought to the table on a dish. His head rolls sideways. I see drugged blue eyes. He is conscious. Michel! Michel! I leap to my feet. My knees collapse and I stagger, almost sinking to the ground. He lifts a limp hand. I put out mine and we brush fingers as the gurney rolls by, disappearing again into the same white room – or is it a neighbouring one? 'Are you all right?' I call, but the doors have swung shut. This time they are closed from within and, try as I might, I am barred entry.

I request 'the ladies' room'. In the glass I look like nothing more than an alley cat who has been in a scrap or a pirate returned from the high seas. I wash my face in cold water to alleviate the swimming tiredness – I am punch-drunk with it – and to clean off the blood smeared all over my cheek, neck and collar. With warm water, I prise apart the viscid seal, releasing the sight in my left eye.

Back in the corridor once more I become obsessed with the notion that I must inform someone of what has happened. But who? I wouldn't want to alarm *les filles*, Michel's twin daughters, and I certainly won't disturb my mother in her bed in England at this hour but, in my aberrant state of mind, it has become essential to inform *someone*. Eventually, I decide upon Bob, Michel's Australian business associate and dinner companion. I root about for the number in a local directory and wake the man from deep sleep. He is groggy, barely lucid and clearly completely baffled by the sound of my voice.

'It's Carol.'

'Who?'

'Michel's wife. We are here in Monte Carlo at the Princess Grace Hospital,' I am yammering. 'Accident. Hole in his sock. Looks like a fish. Jumped like a fish. But he's not dead. He's going to live.'

'Yes, well, thank you for contacting me,' he growls sleepily. 'What time is it, for Christ's sake?'

The day is alive and kicking in the Principality of Monaco when we step outside the hospital into a blindingly bright summer afternoon. The warmth of the sun against my damaged face, which feels as though it has been twisted out of all recognition, is salving. Hand in hand, awaiting the taxi that has been ordered at Reception for us, we stand. We are going home. Michel has no internal injuries, we have been assured. The lower corner of the rearview mirror breached his flesh and sunk deep, skewering him. All traces of glass have been removed. The wound has required fourteen stitches. He has been given pre-scriptions for painkillers, tranquillisers and has been injected against the risk of infection. He has been instructed to rest. The impact shock will take time to heal. The specialist recommended a night or two in the hospital but was willing to release him on condition that he returns for a check-up, that our own doctor oversees his recovery and that Michel stays put for the foreseeable future. 'No air travel.'

I, on the other hand, have not been given any form of once-over but I have been urged to make an appointment to return in the immediate days to come for the obligatory scan. My pigheadedness has been treated with varying degrees of civilised compassion, but I have been warned that insurance companies, police reports etc., etc. will require the examination. The offending driver, who has smashed both kneecaps and inflicted various other leg injuries upon himself, is to be charged with dangerous driving while under the influence of alcohol, or so I have been informed by a police inspector who stopped by to interview me. Facts have floated over me. I have very little grasp on linear reality. The only reality I can latch on to is the fact that we are both safe and being released.

Seated in the back of the taxi, pressed tight against one another, we are zombies gazing incredulously out upon a familiar coastline where folk are at play, indulging in their favourite water sports. The fact that it is an ordinary day like any other seems to be odd. Miraculous, really.

Warning Skies

The taxi delivers us to our gate and from there we climb slowly up to the house; a storm-tossed twosome we must make, puffing and resting, winding our way through the argentate olive groves and thick golden heat. The sky is so acutely blue it looks as though it has been freshly painted. I am seeing it all as though for the first time. Between one day and the next, the season has burgeoned, exploded, or that is how it appears to me. This shimmeringly hot early afternoon is as intoxicating as any hallucinatory experience. I drink it in intensely, addictively, through drooping eyes that kept vigil with death, and a nervous system that is so shot it is on overdrive. There is no sign of Monsieur Q. He must be elsewhere on the land, attacking the perennial chores. But no, it's Sunday, isn't it? I fold in the shutters in our bedroom, closing out the flaxen shafts of day, sliding us into *dies non*. Clothes fall to the tiled floor and we fling ourselves into bed, rolling into one another, crashing up against flesh and hair and body perfumes like waves against a windbreak; scuffling for contact; making ourselves our universe; clinging tight to one another as though our salvation, our ability to weather this trauma, lies here, here within this bowery where we have known so much joy; stroking, touching, locating body parts as though to reassure ourselves that we are both still whole and functioning, still capable of normality.

Here we pass the better part of the day. As evening draws in and I am woken by distant church bells signalling the call to evening mass, I rise, go out, walk barefoot on the warm slabby tiles, absorb the view, sink into the pool, relishing its silky coolness, doggy-paddling to and fro, trying not to get my face wet. I look a perfect sight.

During our *petit séjour* in deepest Monte Carlo my rescued bird has perished. I find him lying on his back, stiff, legs extended heavenwards, erect as open scissors with minuscule feet curled at the extremes into arthritic claws. His feathers are dishevelled as though he has been pecking at himself, angry and self-flagellating after aborted attempts to get airborne. His broken wing sweeps the chalk-shitty floor of his makeshift hutch like a torn curtain.

When Michel wakes, we bury our silent songster in the garden.

I wrap his remains in white kitchen roll, shrouding him in a make-believe swan's down cloak, while Michel digs out a shallow grave down by the lower cherry tree and there we lay him to eternal rest. When the mound is covered over, patted firmly down and surrounded by stones, I place several sprigs and one flower upon it from the star clover plants that I have retrieved from those self-seeded in our flowerbeds. (I choose them for their heart-shaped leaves.) In my state of shock, this feathered creature's departure upsets me profoundly. We never confirmed whether or not he was a warbler, we never gave him a name, we never heard him sing. Orpheus.

During the days immediately following the accident, I attempt to screen us from the outside world and the onslaught of telephone calls and affairs to be addressed: the Nice *gendarmerie*, Monaco Accident Enquiries, my insurance company. Owing to our proposed, now postponed, mini-adventure to the Camargue, the cupboards are almost bare. Both automobiles are in Monte Carlo. We have no means of transport. We have no cash; the taxi that delivered us back from the Princess Grace Hospital emptied our pockets. Quashia, shocked to find us in such a condition, walks to the village to stock up on provisions for us. When he returns he digs up fresh lettuces and radishes, tomatoes, of course, and gathers herbs, washes the lot under one of the cold-water taps in the yard and, in order not to disturb us, leaves everything inside the front door, out of reach of the thieving mutts.

I receive a call requesting that I pay a visit to a yard close to the border between France and Italy, the garage annexe where my sports car is being stowed, pending a decision on its future, to sign identification papers and remove all possessions. Several police officers motor by to interview us, asking questions and then more questions and requesting signatures on pages of forms. A telephone call from a very fraught Frenchwoman reveals the mother of the young fool in possession of the offending vehicle.

'The police told us your husband could have died,' she sobs. 'My son has no father,' she offers as a form of explanation. 'Will you be pressing charges?'

The question catches me off-guard. It had not occurred to either of us to do so. Our thoughts have not travelled such a distance into the future. We are still wrestling with the recent past.

I tell her that I have no answer to give her, that we are recuperating and that my husband will heal. 'He isn't going to die,' I say gratefully.

'May I call again?' She is weeping uncontrollably. 'My son will be six months in hospital. My only boy.'

I tell her that I am sorry for her son but I judge it unwise for us to maintain contact. Bob, from Monte Carlo, rings, wanting to know whether I telephoned him in the wee small hours or was it a dream he'd had? 'After Michel and the other guys left my pad I sat up late watching movies. It'd been a disappointing evening and I had a few,' he confesses rather sheepishly.

I confirm that I did call and I apologise for my gibberish dawn intrusion.

'It's a fucking shame the budget for the project fell apart. We all tried our damnedest to get the bloody thing up and running and I know better than most how desperately Michel needed it to save his company from closure, but sometimes the pieces just don't come together. How is he, by the way?'

It takes me a moment to reply. 'Sleeping.' And that is a fact. Michel spends hour upon hour sound asleep in our room, shaded by the slatted shutters. In a no-time world of pillows and penumbra and plays of light. Dusk aeonian; infinitum. I pass by regularly and find him curled up beneath the duvet, breathing heavily; a creature speared; a hibernator hunkered down beneath a substantial bed of leaves in darkest winter. I sit beside him, careful not to disturb, and gently stroke the crown of his head; his soft curly hair still matted with blood. How long has he been struggling with such financial difficulties, and why hasn't he shared them with me? He mustn't worry. The contract I have recently completed will provide us with sufficient to run our lives for several months to come, as long as I don't go investing in vineyards, that is.

When he wakes and eventually rises up out of our room he settles on to one or other of the terraces drinking tea and gallons of water. Michel is not a man who enjoys tea but he finds it comforting now, he says. I boil more water and keep quiet about what I have learned. He sits beneath a parasol, out of the sun, to safeguard his wound, staring seawards. He seems distracted, only vaguely aware of our exchanges, and he stares into me with a quizzical expression that worries me, as though he is not entirely sure of my identity.

His stare is unnerving.

'Michel?'

He knows my name and the daily details of our life together. I think so. I pay close attention to the minutiae in an attempt to confirm it. Quashia comes looking for him, needing advice about some aspect of the shed and Michel deals with it without a hitch. He remembers that we are building a shed. He has not forgotten his construction skills. There are no missing elements as far as I can tell, no memory loss, but he is unresponsive. Sentences do not seem to penetrate. It is as though he is concentrating on another dimension of sound. Somewhere else, deep in thought. A confused ruminant, striving to figure out a puzzle. Is he listening to an inner voice? Is he grappling with images of the accident? Is he worrying about his workload? He does not bear a troubled face. He is simply not present, and does not engage in conversation. And when the phone rings, for now the word is out that he has been injured, he waves the callers away. He wants to speak to no one. I shield him from the world. And I shield him from what I know.

As for my own wounds, I am more or less intact. My face is a mesh of scratches and bruises and bumps; my left eye has puffed up like a rhizome and I have the irritating sensation that there is a mountain directly in my field of vision that won't scratch away – it is the lesion above the cheekbone swelling up – and I am plagued by a nagging headache, but otherwise I am in workaday shape.

Perfunctory matters are beginning to call on our attention and it is clear that I must take the reins. Two cars in Monte Carlo. None here, and we are several kilometres from the nearest bus stop; there is no other form of public transport in the vicinity. A letter from the olive organisation in Marseille which oversees tree plantation and olive produce has arrived. They are requesting an appointment for Monday of next week here at the farm; they wish to send a financial controller to visit us, to clarify a few outstanding queries. A form Michel has furnished appears to be incomplete, unsatisfactory. As far as I know we have never submitted any accounts to these people, though we are registered with them, so I cannot get to grips with what the letter is about. I put it aside; I'll show it to Michel later and if he is not sufficiently recovered to handle the meeting, I will postpone it. Due to the augmenting heat, the swimming pool needs cleaning again. The firm contracted to carry out the work on a weekly basis is still not answering its phone. I am wondering if Michel has clocked the developing algae. He hasn't stepped into the pool since we returned. He is constantly cold and is suffering from bouts of violent shivering. Shock, I assume. We both have pending appointments at the Princess Grace Hospital and no means of getting to the principality. We will need to hire a car, for we must attend. It is a fact that I shall have to undergo the scan I so cussedly resisted.

Three days after the accident, I rise early, swim in the slippery green water and, armed with straw hat, walk to the nearest village before the sun has rounded the mountains, to take the bus to Cannes, where I rent us a replacement vehicle. From there I drive directly to the agricultural co-operative of which we are habitués and ask for Laurent, the young assistant who usually helps me unravel our farming dilemmas. Laurent is off sick, I am informed by the doleful biddy who keeps the till and rarely gives us the discounts we, as regular clients, are entitled to. It is unlikely that he will be back this year, she announces, while pressing her glasses up the bridge of her nose.

'This year? But it is only June!'

The cashier's hangdog countenance, a harbinger of life's bad blows, is interrupted by a lanky, peaty type with hands of horn who leans in from behind me, asking, 'Lend me your Bible, will you, love, for five minutes?'

She swivels on her chair, picks up a weighty paperback, delivers it to the client, muttering, 'Bring it back,' and then informs me that Laurent fell out of a tree, fractured his collarbone in several places and damaged a group of ligaments in his shoulder which have rendered him unemployable for the foreseeable future. I offer words of condolence to be transmitted to him, which the woman promises to deliver personally when she visits him at the hospital the following afternoon.

'And what about you, madame? You look a right old sight yourself.'

I shrug off discussion of our recent events, mighty grateful that our injuries will not continue on into another year, and am directed to the replacement employee, Alexandre. 'You'll find him in the hangar with the bird seed and dog food at the bottom of the yard.'

I thank the teller and weave my way through the string of trucks and farmers at work charging or unloading produce in search of Alexandre. From the dark caverns of the warehouse strides a lean, athletic man in T-shirt, shorts and solid boots, in his late thirties, disarmingly good-looking with a beard that under different circumstances might be described as 'designer'. He is smiling broadly and shakes my hand with the force of a labourer.

'How can I help you?' he grins.

'Four dozen tins of dog meat, please, and fifty kilos of mixed biscuits.'

While he freights these to the boot of the sprucely cleaned hire car, I explain my pool dilemma. Alexandre listens politely, all the while studying my face, which makes me self-conscious.

'What is the name of the firm?' he asks.

I furnish him with this detail and he laughs loudly. 'Sorry, but they went out of business a couple of months ago. You'll need to find someone else.'

'Yes, but where? It's almost high season. It promises to be a long hot summer . . . every other *société* will be fully booked.' What I refrain from mentioning is that I have paid our contracted company six months in advance; a loss of approximately £1,000.

'Jacques!' yells Alexandre towards the yard, and a tall burly fellow in his early forties, equally fit and in his prime, stacking sacks of dark earth on to a battered truck, waves and continues with his task. 'He'll clean your pool. No need to look further.'

When my shopping has been packed, I cross over to the man called Jacques and introduce myself. He, too, is robustly handsome and as tanned as a gypsy. He quotes me a price which is out of the question and then smiles, promising to drop by the farm later to check out what the job involves.

'Well, come after five, please. We have an appointment earlier.'

'He'll sort you out,' winks Alexandre, who has rested an arm on the cusp of my back.

I have the feeling I am about to be stitched up. The two men grin at one another, secure on their turf; overt male bonding in the company of a woman, and a foreign woman to boot. I thank Alexandre a touch archly and silently resolve to give Jacques the brush-off when he drops by later.

Alexandre leans in through the open car window. 'You're very pretty. What happened to your face? You certainly got walloped.' I grunt and reverse the hired vehicle at a lick, causing him to jump swiftly out of the way. He watches my departure with amusement.

I return home by the open parkland, which remains cordoned off and sadly lacking in dogs, children or games-players. I zoom up the drive to collect Michel. He is scribbling notes in the shade beneath one of the banks of cypress trees. We set off for Monte Carlo, the land of skyscrapers on the strand. Once there, passing at a distance Monaco Ville, the exalted rock upon which the Grimaldi family's palace is sited, we go in search of Michel's abandoned powder-blue Mercedes, which he claims to have parked in a tunnel beneath a flyover, close to a flight of steps. But when we arrive it is nowhere to be found. 'Are you sure that's where you left it?' I ask him. He is quietly adamant.

Either it has been stolen – highly unlikely under the scrupulous gaze of the Monégasque police force – or impounded for illegal parking. With the aid of a member of the aforementioned super-efficient law-enforcement team, we track the car down in no time. It has been impounded. A local rescue service installs a new battery. We cough up for that, and the astronomical sum requested for reclamation of the vehicle, and organise garage space at one of the hotels until I can return for it by train later in the week. Michel is still not able to drive; his vision is mildly fuzzy.

Our visit to the Princess Grace Hospital delivers us

both with heartening news. Our check-ups confirm that neither of us has suffered any permanent or long-term damage. My scan, mercifully, is clear. No stitches are to be administered to my face. 'The cut is closing up nicely by itself, we'll leave it be.'

Michel's wound is redressed – the stitches will evaporate within a few days. The injury will heal, though the doctor warns him that he will be scarred, that he is still suffering severe shock and that at all costs he must rest. 'The shock will take a while to settle. Try not to travel and avoid all stress.'

Both are tall orders for the silent, sleeping passenger at my side.

We have cleared the toll booth west of Nice and I have chosen a tranquil, scenic route through the countryside to the farm. I don't own up to it but the journey on the autoroute was nerve-racking. Every thundersome lorry or fast-moving saloon left me trembling, with the crash replaying in my psyche. Charles Aznavour is singing sotto voce on the radio. My thoughts are drifting from one place to the next, from the music to my work, which I haven't touched in days, on to the financial trouble Michel is in and how deep his shock might be – I was given no opportunity to speak privately with the doctor – when a lurking damson cloud directly in front of us, some miles distant, draws me into the present. It is a wall of smoke.

'Is that a fire up ahead?'

Michel opens his eyes.

'Any idea where it is?' I ask, selfishly concerned for our own realty.

Michel does not reply immediately and I throw a swift glance in his direction to confirm that he has heard, that my question has sunk in.

'Difficult to say,' is his eventual response.

When we arrive at the dip in our high lane, where the road curves, we come upon Jacques waiting outside the locked gates. Beyond, the dogs are jumping and barking insanely. Lucky is hurling herself at the metal like the Hound of the Baskervilles while Jacques is sanguinely studying the sky and seabirds wheel fast overhead.

I throw open the car door, hurry to unlock the gate and attach Lucky to the chain we have hitched to the trunk of one of the lower cypresses to confine her within the boundaries of our property.

'Sorry if we've kept you waiting. Keep still, Lucky!' I am wrangling with the Alsatian, who is practically rabid to get loose. Michel, I notice, has not stirred. He remains staring impassively ahead from his passenger seat.

'Let me,' offers Jacques.

'No, she's ferocious until she knows you. Watch out, she'll bite! But don't worry, when she makes friends she's as soppy as a puppy.'

This able-bodied gardener pays me no heed. He slips his fingers through the dog's collar and she sinks submissively at his feet. Jacques bends to caress her. She is putty in his hands, thumping her tail, legs apart, open-bellied with animal happiness. I am astounded and pause to take in the scene.

'She'll be fine.' He pulls on the cab door of his truck and the dog leaps in after him. They ascend the drive as a trusted twosome. I follow, drawing the gate to once the hire car is in.

'Did you see that?' I ask Michel.

'What?' he replies.

'Are you in pain?'

'I need to lie down for a bit.'

By the pool, the three dogs are playing rough and tumble with Jacques' sneakers and tugging at his jeans. He strokes them with absentminded affection, staring beyond the valley into the middle distance. 'You seen the fire?' he calls to me as I pass, running to unlock the house and escort Michel inside.

'Saw it from the road. Any idea where it is?'

'The very limit of the Var. Fifteen minutes from here. I think they caught it, but look.' He raises his arm. 'There's another started up right behind it. We've got friends who live there.'

'I'll be right back.' I am anxious to tend to Michel, who looks exceedingly pale but assures me that he is fine, waves me away and shuffles through to the bedroom.

Returning downstairs, I turn my attention to the business of the pool.

'It needs a good clean. Want me to get stuck into it right away?'

I hesitate. 'It depends on the price, Jacques. We can't pay . . .'

He revises this morning's request to a sum almost 50 per cent less if we settle in cash. I have grown so accustomed to the local black market that I rarely argue against it these days – if I did we would never achieve anything. We shake hands on the deal, settle on 'once a week' and he strolls casually over to his truck to unload pool brushes, nets and metres of blue squidgy piping.

'Do you want a beer?' I yell, as I move off towards the summer kitchen.

'No alcohol, thanks, it's too darned hot. Some water would be terrific.' He pulls off his T-shirt, revealing a taut, sinewy torso in a singlet, tugs a cap from out of the back pocket of his jeans, shoves it down over his reddening face and rubs the sweat from his forehead with the pulse of his wrist. 'Fires at this time of year! It doesn't bode well. This'll be just the beginning. We're in for a long dry spell, I'd say.'

I am sitting alone on the upper terrace, a glass of white wine growing warmish at my side, watching a crimson red sky darken to ash grey as the sun sets. Helicopters and Canadair planes have been buzzing back and forth for the last two hours. Now they have disappeared and the bats are swooping low, zipping and cornering like military jets through the embers of daylight. Dusk is everywhere; in the corners of things; in the nocturnal penumbrae that are emerging; in the silhouettes; in the eclipsing light round the pruned heads of the orange trees.

Michel is still sleeping, which is why I am upstairs and not laying the table down by the barbecue and the pool. I have thrown a couple of plates, pieces of cutlery, basic stuff, on to the small teak table up here, for when he awakes.

I cannot deny that I am worried.

His arrival is so silent, so disembodied, treading

delicate bare feet on the tiles, his arms slipping like vapour round my shoulders, that I am hardly aware of his presence. I smile warmly, a little desperately, I fear. 'Hungry?'

I knock together pasta and salad and we eat our meal facing out towards the bay. From behind the shoulder of pine trees on the curved evergreen hill in front and to the right of our property, a dandelion-head of cloud begins to unfurl, pinking, bleeding into an eerie, unnatural sky.

'Is that another fire somewhere?' I whisper.

We peer out along the horizon towards the Var. The cloud, rose-toned now, is tinged from beneath by flames. Flames that are travelling the coastline towards the west, towards Fréjus, reluming sections of the sky as they gain ground, billowing like a miniature atomic fallout.

Michel estimates that the breadth of this ferocious conflagration is somewhere between ten and twenty hectares. A wall of destruction burning westwards. We watch on, passive spectators. It is curious how when our own investment is not threatened we feel distanced, dislocated from the event, though we have known the horror of fire bearing down on us here; a roaring, ravaging brute force. The planes, the 'copters cannot fly after sundown. Only foot-soldiers are at work, the ground-force fire brigade. In the fray, barely twenty miles from our dwelling.

It is Friday, not that it really makes any difference. We have woken to a sky that is wreathed in fire clouds, sombre and ominous, hanging there as though shipwrecked. I sniff the distant land burning; charred whiffs on the wind. There is a vibe in the air, a mood along the littoral, of mourning. I am intending to return to Monte Carlo before lunch to collect the blue Mercedes and sign the necessary papers for the wreckage that was my own means of transport. I'll drive the hire car to Cannes, return it and from there take the coast train bound for Italy. Michel has expressed no interest in accompanying me.

I hurriedly shoot off a couple of urgent e-mails and run to the bedroom to collect my handbag. There, I find that Michel has laid out three neat piles of clothes: several pairs of clean socks, trousers and jeans, half a dozen short-sleeved shirts all neatly arranged on the bed. I go outside and lean over the balustrade searching for him in the pool but the pool is deserted, its water crystal clear. Jacques has done an excellent job. I hasten down the steps that adjoin one of the outer walls of the house, looking for Michel. He is nowhere to be seen. I race round to the back of the house, scanning the grounds for Quashia, who I see at work, mixing up cement, in the vicinity of his shed. I look left and right for Michel, who may be guiding him, but I cannot spot him. I run up the stone steps that lead to the wooden cabin and Michel's palm grove, behind Quashia's *chantier*, his construction site, but there's no sign of him. Back-tracking, I pause at Quashia's level and step quickly across what was grass and has now been denuded and calloused by his work to ask after my husband.

'*Bonjour*, Carol, what do you think?'

The stone Quashia has been quarrying from our

hillside to build his phenomenal wall is limestone and as porous as sponge. Centuries of lying submerged beneath our ochre-red soil has rendered it a glorious colour. As he drills, it splits quite naturally into chunks the size of small washbasins which have a luminous amber tint and, mounted, look mightily impressive. When the row of young fruit trees are in blossom, if they survive this onslaught, it should be a splendid sight. I consider a quip about the Great Wall of China and then decide to leave it.

'*Bonjour*, Monsieur Quashia – yes, it's really coming together. Have you seen Michel?'

He throws his spade to the ground, pulls out a handkerchief, wipes his brow, swabs beneath his hat and strides in his brogues to embrace me. Arms outstretched, I note that he is wearing rubber kitchen gloves: one Robin Hood green and the other livid pink. 'He was up here a while ago. He wanted to go back over the measurements and placings for the pillars before he leaves—'

'*Leaves?*' I holler, and hurry away.

'Carol, when you pass by the builders' merchants can you pick up another dozen bags of cement and twenty cartridges of ten-centimetre metal roll for the wooden beams?'

I nod, without turning back. 'Tomorrow, Monsieur Quashia. Can't today.'

I eventually find Michel in the garage, rummaging through shelves straining under the weight of old scripts and programme flyers and floor space packed with stacks of rubbish and boxes and containers and tools and machines, not to mention Quashia's gallimaufry of gizmos and rainy-day magpie-pickings. Looking for what?

'What are you doing?' I quiz, fighting to keep any nuance of accusation out of my voice.

'Searching for the leather suitcase. The sooner that wretched shed of Quashia's is finished the better. This place is worse than a jumble sale.'

The leather suitcase.

Michel and I travel so frequently we have acquired between us a veritable collection of luggage – overnight bags, computer holdalls, tote bags, weekend cases, briefcases, Gladstones, little wheely numbers for carting scripts and video cassettes without breaking our backs – but we own just the one leather case between us. It is a very capacious and rather impractical object and is dragged out only for long-haul, long-stay trips.

'Why?'

'Because I need it.' Dust is rising and settling, displaced objects are slamming to the floor, dropping around my husband, the world's tidiest man. He straightens up and looks about him, not in disgust, that is not his style, but dismay. 'We will have to do something about all this. Have you seen it?'

'It's next door, in the central-heating cave.'

'What is it doing there?' he calls as he makes his way past the open door, hanging by its last-remaining hinge, into the underground rock cave where our antediluvian heating system, which is crying out for a service, lives. Spotting the case instantly, he extracts it from beneath the sheets and mattresses that are meant to be protecting the detachable hard top of my wrecked coupé, knocking over a saucer of rat poison in the process. 'What are you going to do about this?' He points at the roof.

'I don't know. I hadn't given it a thought. Is it important? Where are you going?'

Michel carries the suitcase outside into the sun and tosses it on to the tarmac. A cloud of dust rises as he goes in search of a sponge and cleaning materials. I stand near the luggage, by the garage, dazed; dazed by events, dazed by the sun, blinded by its light – my sunglasses are in the house. I do not know what to say. This man who yesterday seemed to have been stunned into comatose silence is now chugging through the morning as though it were he who had been fitted with the new battery. And where is he going?

'Where are you going?'

'To work.'

'Work? Do you mean Paris?'

'Let's not discuss it.'

'Why not? Michel, it is only a few days since—'

'Carol, I have to go back to work and I don't want a debate about it.' And with that he picks up the empty case, carries it round to the covered walkway that skirts the pool, up the exterior stairs and into the house. I am flummoxed. And a little frightened. I decide to leave him, but I am now deliberating about my planned excursion to Monte Carlo. Perhaps I should forget it for this morning. Instead, I could nip round to the builders' merchants for Quashia and see how Michel is when I return. That is what I decide to do. I retrace my steps, following the same route

Michel has just taken to the upper part of the house but, as I am entering the front door, I spy him on the verandah leaning against the table we ate dinner at yesterday evening. Beyond him, in the lower-middle yonder, the skyline resembles a turbulent seascape with its blackening clouds and streaking fire scars.

Michel's back is to me, his head lowered. I hesitate. Should I continue on into the house or should I go to him? I choose to go to him. I approach gingerly and pause about five yards behind him, hovering there. He doesn't appear to be aware of me. His head remains bent. Is he in distress? Might the view beyond equate to the chaos in his mind?

'Michel, listen, I know there are financial difficulties, but—' That is it, that is all I manage before he pivots a 180-degree turn with a force, a missile of emotion, the like of which I have never witnessed from him before. Then he bends, lifts up a chair, an ordinary wooden garden chair, over his shoulders and hurls it. It spins and flies over the balustraded railing, falling to the terrace beneath us where it lands, splintering into pieces, sending the dogs scurrying in terror, leaving its metal frame to roll and rest in contortion.

I step back, horrified. Now I really am afraid.

In our years together, since we first met in Australia, we have fought only twice. Bickered, of course. Disagreed on many occasions. But physical outbursts are not tools or recourses of Michel's. He is a man who is never violent, never drives his negative emotions over the edge, unlike me, with my actress's sensibilities. I stare at him, longing to go to him, to hold him, to protect him and heal him, but I dare not.

Because I don't know where this is leading. I don't recognise this person here in front of me. And because I am inept.

Slowly, he sinks into one of the three remaining chairs, a worn-out man. I move in a little closer.

'I am due to attend an international television festival at the end of next week. It is an excellent opportunity, catchment, for the series I have just completed. There will be many clients in attendance. I cannot sit here and let this opportunity ride by. My company needs the sales. I must go to Paris and prepare my papers.'

'Can't someone – Isobel? – represent you?' Michel has two women working for him in Paris.

'It's not the same.'

'Where is it being held?'

'The Philippines.'

I step swiftly to the table and settle at his side, opening up the parasol as I do so, to protect us, him, from the sun. The heat is crucifying.

'I know that nothing ever stops you from what you are set on doing; certainly not me,' I tease, resting a hand on one of his, noticing how cold his fingers are. 'And I don't want to sound like a nag, but you have a head injury. The flight to Paris would be risky, air pressure and all that, but what is it, seventeen hours, to the Philippines? Please be realistic. Whatever professional difficulties you are facing, you heard what the doctor said.'

He doesn't answer.

'Michel, you are not well enough to endure such a journey. I won't let you leave. If you want to give me your address book I can send faxes to your clients or Isobel can contact them.' Still no response. 'I was planning to collect your car later. Why don't you come along and we could pop into the hospital, see what the doc—'

'I'm going to lie down.'

Quashia is calling. Michel disappears inside.

Walking round the back of the house, the protected side, I pass Lucky and Bassett. They are suspended upside down, slumped against the cream walls, clinging to the shade like expiring insects. Monsieur Q. tells me that he cannot work in this heat and that he will stop now. I nod, barely listening. 'I'll start earlier and work in the evenings but noontime is out of the question. I've never known heat like this.'

'Whatever works best for you.' I pat him on his woolly hat and we both grin. 'What are you wearing this for? It's stifling. Why don't you get yourself a boater?'

'Or a pith helmet! This one's moulded to my crown now; it fits me. How's Michel? Is he leaving?' He reads my troubled eyes.

'I hope not.' I turn my head. Below, I hear the phone ringing.

'He should rest. You both should. Zipping about like fireflies.'

'I must get that. It'll disturb him. I'll see you later.'

'Don't forget my shopping!'

By the time I reach the house Michel has answered the phone. It is the first call he has intercepted since the accident. I find him replacing the receiver.

'You could have left it, I would—'

'The answer machine was off.'

'Sorry. Who was it?'

'The olive people in Marseille. Apparently they sent a letter requesting an inspection of the trees this coming Monday.'

'Yes, I forgot to mention it. I . . . what did you say?'

'I told them to confirm it. The controller will be with us by midday.'

I take this in. Michel always deals with these matters. 'Does this mean that you . . . ?'

'I'll stay over the weekend and take care of this interview – it sounded important and we are so close to gaining our AOC status – and then I'll see how I feel on Monday afternoon. If I'm a bit stronger, I'll leave for Paris in the evening.'

I breathe a heavy sigh of relief for the few days' respite.

It is Monday, eight days since our accident. Although Michel's business trip to the Philippines has not been mentioned again, I am worrying that he might still decide to take off. I am returning from Monte Carlo with the old Mercedes. My mind on my wounded man, I have overshot our exit from the motorway. Having sailed by the turn-off for Cannes, followed by Cannes La Bocca, chugged past Fayence, I am well into the Var district before I come to my senses. In the rearview mirror, I see the outline of an imposing mulberry mountain. Even with my inaccurate sense of direction I know that what is being reflected back to me cannot be a sketch of the Alps. And then it dawns on me: yet another fire, somewhere back our way. I trundle on as fast as this old bus will manage until I find a slip road, then I swing the car, lumbersome without power steering, to the right, hugging an orbital carriageway, circling two roundabouts until eventually I negotiate my way back to the motorway, travelling now in the opposite direction.

I am growing anxious, having been absent from home for too long.

To the left I see a column of flames. They must be 15 metres high. A fire is raging on the crest of a hill. The sky overhead is red-raw as though the heavens are being roasted. Aircraft scud in from the south, crating water from the Med, poppling the vegetation, volplaning to the scene of disaster. A motorway emergency signal is flashing 'Danger!' and informing travellers that the *prochaine sortie*, the next exit, has been closed off; fires are obstructing passage.

My nerves remain unsteady. This old car doesn't have much stuffing left in it. I gird myself, push hard on the gas pedal, desperate to be home before I find myself ensnared.

As I draw close to the next exit, I see the tailback of stationary traffic. It must be 100 metres long. Folk are pressed up against their idling vehicles, hands shielding eyes blinded by light and panic, transfixed by the galloping conflagration, dragging hard on cigarettes, frantic to quit this scene, to be on their way. Are they gazing upon their own homesteads?

I press on, glancing fearfully at the charcoaling hills. The flames are drawing closer, threatening the motorway. I switch on the radio, twiddling, pressing, slapping knobs, searching for any local station, but all I receive is a high-pitched whistle. I switch it off.

Concentrate on getting home.

When I arrive at the farm, it is after midday. I am frazzled, soaked with sweat and trembling. The controller from the central olive office in Marseille has arrived. Michel has installed him at our long wooden table by the pool. I find them there, sheltered beneath the large parasol and the overhang of the *Magnolia grandiflora*.

We shake hands. Yet again I am taken aback by the figure who has been thrown up in our yard. A controller of finances working for a government body? His shoulder-length hair and the two silver earrings pierced into his left ear belie what I at first read to be a rigorous attention to detail and an obsession with figures.

'You must have driven through the fires, monsieur?'

He shakes his head in disbelief. 'Shocking, shocking. All along the route there were fire engines. On the outskirts of Marseille, I passed three caravans of them. The first had eight trucks, then another with nine and the last had six. Later, as I came closer, six kilometres, well, almost seven actually, after the slip road for traffic approaching from the A57, I spied two more convoys of ten trucks each. Forty-three fire engines in total, madame. I understand the government has called for assistance from the Pyrenées where, although the weather is warm, it is cooler. The problems are not as acute and to my knowledge there have been no incidents of arson there this year. The fire service in Toulouse is in a position to send up to as many as twenty-eight fire engines, plus manning crews which could total one hundred and eighty-seven men.' As he talks he is unpacking his briefcase on to the table, lining up four slender piles of papers. He considers these and then divides one of the piles into two and realigns all five so that they are equally spaced out in front of him. Out comes a biro, a rubber and a pencil. Then a calculator. He shuffles these to and fro, rearranging them to better suit his eye. Once more he burrows about inside his briefcase, delivering a pencil-sharpener to the game plan. Now he exhales, satisfied. '*Très bien*, shall we attack the paperwork first?'

Michel has uncorked a bottle of rosé. The barometer is reading 34 degrees centigrade. I glance quickly at Monsieur, certain that here is a man who will not look kindly on the imbibing of alcohol during business meetings, particularly out of doors in the heat. I intervene swiftly. 'I think monsieur might prefer water, *n'est-ce pas?*' After all, this fellow has a two-hour drive back to Marseille. Without waiting for his response I scuttle off to the summer kitchen and return armed with a choice of chilled and ambient-temperature bottles of San Pellegrino and Badoit. 'Or would you like still water? Perhaps you take ice? Or lemon squash instead?'

Our accounts controller glances at the various mineral waters on offer in my arms, then studies the glasses laid out before him on the table. Three wine glasses and three tumblers. He thrums his fingers against his papers and then thoughtfully moves his tumbler slightly to the left of him, drawing his wine goblet closer.

'Erm, yes a little water, of course, but I'll have a glass of rosé as well. Why not? Your husband has gone to the trouble of opening it.'

'Will you join us, *chérie?*' asks Michel.

I shake my head. 'Not unless you need me.' I am still a little churned up by my journey and am keen to get inside out of the sun.

'Madame, before you leave us, I will require you to sign each set of these forms, if that is not too much trouble.'

'Of course not.' I sit down and pour myself and both men glasses of water.

Monsieur sips his drink and turns his attention to Michel. 'Shall we begin with the paperwork, get that out of the way and then we can pass along to the business of the trees. Will you not accompany me in a soupçon of rosé, monsieur?'

Michel pours himself three-quarters of a glass. I shoot him a glance. I have no idea what if any of the tranquillisers or painkillers he has swallowed today. I take comfort in the fact that the answer is probably none, given Michel's aversion to medicines. I am still not quite sure what the purpose of this meeting is and I wonder if Michel, during my absence, has managed to find out. Dare I ask?

Monsieur, who has already downed his glass of rosé, lifts his pen and begins with the first set of forms. 'Name?'

Michel patiently repeats our names. For a reason that I can no longer remember we are registered with the olive bodies under our two individual names, not under the umbrella of the married one, and this seems to bother the controller.

'This is regrettable, monsieur; it could entail another set of forms,' he concludes fretfully. Michel raises the bottle and positions it over Monsieur's glass. 'Yes, thank you, I don't mind if I do. Two surnames, not one . . .'

The hitch involving two names is then dealt with in a jiffy and we move on, but I cannot help feeling that the questions he is posing are ground that has been trodden and retrodden on numerous occasions in the past. Michel looks exhausted. I find myself losing patience as this fellow downs yet another glass of rosé and painstakingly fills out in spidery little writing line after line of tedious data.

'Now, how many parcels of land do you own in total? And how many of these parcels have olive trees growing on them? And how many parcels had olive trees growing on them when you purchased the farm? And how many of these parcels of land do not have olive trees? And how many parcels not yet exploited do you intend at some point in the future to exploit for *oléiculture*? How many of the trees have been planted within the last five years?'

I see Michel's eyes glaze over. His face is ashen. He looks as though he might collapse from his seat and crash to the ground. Lucky, who has been chained up for the best part of an hour over by the garage, is yapping dementedly.

'Monsieur, sorry if I am . . . erm, I haven't quite understood what precisely is the point of this meeting?' I brave.

Le Monsieur lifts his head, drains his glass, leaving it available for a top-up, and replies. 'Olive trees.'

'Yes, but what about them?' I press.

Michel empties the remainder of the bottle into Monsieur's glass. Monsieur is beginning to look as shiny and florid as a scoop of raspberry ice cream. A Canadair plane zooms across the rooftop. We all raise our heads. A fire in the vicinity. They are drawing closer.

'I am here to count the trees.'

'You are here to count our olive trees?' I repeat.

He nods.

'You have driven from Marseille, a two-hour drive . . .'

'One hour forty-five minutes,' he counters.

'. . . to count our olive trees. We have two hundred and seventy.'

'That is the figure that has been declared, madame, but it is my job to verify it. A false declaration could lead to . . . You'd be surprised just how frequently there are errors.' He suppresses a hiccup and swiftly reaches for his tumbler of water.

My patience is fast declining. It is past one o'clock – lunchtime; I have an injured and worried husband; the sun is at its zenith; the heat is torrid, deathly still yet buzzing; the cicadas are screeching like overwrought children; Lucky is going nuts, and now Bassett has joined the chorus.

'Well, let's count them, and—' Upstairs the phone begins to ring. I rise. 'We have declared two hundred and seventy trees. In fact, because the gardener and myself have stuck a few striplings in the ground, scions, shoots from old trees that we are experimenting with as transplants, there are in total two hundred and seventy-five *oliviers* on our land. We decided, though, that the scions were too insignificant to include. I hope that does not count as a false declaration.'

The man stares at me from across the table. He looks a little the worse for wine.

'Have you lunched, monsieur?' He shakes his head blearily. 'Why don't I prepare a snack for you and my husband while you wander off and count the trees?'

Michel stands up beside me. His movement is slow, weary. He touches his head. 'I'll lend you a hand, *chérie*.'

'Apologies, sir, but I'll need you to accompany me,' declares Monsieur to Michel. 'In that case, I will accompany you and my husband can make us all a sandwich.' I insist, growing concerned for Michel, who I fear should be lying down, not traipsing about the garden in this temperature counting trees.

'Monsieur is the principal signatory on the declaration forms. It would make life very much simpler if he accompanies me.'

I am on the point of arguing but I can see that Michel does not wish me to. Our visitor continues, 'Madame, if you accompany me and if there were a discrepancy in the figures, we would need to go through the entire process again, from the beginning, with Monsieur.'

'Why would there be a discrepancy? There are two hundred and seventy trees!' I am at my wits' end. The phone has started up again. I am beginning to understand why Michel insists that he handles the bureaucracy. I smile tightly and assure them that I will be back to add my signature when the trees have been counted and the forms filled in. The men disappear off along the terrace towards the farthest of the olive groves. I clear away the empty wine bottle and hurry inside.

It is three o'clock. The plates of nibbles I have laid out are beginning to dry and curl. I carry them in from the wooden table and leave them in the cool, shuttered light of the summer kitchen. I cannot think where the men have got to. I have been up behind the house twice already, calling to them, but there has been no reply. Now I am concerned. Not least because when I brought down the plates of food I found a cork and the dregs of a second bottle of rosé. I call again. Still no response. Might an incident have occurred? Eventually I see them, hiking towards me from the farthest extremes of the estate, close to the wilderness area, the *garrigue*, owned by the Hunter on the Hill. Both men look shiny with exhaustion. I hurry to greet Michel. 'Are you all right?' He nods, puffing as he climbs.

The other fellow, whose hair is sticking up in wispy clumps, looks as though he has been living like a savage in one of the neighbour's hideouts. He is tomato-red, his eyes are bloodshot and he is panting like a dog. 'Not good news,' is his opening gambit.

'Why not? Is everything all right?' My attention is on Michel. Might something have happened to him? 'How's your head?' I ask in English. His dressing has come unstuck in the sweltering heat, where he has been perspiring. 'Why don't you lie down? I'll handle this.'

'Unfortunately, madame, the news is very bad. I am afraid that you and your farm are no longer eligible for the ticketing which would allow you to put your produce forward for AOC consideration.'

'Why not?' I bark.

'You lack the requisite number of trees. The minimum for eligibility is two hundred and fifty, and—'

'We know that!'

He lowers his eyes, painstakingly. 'And you possess two hundred and forty-nine trees, hence you are one tree short of eligibility.'

I stare at the man open-mouthed and then turn to Michel. 'How much wine have you both drunk? Or, more to the point, how much has he consumed?' I am speaking in English again.

'The fact of the matter is that you have submitted a false declaration, which is a very grave affair. These matters go all the way to Brussels. It is my unfortunate duty to cross your farm off our lists. You cannot be granted AOC status.' He hands me our land plans, now creased and wilting from the blistering noontide. I take them from him, racking my brains to save the day.

'Quashia's plot! I bet you haven't included the tree in the cottage garden?' I cry like a madwoman. 'Look, see, here, this small parcel of land across the lane where our gardener lives. One tree! You can stop your car on your way out and count it. *One!*' Monsieur glances at Michel and peers over at the plan, where I am rapping my finger.

'Er, no, we didn't think of that one.'

'That makes up our quota of two hundred and fifty for starters! Now, how about the four reclaimed trees at the summit of the hill? The very last of the land to have been cleared. Just above the highest of the recently planted saplings. Did you count those?'

The accountant is now looking sheepish and very rocky on his feet. 'Erm, *non*.' 'Two hundred and fifty-four! We're getting somewhere! I am surprised our total wasn't two hundred and seventy times two!'

'Sorry?'

'Seeing double, sir! At least then your vision would have gone in our favour.'

'*Chérie* . . .' Michel warns me cautiously.

An aircraft sweeps in from the coast and disappears into the elevated woodlands. 'When we bought the property it was registered, *cadastré*, as possessing sixty-four olive trees. Many of your colleagues have visited here and inspected those trees, which have stood on this hillside for centuries. I mistakenly stuck in six of the *tanche* variety. Then we purchased, from one of your registered nurseries, another two hundred youngsters. Those trees have also been inspected and a copy of the receipt of purchase was filed with the plantation office in Marseille. Need I continue? Would you like your sandwich now, or would you prefer another glass of wine?'

'*Chérie*, Monsieur here is responsible for the inspection of the quantities of oil we produce. He will be dropping by to see us on an annual basis. I think it would be wise if . . .'

'I tell you what,' says Monsieur with exerted bonhomie, sweat dripping in runnels down his face. 'Let's pop over there out of the sun and we'll get the papers signed. I'll register the figure as two hundred and sixty-four – the originals plus the newly purchased saplings. The rest I'll mark down as a miscalculation.'

'*Miscalculation*? No!'

'Please, don't worry. I'll count them all again next time I'm here and I'll add the others to your list then.'

Another aircraft stripes the heavens and our treetops shiver. Could this be the first sign of an approaching mistral? Fanned by searing winds in the Var the fires would bolt in this direction.

Exhausted, stressed, I am like a dog with a bone. 'There are two hundred and seventy trees declared because that is the number we possess, aside from the weeny transplants. Why can you not register the accurate figure?'

'To do so would involve beginning again, madame. I would need to recount all of them this afternoon,' he answers. 'I don't want to be driving in this . . .' his eyes lift skywards. 'I need to get back to Marseille.'

And so the forms are adjusted and I grit my teeth as I add my signature alongside Michel's to a figure that is short of the aggregate on our working plantation. I wonder if this oddball controller of numbers ever stops to ask himself why he so frequently discovers errors. But I hold my tongue as he gobbles down his sandwich, bids us a good afternoon and sets off triumphantly, if mildly hung over, for Marseille, the oldest (or could it be the second-oldest?) of all French cities. No doubt he'll be miscounting the fire engines along the way.

Together, Separately

It is the *estivale* season; full-blown summer. The coast is clogged, fraught with traffic and trippers; late-night jazz and blues bands are jamming in sultry gardens while the drug-inducing beat of techno booms from discos and clubs all along the beachfronts and up into the arid hills. Diurnal city folk turned holidaymakers are metamorphosed into barflies and nocturnal swingers: partying, boozing, boogying the nights away: *les nuits estivales*.

Stifling hot nights. Sleepless nights of nakedness and sticky heat.

Monsieur Q. begins his work at five in the morning and packs up at half-past ten to avoid the sun's worst. I am awoken by his machines coughing into life and I climb out of bed to make us all coffee. He returns at four and continues on till seven, when we begin the hosepipe rounds. The rhythm of our days is governed by his hours and he is governed by the climate. The only blessing of these sun-baked, drought-threatening conditions is that the mosquitos are staying away. We are not troubled by the buzz and itch and sting of them during the endlessly long evenings; evenings with sunsets that bleed like broken eggs and spilled jam across the skyline. We sit out in shorts or sarongs, eating our late-night meals, side by side on terraces illumined by oil lamps, sharing the mundane but treasurable rituals of married life; insignificant details, except that I cling fast to them because Michel has gone away in his mind, moved elsewhere.

During the weeks since the accident, weeks of brain-pulping heat, he has been sitting in corners, beneath trees, seeking out the garden's purply shade. He gazes about him or stares, frowning, at the ground, his body slightly bent. What is in his thoughts, I crave to know. I have never seen him so inactive. This stillness, this profound reflection, unsettles me. He is growing ever-more distant, silent and self-protective. I am losing him.

From overhead terraces, a wordless, worried observer, I watch him. Every now and again when he lifts his eyes in my direction, I smile encouragingly. He nods in response, in a vague sort of way, as though I have not totally penetrated his consciousness. He is housed within silence. He collects pine cones, turns them over and over in the palms of his hands, contemplating them. Twigs, small branches, leaf formations; lays them out on the walls and chairs. He stares into trees, apparently studying their history, their forms, colours, their tree-ness.

I approach the Italian cypresses where, head craning skywards, he squints into the bright light of morning.

'How about this?' I offer, gesturing towards the elevation of slender evergreens, 'in Iranian mythology, the cypress was the vegetal representation of fire, of flame, and reminded man of the paradise he had lost.' Michel glares at me as though I am mad and I retreat to my den, leaving him in peace, to listen to the fire engines hee-hawing their way along the coast, closing my eyes in prayer, knowing that they are hurtling towards yet another act of arson. Provence's natural heritage is being threatened. Under fire. Paradise lost. To date, some 6,000 hectares have been burned.

For want of distraction and because I know that the sum earned on my last contract is our only income, I galvanise myself into work, attacking my script adaptation with souped-up energy, and when I am worn out I peruse my Provençal dictionaries and local studies – they are a real tonic to me. I become hooked on media reportage. Watching the news one evening on TF1, France's main television network, I learn of the first casualties in the fires. Fires that are still burning, in which many have lost their homes. Tourists and locals alike are being evacuated as campsites capsize beneath the destruction. Film crews in low-flying planes and helicopters record the charred plains, blackened forests and gutted habitations. One lone piglet, a month-old *sanglier*, is seen pounding through a desert of ravaged trees and sooted earth. The creature spins about in terror – it has lost its sounder, been deprived of its neck of the woods – then scampers for its life. A sole survivor, ignorant of its role on the national stage as a poignant image of a timeless landscape reduced to featurelessness.

Walking to the pool the following morning, passing Michel's old blue bus, I find it covered in a confetti of mauve-grey ash. Quashia mentions the news programme, delighted that the wild boars who frequent our grounds have gone into hiding. 'Or been destroyed in fires,' I add. The piglet had appeared so vulnerable, so unrelated to the beasts that rampage our land.

He asks if I want the car washed. I shake my head. Best to conserve the water. Not that we have a shortage, but who knows if these bone-dry conditions will endure? The latest development in the saga of my own smashed-up machine is that the insurance company have instructed its repair. It is not a write-off, they decree, but the works to make good will take several months. For the time being Michel is still not back at the wheel and my only excursions beyond the gates are for life's necessities and trips to the local village to pick up the daily newspaper, *Le Monde*, so I make do with the transport we have. My concerns lie elsewhere.

As July pushes forward we shift to a more southern European tempo, adopting Spanish habits: long siestas throughout the afternoons, dining towards midnight. Even the dogs won't take a bite until darkness descends and the heat has diminished. They pass the days like mummies, slumped in corners of the terraces or slinking from shaded wall to shaded wall. The phone rings rarely; folk have accepted that Michel requires solitude.

Fires are burning across the Var and now the countryside around the lovely old *village perché* of Eze towards the Italian border is also alight. Clouds shot through with red zig-zags, warning of the destruction raging elsewhere, converge in the sky from two directions at once. Gazing out to sea from the terraces, the Mediterranean has a sludge-brown, oily sheen to it. So far, thank God, our little pocket inland of the coast remains fire-free. Our olive trees are not yet at risk and, for the present, we are safe, but any security I feel has no more substance than the moths and flying insects that appear at sunset.

While Michel recuperates, Quashia and I do our best to keep the land irrigated. My days are about the back-breaking heat, about keeping at bay the desiccating power of the sun and about my husband's convalescence.

One morning, before breakfast, I am watering the junior olive grove adjacent to the orchard, where a few drupes are slowly fattening, speculating upon whether, given Michel's health, this year's scarcity might not be a blessing in disguise, aside from its effect on our AOC status, when I catch sight of him lower down the land, rummaging about in the rose garden. At first I assume he is weeding, rooting with the trowel, but then I see him retrieve a tiny object from the earth and slip it into the pocket of his shorts. I call to him but he does not hear me. Lucky is trailing after him, back and forth; a loping loyal shadow, and when Michel pauses for a moment, she drops contentedly at his feet. I release the hosepipe in my hand and watch the pair of them. The Alsatian, whose sleek coat gleams in the early-day sunlight, transformed from the battered creature we took in, her black hair tipped with grey now, cuts a fine figure; she is stronger, healthier, more alert than her abused, adolescent self. She is at peace here. But what of Michel? The incision, the wound, the mirror's stab will heal. It will leave a scar but Michel will not be disfigured. It's *him*, the man, I worry for. I barely know him. I haven't understood what is driving him so far away, and I am struggling to find a handle to guide or partner him through the forest in his mind.

A little while later, after my morning swim, while

our coffee is brewing and Michel is showering, I empty the pool-skimmers. There, in the basket, lies a praying mantis, lifeless amongst the swirl of trapped petals and leaves. I scoop him out and lay him on the tiles. Michel, with coffee pot, comes to look. On our knees by the poolside, we investigate him. His brilliant-green, stiff spindly body against the mauve bougainvillaea petals is arresting. Michel cradles him in his palm and studies him. Upstairs on the seaview terrace, I find another, a living one, crawling along the balustrade. Because I am a little uncertain about whether or not the insect will bite or sting if I handle him, I lift off my shoe, encourage him on to it and then, with one foot bare, hobble to Michel, who is sitting downstairs at the long wooden table arranging a collection of seashells into patterns.

'Where did those come from?' I am slipping the insect off my shoe. It prances on to the table and freezes. The shells are from an island in one of the Fijian archipelagos. We collected them from a beach there, Sunset Beach, before we were married. When we returned to Europe we spread them out on a wall in the garden; the winds and rains have since driven them into the flowerbed where they have lain buried until this morning when Michel retrieved and washed them.

'I shall do something with them.'

'It'll be fun to use them. What will you do?'

'Not sure yet.'

'I had forgotten about them. Look, here's a living mantis. The partner, perhaps, of the drowned one.' The entire length of the insect's twig-like body has begun vibrating. He is alert to us, his forward-facing eyes transfixed by us, weighing up the danger factor. 'His eyes look magnified, don't they, like a pair of binoculars?' I murmur. And while the mantis takes stock of us, I observe Michel's interest, his rapt attention. 'See how green he is,' he says. 'Green as lime soda.'

Later in the day, while I am on a shopping expedition in Mougins, hurtling from one errand to the next, queuing to park, charging into shops, paying bills, ordering building materials, anxious to complete the tasks and hurry home, my head begins to swim. My cut eye is throbbing and I am dizzy with heat. Instead of dashing back, I decide to pause awhile and drink a *citron pressé* at one of the cafés in the heart of the old village. Here, beneath the shade of a full-leafed plane tree, I settle with my dog-eared notebook to watch the world go by and chill out by the gently babbling fountain. Here, where the local town hall is housed in an ancient chapel that once gave refuge to the Order of the White Penitents, I remind myself how long it has been since I have visited this pretty *place*, and since I have nothing in particular to do, on a whim I decide to pop into the Musée de la Photographie.

The gallery of the photography museum is deserted. Grateful for the hushed stone rooms, I drift from space to space, peering at black and white aerial pictures taken of this renowned canton at the turn of the last century, back when they were building our villa, wending my way up winding stone staircases, ignoring the rather splendid collection of antique cameras – might those interest Michel? – searching out photographs in the permanent exhibition: Picasso and his life on the Côte d'Azur as seen through the eyes of several highly esteemed twentieth-century photographers. Much of Picasso's life was a love affair with Mougins. He first came here with his dark-haired Dora Maar and, after many years of living and painting in a number of neighbouring locations around the coast, died nearby in a house that he and his last partner, Jacqueline Roque, shared together. When we bought our farm, before we planted our young olive trees and when I had more time on my hands, I used to while away hours in the Château Grimaldi in Viel Antibes. At the end of the Second World War, when Pablo was living in the holiday resort of Golfe-Juan with Françoise Gilot, he occupied a section of that spectacularly sited castle as his *atelier*. Today, it is the old town's Musée Picasso.

I find the permanent collection on the top floor and drift from photo to photo, gazing hard into the artist's life – solitary moments, others in the company of friends and lovers – as if I might find the answer to a question I haven't even formulated, until I find myself standing in front of a portrait, signed by Robert Doisneau, one I have never seen before. Its subject, of course, is the painter. Eyes blazing, direct to the camera, he is playfully displaying a praying mantis perched on his fingertips.

My thoughts inevitably settle on Michel, on how I might awaken in him a passage to health, recalling his response to the insects this morning. Might his affinity with colour and form be his lifeline? I hurry off home with my bags of shopping, feeling upbeat and encouraged.

It begins with a single wing; a strikingly marked, brilliantly coloured butterfly wing that I almost disintegrate underfoot in my den. It is the size of two of my fingernails and distinctly triangular in shape. I pick it up and look at it through my magnifying glass. Oranges, browns, white, a fine strip of red; each colour outlined in black, like eyes decorated with kohl; almost arabesque in the intricacy of its design. I place the fragile appendage on my desk and look it up in one of my books of Med Wildlife but, unable to trace it, I give up and deliver it directly to Michel, who is reading in a chair in the garden. Or rather, not reading. He has a script open on his lap but he is dozing, eyes narrowed, then wide awake, staring into the middle distance. I drop down on to my haunches at the deckchair's edge.

'How are you feeling?' I whisper.

He turns his head towards me as though he has never seen me before, furrowing his brow. 'Fine.'

'Look what I found.'

He takes the bodiless matter and presses it like an exotic stamp into the palm of his left hand. I watch him hard as he scrutinises it. 'Can I hold on to this or do you want it back?'

'No, I brought it for you. It's beautiful, *non*? I wonder what happened to the butterfly, though. She couldn't fly, could she, so disabled?'

'So disabled,' he repeats distantly. He shakes his head and I leave him alone with our find.

Before evening falls, while I am in the vegetable garden gathering courgettes for our supper, the telephone bell interrupts my dusty work. Keen to reach it before it disturbs Michel – the portable handset doesn't work this far from the house – I drop my basket, struggle out through a web of olive netting Quashia has suspended over the caned framework to protect the lettuces from rabbits, muttering that we must organise ourselves a less convoluted barrier, and charge to the phone.

The monsieur asking to speak to me is a complete stranger. He has been given our name by the bee-keeper who was to have become our beemaster. Quite some time back, he and we had struck a deal whereby he would winter a dozen hives on our land and in return we would receive a very modest share of the honey gathered. Alas, due to the unexpected poor health of his wife, he was unable to honour the arrangement. Although the distance from his apiary to our farm was a mere forty kilometres, in his troubled eyes our property had grown too remote; the travelling would have involved time he needed to allocate to his spouse's failing condition. At that stage, after almost a year of hunting for a suitable candidate, we decided to relinquish the dream of beehives on our land. So this present caller takes me quite by surprise.

'But it has been an age, monsieur,' I cry, 'since we heard from your colleague! I thought he had forgotten us.'

'Ah, we *apiculteurs* are always so busy with our bees. *Desolé.*' His voice is high-pitched yet soft.

'It doesn't matter at all. My husband and I would be delighted to house your hives here.'

'Madame, we will need to inspect your grounds

first, and decide whether they are suitable for our little girls.'

'Yes, of course, excuse me. Please come and scout about all you want.'

We arrange a rendezvous for a Sunday towards the end of July. He will be motoring down from high in the Alps, where he and his wife are building a chalet, and so cannot be precise about his time of arrival. 'It's tricky to organise anything when there are so many tourists about,' he sighs. 'Fortunately, we won't be transporting the bees.'

When I express my concern that his village is a long distance from us he assures me that he traverses north to south and east to west of the Alpes-Maritimes in search of the ideal *placements* for his bees. 'In summer, I like them within range of the best lavender sites. So, see you in two weeks, then.'

'I didn't catch your name, monsieur.' I reach for my pen and open up my diary.

'Mr Huilier,' he says.

'Excuse me?' I feel certain I must have misheard.

'Mr Huilier,' he repeats.

'Are you joking?'

'Joking?' He sounds affronted. 'Madame, that is my name as well as that of my *chère* wife.'

I fear I have put my foot in it and damaged our oh-so-slim beekeeping opportunities.

'Well, Monsieur Huilier,' I rush on breathlessly, 'We look forward to meeting you. It's been a pleasure. Please telephone us when you reach the motorway exit and my husband' – I throw a glance in Michel's direction but he is not paying attention – 'and we'll give you directions. The farm's not easy to find, but don't worry, if necessary, I'll come and meet you.'

He seems reassured and we hang up.

Monsieur Huilier translates as Mr Oilcan or, possibly Mr Oil and Vinegar Cruet or Mr Oil Manufacturer or Mr Oil Dealer.

'That was a call from Mr Oilcan, the beekeeper,' I shout to Michel, still wondering if this is a hoax. 'Perhaps we will have bees after all.'

Almost as soon as I replace the receiver the phone rings again. It is feedback from Guillaume Laplaige.

'I have been expecting to hear from you,' his raspy voice accuses. The truth is I had temporarily dismissed the vineyard, lost his phone number, misplaced the magazine. It is somewhere, but what with one thing and another . . . I apologise profusely.

'I am five minutes from your holding and thought I'd drop by.'

I dither, considering the intrusion.

'I have identified your vines.'

'We are a little tucked away, and my husband—'

'I'll find you.' The phone goes down and within a quarter of an hour, a royal blue car comes flying up the drive. A lovely old Peugeot in mint condition. I am no specialist but it must date from the 1950s.

Mr Laplaige, the wine-variety expert, hauls himself out. Bent as a question-mark, he shuffles across the *parking* supported by a gnarled cherrywood cane, smiling broadly between pixie ears, greeting me with his thick, scratchy accent.

'Splendid car, monsieur.'

'Old cars are my weakness. You might want a few

chickens before I leave,' is his opening gambit, followed by a request for a glass of port as a petit *apéro*.
He wears a tomato-red checked shirt with sleeves
rolled to the upper arms and blue dungaree pants, the
quintessential uniform of the French land worker,
with olive-green braces bearing embroidered hunting
motifs: rabbits, hares, eagles in flight. There are green
Wellingtons on his feet and a navy beret sits flat
atop his crown. He is eighty-one years old, he informs
Michel proudly, and works his vineyard, his *domaine*,
single-handed. He has never married. In earlier days
he ran the place with his brother, who is dead now.
His fingernails are ridged and tobacco-stained; they
remind me of miniature tortoiseshells. He downs his
port in one and then suggests we 'get on with it'
because he has a long journey home. We cross the
land slowly in the shadowing light to the stone ruin at
the extremity of our estate. He talks as he walks, aided
by his cherry walking stick.

'I am fairly certain that the vineyard on this terrain
was established in the 1930s, could be the forties, but I
doubt it, what with the war and the restrictions during
that period. Pre-war is my verdict. The fact of the
matter is that what you have here, well, the *pieds*,
the vine plants, could never be used for wine-making
now. They are far too old.' He bends to finger several
of the stalks.

'But we could use the same variety of stock,
couldn't we? If it produced excellent wine?'

'Please let me finish, madame. I was about to say
that what has been produced on your estate was
rubbish.'

'Rubbish? But the quality of the olive trees . . .'

'It bears no relation. My guess is that it was drinking wine.'

This confuses me.

'These days wine production has become something of an art. In the last century, when your vineyard was established, many landowners planted to produce anything that was vaguely *buvable*, drinkable. I suspect that it was doled out to the land labourers to quench their thirst and to accompany the meals supplied to them by the *patron*. In fact, the varieties of vines you posted to me are rarely if ever used today. I would have a job tracking them down. However, I can supply you with first-class stock that would produce wine suited to this district and that you would be very proud of.'

'I see.' A little disappointed, I thank him for his trouble. He refuses any form of payment and I assure him that when we are ready to plough and plant these parcels of land we will be back in touch.

'It's a good location, the soil is fine; you'd do well here with a hearty grenache.'

Returning to his car, he pauses to shake hands with Michel on the grand terrace that leads from the original flight of stone steps.

'That's a mighty fine ascent,' he remarks.

'Yes,' agrees Michel, 'we discovered that stairway when we first cleared the grounds.'

'They rarely construct them like that any more. You know, you could return it to its former glory by mounting a climbing iron pergola and planting it up with vines. Full southerly sun, excellent exposure. I know someone, Pascal Pear, you won't find a finer blacksmith in the whole of France. I'll tell him to get in touch.'

I escort our wine expert back to his snazzy blue automobile, after one more swift port for the road, giggling to myself. We have found a beekeeper called Oilcan and now it's pear-shaped ironmongery. Before settling in the driving seat, Mr Laplaige indicates the rear, which is packed with straw and, on closer observation, a battery of half-a-dozen, exquisitely marked red and turquoise chickens brooding atop the stacks.

'Rare birds,' he declares. 'Excellent layers. I can leave a couple with you for a very fair price.'

I am relieved that Monsieur Q. is not about because he is regularly requesting the addition of chickens to the estate, but with our hounds it would be a catastrophe.

'I have dogs and a hunter amongst them. Otherwise, we would love some.'

Laplaige shrugs. 'Wine, chickens, olive oil and cars, what more can life offer? Think about the *pieds* for the late autumn or spring. I can supply two thousand at a fortnight's notice.' He shakes my hand with the force of a soldier, bids me *au revoir* and steams off down the drive, exhaust roaring.

Twilight falls.

I take a lone stroll back to the stone ruin where the 'rubbish of a vineyard' was once in propagation and land labourers drank thirstily of plonk.

One exterior wall, a surprisingly well-preserved *tommette*-tiled floor, a fireplace with chimney plus two outhouses are all that remains of this dwelling. Wild vines are shooting all along its foreground terraces. I wonder what will become of our plans to restore the vineyard now.

Michel and I believe that this ruin was, once upon a time, a cottage or croft, a *cabano* in Provençal, occupied by the estate's gardener or, more specifically, vine-tender: a vine-worker's bothy. What remains of this stone residence today, without door or windows, is on two levels and, from the upper storey, boasts stupendous views. Framed by towering pines and our Methuselah of a Judas, the vista sweeps all the way down into the valley, beyond our pool, to the sea. The habitation has long since lost its roof, though we frequently unearth its broken tiles buried around the grounds. When I stand within it, I occasionally reflect upon its occupant, about his history and lifestyle. Would he have had a wife or been a solitary vine-keeper? The open fire would have served as a stove, heating capacious iron pots bubbling over with steaming soup or a delicious *pot-au-feu* awaiting him at suppertime.

Abutting the living quarters are the rubbled husks of two outhouses. To what use would they have been put? Beasts' sleeping quarters or inclement weather shelters, most likely. The last time Michel and I stood up here on this site together we pondered what livestock was kept on this farm and what occupied these crude stone sheds. We dismissed goats, though they are common in this area and have been for centuries, because their habit is to range freely and eat everything in sight, which would have destroyed the vineyard and damaged the olive groves. In the olden days olive leaves were occasionally doled out as winter fodder for sheep and goats. Dogs would not have been given separate sleeping quarters. All horses on the estate would have been lodged in the stables alongside the main house. This stony hillside is so unsuited to the rearing of equine species that we were surprised anyone would have entertained the idea, but there are stables – Madame B. bought the place as a birthday present for one of her daughters who was passionate about riding – and in earlier times, when motor-powered carriages were new-fangled machines, horses were the principal means of transport. So, what else, chicken coops? 'Possibly, but I believe at least one of them stabled a donkey,' Michel had argued.

A donkey, yes, to transport materials and the annual harvests up and down these slippery, tortuous slopes.

'Perhaps we should get a donkey,' I joked.

'*Chérie*, you refuse to entertain the idea of a goat because you say, quite accurately, that it will eat everything in sight. Believe me, a donkey will be worse.'

'But we have no means of bearing heavy equipment up to the crown of the hill and when the small trees are ready for picking . . .'

'We'll find a solution, Carol, but no donkey.'

I smile now at the memory of this light-hearted exchange. And sigh.

We have given so much of our energy and limited resources to the renovation of the Appassionata farmhouse, to the restoration of the ancient groves, to the afforestation of terraces that were lacking *oliviers* and to production of our golden oil that we have never really taken time to discover how the rest of the farm operated, how its inhabitants lived and what else we could create on this agricultural canvas.

Michel and I have dreamed that, one day, we will erect in place of this ruin, but built out of its spirit, a space that could be used as a library or workshop, whichever need was greatest. Standing here now in the dappled shade of an overhanging fig tree, self-seeded in what would have been the sleeping quarters of the bothy, watching the sun set beyond the hills, I ask myself what it is going to take to assist Michel's recovery, aside from time. So far he has expressed little interest in the prospect of beehives arriving; his office in Paris telephones on a daily basis but the calls serve only to deepen his gloom, if gloom is what I am observing. So what else can I promote? He has always enjoyed a lively interest in architecture, he loves the business of design, the overall structure of buildings, and I have been observing flickers of fascination in response to arrangements of objects and their shapes and colours. Would a major project such as this give him a goal? When it was finished, it could become his work base. He could transport his editing suite from Paris and complete his programmes at home. He would be safe here; he could take all the time he needs to heal. I would care for him. Yes, the reclamation of this cottage should become our priority. I determine to find a way to finance it.

Every day it grows hotter. And hotter. And there are increasing incidents of fire. The wind is turning in this direction. I see it on the sea, white horses scuffing the waves, frissons in the upper reaches of the trees. Fanned by the mistral whistling down the Rhône valley, the fires rage and spread. But miraculously they are still keeping their distance. Choppers beat through the heat. The sky is a traffic jam of activity. Clouds like silent peach-toned explosions curtain the horizon. In spite of their opaque menace, in a detached way I find them lovely; a ballet-without-music, a caravan in passage across the heavens; graceful, soundless and ominous.

Jacques, thick-bodied, muscular, taciturn, cleans the pool in his leisurely manner and watches the sky. He reminds me of a shipwrecked mariner waiting for rescue. He can pinpoint exactly where the conflagration is centred. He tells us they all start with arson. Every year, without exception, in the dry summer months, tiny bands of pyromaniacs descend upon the coast with the express purpose of setting light to the vegetation. They wait for the winds, ignite a match and watch the forests combust, seeking a thrill beyond our comprehension. 'Less than two per cent of the eruptions here are accidents or caused by negligence,' he says. Last week, 30,000 hectares of coastal forest and heathland were burned to ashes. Homes are being evacuated.

The hawking roar, the guttural bray of rushing fire engines and the persistent refrain of the Canadair planes are beginning to blur into an unbroken, unbearable Muzak while inquietude and rising-decibel panic are fast becoming the most-played phrases of summer. The air gives off an aroma which is repugnant. Cinders fall from the metallic sky like autumn leaves. They lace the pool's surface and catch in the corners of the balustraded terraces. Cinders of what? Carbonised life and nature.

It is four months since it has rained, and almost as many days since Michel has uttered more than a sentence. A ghost of his former self, he behaves as though stunned, perplexed, puzzled, as though he quite literally does not know what has hit him. The growing collection of objects he was squirreling together – our butterfly wing, various curiously shaped cuts of wood, a rusted lock he found when I took him up to talk about the reconstruction of the ruin, shards of painted terracotta tiles, broken casseroles – has been cast aside. Lacklustre odds and sods they have become, discarded in the bone-dry grass, offering no further inspiration. I find the shells back amongst the flowers. I am dismayed; I had begun to believe, to hope that here lay a path forward for him, an ingress back to his creative self.

Now he has retreated into figures, scribbling long sums in teeny notepads, and he wears a worried expression. I make a discreet call to the specialist at the Princess Grace Hospital. I trot out my concerns and he listens patiently. 'Should I bring him to you?' I beg.

The doctor assures me that Michel's condition is quite in order given the force of the impact.

'Do you think a project might assist him? I was thinking of rebuilding—'

'He needs rest and your patient support.'

'Professionally, he's under financial stress but he's not talking about it.'

'Give him time and all will be well again. He will be back to his old self.'

Can we return to our former selves, I wonder, replacing the receiver, after crisis or trauma? I am not sure.

We wake to air suffused with the smell of charred land. But now the sky is silent. Too silent. Eerily so. I am going to Nice, to an art shop in one of the narrow back streets of the old town. On my way out of the door, Michel halts me. 'I shall be leaving after the weekend,' he announces calmly.

I wait.

'I must get back to Paris.'

'But it'll soon be August,' I counter. 'The capital will be empty. You might as well stay for the holiday season and return in September when France goes back to work.'

'I shall spend August in Paris. I have contracts to catch up on.'

'Why not fly up, collect the files you need and bring them back? Or I could go for you. Run your business from here. I won't disturb you.'

'I shan't be coming back, Carol.'

I stand by the half-open door, one foot on the mat, speechless, barely grasping what I am hearing. I move to close the door, to re-enter the hall, to discuss this. My heart is pounding.

'I'm going for a walk. I'll see you later.' He turns and disappears through the French windows on to the patio beyond our bedroom, beyond our breakfast corner and out of sight. The sentence 'I shan't be coming back' beats into my brain.

Down at the coast I call in on a friend who lives in an apartment by the waterfront, above the harbour where the ferries depart for Corsica. We sit on her vine-shaded terrace in dappled light, not conversing much – it's too hot – idly gazing out over the port, drinking iced tea, watching the comings and goings. I long to unburden myself, to share my sorrow and fears, but a desire to protect Michel stays my words. Discussing his state of mind, his professional insecurities, feels like betrayal. This woman works in television, too, and so I resist my longing to open up. Suddenly two Canadairs appear from out of the sea just beyond the yachts, roaring up from nowhere like monstrous reptiles in a horror film. A thundersome clatter they create right overhead as they zoom inland. Without even so much as a glance upwards, my friend remarks, 'More calamities, I suppose. Do you want another glass of tea?'

I am shaken by her casual comment and ask myself if this constant state of alert is not desensitising us. If we live side by side with danger for long enough, albeit screened from it save for a smoke-louring sky, will it become our norm?

My heart is settling into an unquiet state of alert.

When I return home Michel is nowhere about. I leave the sketch pad and crayons I have bought for him, as well as several rolls of film for his camera, on the table in the summer kitchen out of the late-afternoon sun. I phone our new acquaintance, the apiarist, to confirm his impending visit for the Sunday after next. I am half-expecting the number to be erroneous, to return me an out-of-order signal, but I am desperate to find any evolution in our daily life that might ignite my husband's attention and anchor him at base. I fall upon Mrs Beekeeper, or more precisely, Mme Huilier. She answers the phone with a chirpy '*Allô*'. I give my name and she sounds genuinely delighted to hear from me.

'I would like to confirm our rendezvous for Sunday week.'

'Ooh, yes, ten o'clock. We are *so* looking forward to it.'

I am warmed by her enthusiasm. The meeting had been arranged for eleven, but no matter, I reconfirm it for ten and reiterate that they should check in with us and we will direct them to the gate. 'There will be cold drinks awaiting you after your long drive,' I assure her.

'*A bientôt*, madame,' she trills.

I dig out my aged bee tome and start boning up on the subject of apiary once more. I pay heed to the bees working our land; alighting on flowers, gathering nectar, pollinating; pointing them out to Michel, sharing what I am learning, hoping to engage him too. He has expressed some interest in the beekeepers' impending visit and I attempt to build on that.

'Bees do not pay calls everywhere. The white-forked blossoms in our olive groves, for example, are never visited or fertilised by bees. And what of the fig tree? It has no blossoms, or so I had mistakenly concluded. I have frequently asked myself how a fig is pollinated and I have discovered this most extraordinary phenomenon. Figs do have flowers; they lie buried within the early fruit. But it is only the fruits with female flowers that mature into edible figs. So how do the bees access the flowers?'

Michel ponders my question, but he cannot provide an answer.

'They don't!' I cry. 'Bees have no business with the fig tree. There is a special wasp, a fig wasp, that fertilises fig fruits. These wasps have evolved a symbiotic relationship with fig trees. The female wasps, who are tiny, about three millimetres in length, crawl inside the growing figs to visit the flowers which line the interior of the fruit. Some flowers are pollinated, others receive eggs. Once the eggs have hatched, the male wasps, who are wingless, fertilise their new-born sisters and then the girls fly off to find other trees, where they begin the process all over again. Twenty times as many females as males are born. I guess their workload is greater.' I laugh. He smiles, and I am encouraged to add, 'Why not shoot a documentary about the myriad forms of propagation right here in the garden? You'd be working from home . . . I could write the text.'

But Michel does not bite, does not pick up on the suggestion. So I don't bother to mention that the fig wasp exists in Asia, southern Europe, Australia and California and pollinates *Ficus carica*, the common fig trees growing everywhere here. Nor that it is thanks to the Phoenicians that fig trees grow so prolifically in the occidental world, which could also be claimed of the olive tree. Although Michel has not jumped at the idea of making a film together, I steal this companionable moment to ask, 'Won't you stay here one more week to meet the beekeepers?'

Suddenly I see the clouds darken his thoughts again. It turns out that he thought the apiarists' visit was this coming Sunday. Is his grasp of time slipping away from him, or is it a simple error?

'Why don't you stay on till the end of the month then and meet them?'

'I don't know.'

Later, when we begin to prepare our supper, I find the sketchbook and crayons and rolls of film lying on the floor under a chair by the wastepaper basket in his office. I shove aside my dejection, determined not to be defeated.

Michel stays on.

And for many of those days during the latter part of July, he appears fitter, more accessible, less lost within himself. We grow closer. But what I have yet to learn is that there are good days and regressive ones. His progress is not linear, not uninterrupted or consistent. I remain constantly on the look-out for subjects that might enthral him, might link him with the here and now.

Towards the end of the third week of July, I read in one of the French newspapers that we, in the southeast of France, are facing a *stress hydrique*. The *hygrométrie* for our region is at 16 per cent. I show Michel the article. What does it mean? He does not know. I suggest we investigate.

A hygroscope, or hydroscope, is an instrument used for the detection of humidity in the air. Sixteen per cent, its current reading, is the equivalent of, say, an area as hot and dry as Marrakesh at the end of August. Just for fun, we look the word up in my English dictionary and also discover 'hydroscopist': a water-diviner, a dowser. This spurs me to telephone our own water-diviner, Claude, with whom I have not spoken in a long, long while. My timing is not good. His wife had a stroke and died in her sleep a matter of days ago. I offer my sympathies and he promises to be back in touch when life is more upbeat.

Then I call René, who is delighted to hear from me and talks as though I had scratched him from my address book. I refrain from pointing out that he has stood me up twice in our recent history.

'It's too hot to go out fishing with my boat so I've been driving inland, avoiding the coast. It's the season of red fruits,' he croons. 'I've been walking in the mountains, most invigorating, collecting wild strawberries and *myrtilles*, bilberries, to make jam. I'll bring you a couple of jars; you'll never taste better. When can I drop by?'

I marvel at the energy of this man.

'How are your olive trees? I bet you regret the fact you haven't treated them.'

'They are fine,' I retaliate. 'We have our work cut out keeping the little ones irrigated, but otherwise . . .'

'For heaven's sake, don't overdo it! Even in the inferno of our summer they don't want to be watered more than once every three weeks or the young roots won't be encouraged to drive deeper and fend for themselves. I'd better pop by and see how you are coping.'

I smile. We settle on a time and date two days hence but, not unusually, René doesn't show up.

On the third Sunday in July, M. and Mme Huilier chug up our hillside in their four-wheel-drive on the heels of Michel, who went in search of them when they telephoned to say that they had lost their way almost an hour ago. This is the first time he has been at the wheel since the accident but he was keen to go and I was glad of his interest. The retired couple arrive bearing a jar of golden rhododendron honey from their *miellerie*. Michel escorts them to the bougainvillaea terrace while I zip inside to prepare coffee because they have refused the cold drinks I'd prepared.

'The rhododendrons are a wilder, more stunted variety of the fabulously bushy parkland plant known to the English by the same name. Here, they are a ground-growing shrub rather like a small azalea,' Madame is explaining when I return with the tray of *café*. The bees collect from the rhododendrons in the Parc de la Mercantour at an altitude of 2,000 metres. Mercantour is a magnificent national park an hour and a half inland and to the east of our farm. The Huiliers' hives also produce honey collected from lavender, pine and white heather but their pièce de resistance is *miel de pissenlit*, dandelion honey, which I confess to never having come across before.

'Oh, you should have seen the dollar signs in our eyes when we discovered we could produce such an ambrosial delicacy, but, alas, the climate being what it was last year, our plans were ruined.'

I am puzzled. The previous summer was extremely hot so I beg an explanation.

'In the mountainous region where we are living we had a dreary summer. So wet and, as you probably know, bees will not be parted from their hives when it rains.' This is Monsieur.

I had not known this.

'The weight of the falling water makes it impossible for them to fly and it can damage their wings. Last year was quite the reverse of this year's atrocious heat. For two weeks during the dandelion-flowering season, it just chucked it down, never let up. Finally, when the sky cleared and the bees ventured forth from the hives, the dandelion flowers were finished.'

'And so were all our get-rich-quick schemes,' chortles Madame, as though it couldn't have mattered less. 'We like to earn a living, of course, who doesn't? But we do this work because we love bees. Oh look, dearest.' Madame has risen. Monsieur follows, and stares deep into the heart of a bougainvillaea bush in full flower. The pair shuffle along the terrace, heads buried in the foliage, entranced by every insect on the flowers.

'See that bee working away there?' Monsieur calls to us. I rise, take Michel's hand and we follow. 'She is *une solitaire*. A loner.'

'A solitary bee. How can you know?'

'Look at the size of her. She is smaller. The *solitaires*, as their name suggests, are outsiders, solitary insects; they hunt alone. They have no hive or social system to protect them.'

'So how do they manage alone?' I want to know.

Monsieur shrugs. 'If forced, most creatures find a way to survive alone.'

Monsieur, who is seventy, was a professional gardener working for a local council. His hobby was beekeeping. When he retired he and his wife decided to take up apiculture as a full-time occupation. Their enthusiasm for their *métier* is heart-warming and contagious. Glancing at Michel I see that he too appears fascinated, engaged.

'We are looking for a coastal spot, where the weather is mild in winter, to place fifty hives. The bees need to maintain a temperature within the hive of between twenty-five and thirty degrees to survive. If the outside temperature is cold and inside the hive it is, let us say, a mere fifteen degrees, they will need to consume their honey reserves to create sufficient calories to keep warm and maintain the health of their queen. The health of the queen is paramount. They wrap themselves in a ball around her and flap their wings constantly like millions of little fans, but it is to create heat, not ventilation. Of course, this is very hard work. It requires fit bees. Their strength is essential to achieve the perfect environment for the queen, who is laying up to a thousand eggs a day. One hive can consume as much as seventy grammes of honey a day.

'Seventy grammes,' I repeat, taking in the information.

'It may not sound like a great deal to you, madame, but it adds up to almost three kilos of honey per hive, each month!' This is Monsieur again. I am a little taken aback by his tone. Madame counters with a discreet brush of his hand.

'We have two hundred hives,' she explains with a broad smile. 'The figures speak for themselves. If the bees consume all the honey reserves throughout the winter we have nothing left to extract and sell. If we can camp them in a warmer climate between October and March they will require less food to protect their queen, to keep her warm; she will be healthier and she will spawn and incubate many more eggs. The position of your farm is ideal.'

'There is one *petit souci*,' returns her husband. 'Where could we station our truck and trailer?'

I am confused by what he has described as his 'little worry'. Our parking area is generous by any standard even while it remains cluttered with Quashia's building materials. I hastily apologise for the mess and assure him that it will have been cleaned up by October.

'No, madame, you haven't understood.'

Oh, dear, I have heard that criticism before!

'The trailer – *la remorque* – in which we transport our hives has been fitted with a costly piece of equipment that resembles a miniature crane. This lifts the hives and sets them down at their winter's resting ground. It delivers the bees to the precise location, you understand?'

I frown. Monsieur is clearly frustrated with me.

'Madame, you don't expect us to deposit fifty hives alongside the car park and leave them there, do you? In any case, it is surrounded by tall cedar trees. There is no passage to the area beyond and it's too close to your house. No, your *parking* will not do at all.'

'What about up behind the house?' suggests Michel.

I nod my agreement, heartened by his positive approach, even as my aspirations for beekeeping begin to wane in the face of Monsieur's negativity.

Monsieur shakes his head. 'Behind the house is most unpromising. Although the bees spend the greater part of the winter inside the hives, if the weather is particularly sunny, as well it might be here, they will come out and fly around for a while. Imagine, if you were enjoying a little al fresco lunch right here where we are sitting now and along come – well, each hive houses twenty thousand bees and we are considering placing fifty hives here, work it out for yourselves. That would be far too many uninvited lunch guests. No, the hives cannot be deposited close to a residence.'

'One million bees to lunch, I see.'

Michel and I scan the land, hoping to offer an alternative. One last attempt before our beekeeping dreams finally hit the dust. Unfortunately, wherever we propose, Mr Huilier solemnly shakes his head. '*Hélas*, I fear that won't work either. The fact of the matter is there is no available approach on your land.' This is Monsieur's résumé. He is ready to give up the ghost until his generous and ample wife chips in with a bright smile, optimistic and determined. 'Why don't we take a stroll, all of us together, and see what is within reach of the crane?'

This is what we do and although we find many areas that they judge ideal for the housing of the hives, *l'emplacement des ruches*, we find no site sufficiently accessible. By this stage, as we arrive at the foot of our grounds by the gate, we are all ready to shake hands amicably and forget the idea, when Michel offers, 'What about right here?'

Once it has been tendered, it seems as plain as day.

Madame is delighted and claps her hands, 'Perfect!'

Monsieur, less enterprising, less open to the bright side, needs to confirm the good news. He struts to and fro, bending like a pecking bird, counting, methodically orchestrating the delivery of imaginary hives, and then comes to a halt, shaking his head woefully. 'We'd never fit fifty hives here. They would be squashed up together like peas in a pod.'

'Oh, *chérie*, why don't we place thirty hives here and take the other twenty to Tanneron?' She spins round, eyes beaming. 'We already have an arrangement there for fifty and there is still a little extra space. Well, sufficient for another twenty hives, I am sure. One delivery here will see thirty safely housed. *Très bon*, that's settled then.'

Monsieur nods half-heartedly. His wife has a point which he is unable to refute, and so it is agreed. Our farm will winter thirty hives and in return they will offer us a few kilos of honey and allow me to accompany them occasionally as apprentice beekeeper. We shake hands on the deal, but Monsieur wants to dot the 'i's. 'Now, so that it is entirely understood: we will not be leaving a million bees in your care, but a mere six hundred thousand, are we agreed?'

Everyone nods, relieved that the matter has been finalised.

'My word, it's hot,' puffs Madame, waving her hands. 'We mountain people are not used to this sweltering heat. Thank heavens for the shade of trees, eh?'

The implication of this innocent remark hits me instantly. No one, including myself, has cottoned on to the fact that we are grouped together beneath the protective shade of two senior olive trees. We are on the lowest terrace at the base of a four-century grove. Winter, the period when the hives would be in situ, is harvest-time, and new year is the pruning season. How would we net the trees with hives all over the place? How could we lop branches when so many bees are directly beneath the chainsaws? I hesitate to bring up these very real drawbacks, to be the one to throw a spanner into the works, but they have to be addressed and, just as matters are concluding positively, I tentatively voice my doubts.

Monsieur grabs at the obstacle and confirms that it cannot work. Madame glances at her husband. I see her grappling for a way forward but try as she might she cannot hatch a counter-proposal. I, who have fed in the objection, now offer a solution.

'But wait, we have no olives this year! There will be no need to net the trees this autumn. And as you well know, it is better to prune olive trees every other year. We pruned all these last February, so next year we could leave this tiny corner alone.'

My proposal is greeted with many whoops of delight. Even Michel smiles proudly and hugs me tight. 'An excellent point, *chérie*, and, next year, we will make sure that there is an access that tracks way up behind the house where the bees can winter in peace and tranquillity.'

In peace and tranquillity. Mmm. Everybody shakes hands like old buddies and the Huiliers set off for their chalet in the mountains, leaving us to enjoy the rest of our Sunday in peace and tranquillity. But how can my heart feel quiet when any day now will be the day set for Michel's departure?

The weather turns cloudy; it threatens a storm. The brittle, sapless sounds are receding and I feel a swish of change coming in. Rain. I never dreamed the word could sound so enticing. The sky is gunmetal grey. Birds are flying fast across the heavens, seeking shelter. The air remains coarse and parched, smoke still rises from distant dying embers and fire engines still echo across the mourning hillsides, but the promise of rain is a blessed relief for everyone, except the tourists roasting themselves on the beaches.

It begins to spit; several generous fat gobs splatting like bird droppings on to the garden furniture. Such a heady relief, and I know that the plants, the crops, farmers, firemen and residents everywhere are feeling the same rush of madness, of exhilaration. 'Rain!' I halloo to the heavens. The dogs are jumpy and rattled, leaping at the doors to enter the house. I charge about, preparing for the tropical downpour, pulling cushions off seats, dragging sunbed mattresses into the summer kitchen, closing down the parasols, shunting away glasses and forgotten coffee cups.

Dry groans of thunder, spectacular flashes of lightning, and then nothing. Nothing from the empty, louring clouds. The change has petered out. The patinated sky evaporates and we are back to the baking, nerve-racking heat. Life becomes about waiting. Waiting for the heat to abate, waiting for a cloudburst, waiting for rain. Waiting to know what Michel will decide to do.

I can't stop eating or pacing and my thoughts are too jangled to settle to my script adaptation. But I am not the only one going quietly mad. Others are irritable, irrational, pixilated. They moan about the fires, the climate, the escalating heat, if they speak at all.

During one of my Sunday-morning trips to the vegetable market in Cannes, I drive by a man yelling, literally yelling, at his luggage in the open boot of his estate car. I see three girls, Japanese tourists, wearing floppy denim hats, holding hands, descending a steep hill in slow motion as though the sun had leached the life out of them, as though they were sleepwalking. Everywhere people are wearing next to nothing. In the *épicerie* in our local village, I encounter some of the septuagenarian and octogenarian church-going ladies, always so smartly attired in their Sunday best, guzzling soft drinks and ice creams, clad in shorts and the skimpiest of tank tops.

Driving along the esplanade early one morning, I am obstructed by a bank of police cars and fire engines parked outside a sea-facing apartment block. Iris-blue lights are flashing; different speeds, alternating rhythms. Against the feverish-yellow coastline, they create a ghostly puce mood.

I park my car at the kerb near the high-rises and ask a bystander what has happened. An elderly gentleman has fallen from a sixth-floor window. I peer upwards. Sweat runs in dribbles from my hairline, stinging my eyes. Dozens of residents on neighbouring balconies, dressed in boxer shorts or towelling robes, squint at the distant pavement, confused and sober-faced, or wave their arms about, screaming, locked in irate debate.

The balcony surrounds are well protected by solid wrought-iron railings, chest-height.

'How could he have fallen?' I muse.

'He jumped,' a woman in the crowd states sullenly.

'It's this accursed heat,' says another. 'Who can stand it? I'd jump too, if I were fortunate enough to live on the top floor.'

The Côte d'Azur has become the setting for a Raymond Carver short story.

Back at home, the ground is so dry it has been bleached of all colour. Bled of life, bled of nutrients. There is talk of impending drought.

Watering, watering, watering, to protect what we have. The crystal sprays falling on the plants release their scents. The evening air brings out perfumes stifled in the heat of the day. Invigorating to ingest.

It is the last week of July. The busiest month of the tourist year approaches, but now the rising morning air has a frisky feel to it, as though it were already September. The seasons are all of a muddle. Let's hope that today it will be cooler, I sigh, but it never is. Day after day, the sun beats down upon us and there is no deliverance.

And then at last, early one afternoon, the heavens open. Fling wide the doors! I hasten to and fro, within the house, throwing open all the windows, shutters, doors, every conceivable aperture, to welcome in the fresh, damp air. I listen to the deluge gurgle and bubble. I skid about the terraces gathering up towels and other poolside clutter. My saturated sarong cleaves like clingfilm to my sticky, sweaty flesh. I tie up the mutts, who are plunging from pillar to post, frenzied and afraid, as though the thunderclaps were gunshots bearing down upon them. I inhale the reeking perfumes of field-filthy dogs, sodden vegetation, soaked dust and drenched earth. I polka to the rhythm of stagnant, leaf-jammed drainpipes sluicing loose with rain. Nature is guzzling greedily like a starved suckling child. I lift my face full into the driving needles of water. Like a diver emerging from the ocean's bottom, I drink deeply the rush of air, licking my lips, savouring every drip. This is a burst of song; my spirits rave like native drums beating.

Inside, Michel sits impassively at the dining table. 'I must leave,' he is telling me once again when I slosh back into the house, feet sopping and squeaking on the *tommette* tiles, skin and hair dribbling and shining from the delicious cloudburst. 'I must leave,' he repeats.

'So soon?' I quiz cagily. 'Do you think that's wise?'

'I have business meetings.'

'Would you like me to come with you? Now the weather has broken we are released from watering chores for a little while. Quashia can look after everything else.'

He shakes his head. 'I'll hire a car and drive to Paris.'

This stops me in my tracks. A puddle is spreading at my feet. He wants to take his files and personal possessions with him because he will be gone for a while. A sick sensation creeps like a bug into my stomach.

'Are you leaving home, leaving me?' I manage, sinking into a chair at his side, ignoring the mess I am making.

'I see fear in your eyes and that doesn't help me,' is his response. 'I need time alone.'

Nothing I say will stay him, no argument strikes a chord; the organisation of his departure unfolds. Two days later he has packed up a hire car and I am the one who cannot fathom what has hit me. Before he leaves he sits me on his knee on a bench in the garden and tells me that it is not that he doesn't love me, but that he needs to go through this on his own. And then he drives away, winding down the path that curves through our silver-dappled, fruitless groves, waving like a man going on holiday.

I see no one except Quashia for two days.

Too Many Strays

The heat returns. It is as though the downpour never happened, as though it had been a mirage, a brief day-dream. The sky is still suffused with droning planes, cruising back and forth, patrolling from on high the parks and forests, always on the alert, ever watchful.

Jacques pulls up in his truck. He strolls over to say hello.

'Good news,' he calls, buoyant in his approach while I can barely raise a smile. 'The recent bout of rain, brief as it was, extinguished the last vestiges of fires in the Var.' He tells me that in one forest a tortoise walked away from the cinders, unharmed. It was the only creature in the area that escaped with its life. While we are talking three rabbits scamper across one of the grass-bare terraces, searching for sustenance. It is five in the afternoon, still broad daylight. They must feel safe; Bassett is pole-axed by the heat and hasn't the energy to harass any living being.

'You should speak to Alexandre about those guys. He'll shoot them for you.'

'I don't want them shot,' I protest. 'We have protected the growth. I prefer to leave them be.'

'Carol, in the nearby parklands and forests the rabbit colonies have contracted myxomatosis and the majority of them have gone blind.' Jacques warns me to pay attention to those on our land. 'The disease is very contagious. The ferals in the parks will have to be trapped and slaughtered due to the risk to walkers with their dogs.'

During the course of our conversation I learn that the reason the lovely parkland to the rear of our farm has been closed off is to protect the area against not rabbits but gypsies. Earlier in the year, while Michel and I were absent from France, 'troops of them with their swanky cars and caravans' apparently invaded the pleasance, setting up home there, 'monopolising the site and despoiling it.' It caused an outcry. 'The local council had the dickens of a job ejecting them. The parkland will be reopened only when a satisfactory barrier to block their re-entry has been erected.' Jacques turns his attention to the condition of our terraced walls. 'They've got worse since I've been coming here. More worrying than rabbits, you have a serious wild boar problem. You should certainly talk to Alexandre about them.'

'Why Alexandre?'

'He is a licensed hunter. He will come and shoot them and that will be the end of your troubles.'

Gypsies, hunting and Arabs are subjects I prefer not to be drawn on. 'Thanks, but that won't be necessary. The *sangliers* have been invading our territory ever since we moved here. We manage.'

'Aren't you afraid?'

I shake my head. At the outset I was scared, particularly when I was alone and they explored close to the house, but after a while I grew used to them.

'You ought to be, Carol. They could attack the dogs

or, if you encounter an angry sow, she could go for you. I don't hunt myself – I'm a fisherman – but if you pot one the rest of the troop won't be back in a hurry.'

In spite of the destruction they inflict, my stand against hunting remains. Michel disagrees. He thinks I am impractical, but he has never forced the issue.

And now he is not here.

'Well, you've got time to change your mind.'

I don't follow.

'You won't be troubled by *sangliers* for a month or two. This time of year they head to the mountains where the ground is less dry and the subsoil remains moist.'

'It's true,' I mumble. 'They have been leaving us in peace.'

I return to my den where I pass the sluggish day-time hours, screening myself from the insufferable heat. I have cast my semi-worked script aside. Instead, I comb my books and dictionaries, feasting on knowledge of this region so dear to my heart. I need to remind myself what holds me here.

The light and the sea; I grow to know them at every moment of the day. Their ever-evolving displays are like conversations I can partake of whenever I care to. And though it seems echoing and empty to me now, our stone house brings relief. It is cool and ventilated even on the hottest of summer evenings, when I lounge about on cushions, all doors open, reading or listening to the uncluttered violin sonatas of Uccellini, struggling to overcome the blank, soulless, melancholy that aches within me. I rise from the cushions and gaze down upon the lamplights of Cannes. Blueberry clouds, like bruises from my heart, pattern the dusky sky. I trace the contours of the sea to the necklace of illuminations along the Estérel promontory, gazing upon familiar sights with altered eyes.

Michel and I have barely spoken since he left. I have lost 6 kilos in ten days. I hardly recognise myself and I cannot stop worrying about him. Without him, my world has grown empty. He has been my pole star.

A letter arrives from Marseille. I stare at its envelope before opening it. Bureaucracy: Michel's domain. It confirms that our farm remains eligible for its ticketing in spite of the fact that we have dispatched an erroneous declaration, having claimed ownership of seventeen trees above the total growing on our land! As I read on, the notification informs me that we will not be penalised; our file will be processed. Fortunately, we are in possession of 251 trees and the minimum requirement, as we know only too well, is 250. I am stupefied. How have they arrived at 251? Our estate is blessed with the declared 270. Irrefutably. I have toured the terraces and counted them twice. The error lies not with our calculations but with the dratted inspector who consumed too much rosé during a hot midsummer's afternoon. However, because I haven't the slightest inkling how to improve this situation, and because my heart is too heavy to face the battle, I decide to leave well alone and ignore it.

Early the following morning, while Quashia is watering the salad garden, he discovers that a length of fence has been torn away from its brick-wall base, our gooseberry bushes have been uprooted and our vegetable beds infiltrated. Some creature has laid waste to our crops. He calls me down from the kitchen to take a look. The damage is certainly remarkable.

'This'll be the wild boars back. The dogs must have scared them off, though, because they haven't touched the potato beds.'

'It's the wrong season for them,' I reply.

'No other animal has a muzzle powerful enough to break through this fence. I fixed it myself, I know how sturdy it was. You have to do something, Carol. Why won't you buy me a rifle?'

Upset as I am by the sight of all our salads and tomatoes ransacked, I refuse his insistent plea and we set about replanting and straightening up what remains. Quashia digs up the garlic, braids the stalks into silver plaits and hands me the garlands to hang up in the summer kitchen. The bulbs are smaller than those on sale at the market or greengrocer's. They could have done with another month in the soil, but they'll still be good, which is more than can be said for the dozens of tomatoes squashed to a pulp and trodden into the soaked topsoil. We planted only fifteen seedlings this year because they always fruit so abundantly and this summer has been no exception: red, glistening tomatoes, plumply ripe from the Mediterranean sun. But now there are precious few left intact. Clambering about amongst them I inhale their piquant scent but not one cane remains undamaged.

'Heavens above, look at this!' Two baby rabbits, weenier than new-born chicks, are cowering fearfully behind the aubergine plants. Delighted by his find, Quashia displays the squabs, squeezing them tight between his blackened fingers.

'Where have they come from? There's no burrow.'

'Those damned pigs have trampled over it. The mother must have fled and abandoned them.'

They cannot be more than a day or two old and, sopping from their hosepipe shower, they look like nothing more than a couple of shreds of soggy newspaper.

'They'll never survive alone. We'll have to rear them here and release them when they're older,' says Quashia.

I hesitate, recalling Orpheus, our warbler, but the choice is to tend them or drown them, and that I cannot face. So dear Monsieur Q. spends the better part of the morning nailing chunks of wood together, constructing a hutch. While their new home is being assembled the duo of slithery grey balls are placed in a plastic lawnmower tray, out of reach of the dogs, where they tremble ceaselessly, as though battery-operated.

Bon appétit, waves my faithful gardener as he descends to his cottage for lunch. 'Michel should be making the decisions about guns, not you,' he adds firmly but without malice.

The following morning, Lucky pitches up outside the wide-open doors to my den with an elongated ebony stone in her mouth. She drops it triumphantly with a clunk, on to the terrace tiles. I rise to see what gem she has delivered me, thinking it could be charred driftwood from one of the recent fires, but it turns out to be a boar's hoof, black, hirsute and solid with a cleft toe. I try to pick it up, to examine it, needing to be certain that this is a wild pig's trotter, but my Alsatian refuses to be parted from her prize. The instant I bend and reach for it, she whips it up again and scoots off to the far end of the patio, clasping the foot tight between her slavering jaws. It is a trophy, her loot, and she is proud of it. But from where have you snaffled it, Lucky? Somewhere close by, no doubt.

On my way out later, I spy a dog in our lower groves. He is a rather attractive beige wiry fellow, medium-bodied and the colour of a llama but a stranger to our neighbourhood. How has he infiltrated our grounds? He runs and hides behind an olive trunk when he sees me speculating about him. If he's a hungry stray, might he be responsible for the damage to our vegetable garden? I hope so.

My route to the farming co-operative takes me by the lovely manor house with its public park. The grassland that was cordoned off to protect the neighbourhood against gypsies is now stationed with fire engines, in convoys of twos and threes. Sitting atop each one, perched on the gleaming metallic-red carriages, are its navy-clad crews; strapping fit, brown as hazelnuts, playing cards in the baking sun, awaiting a call to duty.

Pausing at my favourite bakery, now doing a roaring trade serving ice creams and refreshments to droves of passing tourists, I join the long line, envying families bunched up together in the sunshine, guzzling cones, laughing and fooling, glowing from days at the beach. From the café radio, I learn that in the areas burned out last month, the incendiary investigations have found proof of arson; tyre tracks from one and the same car spinning from the sources of fires in several different locations. Nine fires started within hours of one another. In areas where the worst damage has been wreaked, Molotov cocktails and the remains of yacht distress signals have been dug out of the ashes and debris. To protect against further assaults, preventive measures will be put in place: forests and parks will be closed to the public, in high season, allowing access to no one except rangers; there will be harsher prison sentences for offenders and the burned-out areas will be replanted with less flammable flora such as olive trees, vineyards and other vegetation with a naturally high water content. Queuing, listening to the news, I observe the florid-faced Lautrec woman serving at the counter with her dyed-red hair and flashing fingernails. She is in heated debate with a handsome young fireman who is stocking up with cans of Coke. Even as the tourist season continues to flourish, amongst the locals other moods are taking hold. This proud southern coastland, rich in flora and fauna, its landscapes painted by many of the greatest artists of the nineteenth and twentieth centuries, renowned for its spectacular plays of colour, has been rendered sepia, decolorised or razed to lifelessness. Outrage and desolation fuel exchanges as well as a growing mistrust, frequently present beneath the surface, towards those who are not from these parts. It stokes the fires of racism.

When I pull up at the *co-opérative* a shipment of shiny blue tractors is being unloaded. I pause to admire them. Even if we could afford one, the tyres would never grip on our stony inclines. Alexandre catches sight of me and calls from out of the late-morning shade of his shed. '*Bonjour*, Carol, I see your face has healed. Now you are as beautiful as a beating heart.'

I am taken aback by the poetry in his remark and hide my awkwardness by striding determinedly to the cash desk to order the fencing Quashia and I require for the reinforcement of the ruined enclosure. Moments later, Alexandre is at my side. 'Want me to load the poles and all those metres of *grillage* into your car?'

I nod, handing over the cash for my purchases.

'Alexandre, have you nicked my Bible?' barks the none-too-charming assistant.

'What need do I have of it, Yvette?' And as he slides out into the sun, she shakes her head, tut-tutting as though dealing with an adolescent.

I find the accused in the hangar where the variously coloured rolls of olive nets are stored, collecting the thick wooden pickets for the boot of Michel's Mercedes.

'Building a new fence? You've lost weight. You look a little downhearted.'

'I'm fine,' I reply tightly, moving to lend a hand with the materials before he ushers me away.

'I can do this. Enjoy your ice cream?' He grins. 'It's melted down the front of your top.'

I rub at my T-shirt, embarrassed.

'I promise to make you laugh for five minutes each time you come here. Where's the fence to go? Round your heart?'

'The wild boars have wrecked the vegetable beds.'

'I could rid your property of the problem in no time. I'll drop by and tag their principal *drailles*.'

I don't recognise that word. '*Draille*, what is that?'

Alexandre wipes the sweat from his brow with the back of his hand. He explains that boars will always repeat their routes. *Draille* is their path of entry on to the land. It is born of the old Provençal words *draia* and *dralha*, originating from the idea of cutting a foot-path, a walkway, through cornfields. 'So a *draille* is also the word for the track followed by sheep during *transhumance*, their seasonal relocation to their winter or summer pastures.'

'Do you speak Provençal?' I interrupt.

His eyes light up and he swaggers, tossing his head back proudly, well gingered to have scored. 'When I was a kid, I did. My father, who's passed away now, was fluent. Want me to teach you?'

He sees that I am drawn. This spurs him on.

'So in French *draille* is the path, *le chemin*. Once I identify their routes, I will be able to pinpoint precisely where I must lay food for them: corn, dried bread, fruit – *une bonne salade*! They are creatures of habit. They'll return at the same time each night, and I'll be ready for them!' He concludes with a flourish.

Judging by the nocturnal explosions of dog barking, his theory sounds accurate.

'Usually, it is somewhere around ten o'clock,' I confirm.

'That's in summer,' he warns. 'In winter they will arrive earlier.'

'But I understood from Jacques that they stay away from the coast in summer.'

'The *sangliers* have a nose for when you've watered the olive trees. They will descend from higher ground to snout about the damp earth at the base of the trunks, foraging for underground shoots and bulbs. They will travel up to fifty kilometres a night in their search for fodder.'

He offers to lay the trap and then come by after the first night to see if they have taken the bait. If they have, he will lay out another meal at the same spot for the following evening. This will be repeated for three days and, assuming the family or small herd is tricked each night by the bluff, on the fourth he will bring his gun. 'But,' he emphasises, 'it needs to be a spot far from any residence where there is absolutely no accident risk.'

If the cage traps a youngster, this hunter promises to take it away, raise it and then release it in the mountains. A hefty male will be shot on the spot, as would a 60-kilo or larger female, an older sow. A younger mother will be trapped and delivered to the mountains where she will be released to breed again. If an animal is shot, Alexandre will leave the carcass in our garage overnight and return to strip and carve it up the following day.

'If you want to experiment with the idea of a baited trap, then I'll guide you. Just let me know when you're planning to water the olives again.'

The car is now loaded. I thank him for his explanation and assure him that I will consider it.

He looks me over, smiling, weighing me up.

'I can see you don't approve. Oh, one more thing,' he adds.

I fire up the engine and throw the gearbox into first. Through the open window, Alexandre leans in close. 'You have chocolate ice cream all round your mouth.'

The dog I spotted earlier is still with us. I caught Quashia throwing sticks at him to shoo him away, but he still hangs about the farm skulking behind the gnarled trunks of the centuries-old *oliviers*, peering out from one side or the other, playing peek-a-boo, fascinated by our comings and goings, though he refuses to approach. I have been trying to draw close all afternoon and when I think I am getting the sense of the game, he snaps or whines forlornly, always keeping his distance. I cannot see a collar so I conclude he is a stray. Quashia thinks he sneaks in through one of the boars' entry points.

Later, when the sun has slipped westwards round the hill, my mainstay and I set about the fence reparations.

'I think we should keep that dog,' I suggest as we work. 'He'll help fend off the *sangliers*.'

'We won't catch him. If Michel were here, we'd round him up.'

It is hard for me to see Quashia suffering from the lack of Michel's company. He misses his guidance and friendship and enquires after him repeatedly and his labours require the assistance of muscle and brawn in which I am deficient. I do my utmost but I disappoint him. We drive stakes into the ground, stretch green wires between the wooden markers and make ourselves a brand-new, secured enclosure. Evening is upon us when we close in the last picket and the dogs are pacing to be fed. I am rather chuffed with our efforts but Quashia dismisses them as flimsy. 'This won't solve our problem. The pigs will eventually destroy everything, including the olive trees, if action is not taken. We must drive them off the land. If Michel were here, he'd agree.' He kisses me goodnight and sets off down the hill and I am left feeling inadequate and perturbed by his mood.

'I may have a remedy,' I call after him. I have been mulling over Alexandre's offer, wondering if he could be persuaded to trap the boars and release them elsewhere. Or would they just return, seeking out their habitual *drailles*?

'Nah, you won't solve the problem; you're too soft,' is Quashia's parting shot.

Sitting on the terrace, staring at the stars, a solitary glass of wine at my side, stroking the three companions at my feet, plagued by doubts about my ability to run this place alone, I am suddenly aware that Ella's eyes are encircled with ticks. Their puffy grey skins, engorged with blood, resemble tiny plasticine bubbles. I hate them. They suck the animals' strength, leaving them lethargic and irritated. I must help her. A deep breath and I tweezer the suckers away by pinching each one between my fingers, then twisting and yanking it. The fatter they are, the more feasted and the harder it is to loosen them. It tears her flesh and she moans, resisting me. Once they are released I fling them on the ground and, before they can insect-scurry away on minuscule red legs beneath plastic shells, I squash them mercilessly beneath the sole of my shoe. Ella's blood squirts across the marble floor and she licks at it energetically as if to recapture it. Ugh. Horrid blood clots with legs. I down my wine, wash my hands vigorously and fall into bed, depressed.

The following morning Quashia discovers ticks folded into Bassett's long floppy ears and around his genitals. He calls me to fetch a bottle of alcohol and a roll of cotton wool out of the medicine chest. It helps lessen their grip, he explains. I hadn't known that. Bassie cocks one of his hind legs, buries his muzzle into his soft-belly flesh and tears at his stomach, digging and slurping in a frenzied attempt to free himself of the itchy suckers. I turn him over on his back and ease his legs apart to help him, but he twists and growls and won't let me near his exposed private parts. My little hunting hound is cross with me. His eyes glower at me, clouded with jealousy. He rises and stalks off, waiting for me to enter the laundry room to feed the rabbits, determined that when my concentration is elsewhere, he will bag them or find another way to punish me.

'You'll have to do it, I'm afraid,' I tell Quashia. 'He won't let me near him.'

'If you condone killing insects, why can't we finish off the boars? This is a farm, Carol, it requires such decisions. In the meantime, you had better get to the garden centre and buy these mutts some collars.'

On my way out, I find a yellow leaflet posted in our letterbox by the local council. Due to the extensive damage caused by the boars, it announces, we are to

be offered the services of two top marksmen, professional hunters, for the purpose of ridding our grounds
of the rampagers. Also included in this morning's mail
is the latest edition of our splendid agricultural gaz-
ette. The boars are growing so numerous, it reports,
along the inhabited coastal areas and are causing such
extensive damage within this Alpes-Maritimes *département* that a revised date for the hunting of *les sangliers*
has been scheduled. Chase will be legal as of 17
August. This is a month ahead of all other game. The
change of policy has been agreed upon under the
strictest conditions: there is to be no pursuit by night
or within 500 metres of habitation, and it can only
be exercised with a hunter's licence. The season for
all other game in the southern Alps will open mid-
September. This notification deeply concerns me. Will
the day arrive when a bylaw obliges us to exterminate
the trespassing beasts just as we are obliged to cut
back our land?

I find Alexandre at work in his hangar and am stepping
forward to shake his hand when my attention is drawn
to an old-fashioned triangular wooden fruit-tree ladder
attached to the wall high above his head, beyond the
stacked chicken feed and sacks of manure. 'I have been
looking for one of those for a long time. People rarely
use them these days, but they are lovely and rather
romantic, don't you think? Is it for sale or simply for
display?'

He laughs loudly but not unkindly. 'Romantic?
Well, yes, I could picture you on the top rung and me
on the ground, holding it steady for you. That would

be a romantic ladder indeed. It's not for sale, but if you want it, Jacques'll deliver it next time he is over to clean your pool. A present from me.'

'Oh, that's kind, but, no, thank you. I thought it was for sale. Actually, I'm looking for anti-tick collars for the dogs.'

He shrugs. 'Suit yourself. Three?'

I nod. Open on his desk, a catalogue displaying photographs of rifles draws my attention.

'My passion,' he smiles, flicking pages to reveal cartridges. 'You oppose it, don't you?'

I scuff my shoe awkwardly.

'I thought you were keen to learn about our Provençal ways of life. You seemed interested in the boars' *drailles*.'

'Yes, but I don't want to hunt them,' I counter. 'I know you shoot to eat, but . . .'

'I don't hunt for food. I hunt because I enjoy it and it's a tradition I have grown up with, passed on through generations of my family and my wife's family. Your disapproval was written across your face last time you were here.'

I am at a loss, reluctant to criticise his hobby.

'Why don't you come hunting with me and you will better understand what it's about? The rules are very strict, and we adhere to them. I would lose my licence otherwise. For example, you can never touch a *bête suitée*.'

Again, his French puzzles me.

'A *bête suitée* is a mare with a foal, or any female mammal with offspring in tow too immature to forage for its own food. It is against the hunting code of

Provence to kill a *bête suitée*, for obvious reasons. Each *département* has its own rules. They don't differ greatly but the licensed hunter must adhere to the maxims of his department's organisation.

'I shoot to kill, never to maim,' Alexandre admits. Should he accidentally wound an animal, he must finish it off. He never aims when the animal is in motion. He waits until it is in repose or has paused for water so that there is less risk of inaccuracy.

'Come along when the season has opened – but I carry the gun and in no circumstances will I lend it to you. Bring water, food, carry everything in a back-pack. No shoulder bags. Absolutely no perfume and no garments sprayed with perfume.'

I listen, swayed by the intensity of his passion.

'Good solid walking shoes and socks are essential.' The hunt involves tracking at high altitudes and, on occasion, six or seven hours of marching before any game is located. Although the shooting season opens in mid-September, I would not be invited on the first Sunday; it is for experts only and will be over-subscribed. The week following *l'ouverture*, I can accompany him. 'Will you come?'

I shake my head. 'I don't think so, but thank you for the invitation.' I purchase the dogs' tick-and-insect-repellent collars as well as a spray he recommends. Preparing to leave, I broach the true reason for my visit, 'Alexandre, would you consider trapping the boars for me and setting them free without slaughtering them?'

He shakes his head. 'What would be the point?'

On my way home, I park the car a short walk from

the common parkland. Although the boulders and fire engines remain, the grounds have been reopened. Two local council gardeners are planting dozens of small pines in a deep trench that has been hollowed out round the perimeter. I decide to take a stroll to the lake. I am missing Michel and Quashia is frustrated with me. If Michel were here, what would he advise? Should I call him, burden him with this? I pass a family group conversing in English. They have three pointers in tow, gambolling at the water's edge. A sign states: 'No Feeding the Wildfowl'. In spite of it, the tourists are chucking bread to the ducks. Unfortunately, the chunks are so substantial that the birds are choking on the lumpy offerings. The holidaymakers laugh and throw in more. One bird in particular seems to be in trouble, hooting and flapping. The elder of the men orders his dog into the lake. 'Fetch! Fetch supper!' he cries. The lean, muscular hound, not dissimilar to Bassett, splashes into the pond, crashing through the reedy water, chasing after the frightened incapacitated fowl. The tourists howl with delight, hailing the dog's success until eventually the bird flutters from the water's oily surface and makes its clumsy escape, honking as it goes. The tourists saunter away, satisfied by the amusement they have created. This random example of man's frequent cruelty to beast decides me to adhere firmly to my anti-hunting principles.

As the days drift on, I watch the figs softly rotting, disintegrating in the liquid blue of the pool water, leaving deep mauve smudges on its floor. Michel loves these seedy fruits but I eat them infrequently. I would package them up and send them to him but they are too fragile. Each morning, when I go downstairs to feed the dogs and have a swim, I find clusters of them on the tiled surround and in the pool itself. I raise them up with my toes, playing footsie, as they bob and sink weightlessly beneath the liquid surface. When I fish them out, I toss them into the garden for the wasps to feast upon, but I hate to see them go to waste. I need company.

The stray, who definitely bears no collar, has reappeared. I think he's starving; he looks thinner than when he was last here. I encourage him with food and he edges nervously closer but as he trots up the drive, our resident trio warn him off with a vicious outburst of growlings and barkings. Most malevolent of all is Ella who, though in her dotage, asserts an aggressive display of territorial dominance. A furious energy, a hyped vitality, surges through her decrepit bones. It is rather unsightly to behold, but I feel confident my gang will eventually make peace with the intruder if we can trap him. Our postman offers another opinion. I have not seen the portly fellow in some time when out of the blue he pootles up the drive on his Noddy-yellow scooter and hands me the mail with a bearded scowl.

'As if these weren't enough!' he snaps. I frown, staring at the delivery. There are only two letters, neither from Michel.

'What are you, a refuge centre? That filthy, furry beige thing nearly took my leg off yesterday, snapping and swiping at me. I'll have you in court,' he swears, swinging the bike about and skidding off down the drive.

I sigh, all too aware of how vehemently he detests our hounds and with good reason. There has been a history at our farm of dogs and strays playing Terrify the Miserable Postman, and I haven't forgotten how he set the authorities on us, threatening us with court cases galore if we didn't keep our mutts under control. Should I refrain from encouraging this newcomer who haunts the olive groves?

Jacques says he's a sheepdog from the Pyrénées mountains of south-west France and would be an excellent catch. His tangled, matted coat creates the illusion of a heftier beast but when he finally makes a hit-and-run grab for the food on offer, I see his skinniness. Although ravenous, it is unlikely he would have found the strength to break into the vegetable garden. I find this uncombed scallywag complex and comical and have made the decision that, if we ever snare him, he can hang out with us here. Ella is going deaf, her back legs are giving way and, though her appetite remains robust, she is skeletal. I had been planning to acquire another puppy or two to keep the others company when she eventually departs, to inject new life into the troupe, so why not give board to this ragamuffin, whom I christen Intruder? However, Lucky is not one bit pleased. She is threatened by this camp follower and begins to display signs of her former nature, the beaten brute I discovered shivering in the grass at the foot of the hill: she is becoming highly strung, insecure again, damaged and demanding. She speaks to me with urgent, pleading eyes, moves in close to my calf and nudges her bristly frame against me, begging me not to allow the stranger to usurp her.

'You're secure here,' I whisper, but she is not mollified.

Slowly, Intruder mingles with the gang, but the integration is more fraught than I might have expected. The faithfuls circle my feet at feeding time, growling disgruntledly like a coven of witches. 'I can't let him starve!' I reason, but they will have none of my excuses and while I attempt to appease them, Intruder snaps for my attention, yapping to be fed first, nipping at my heels and calves until he draws blood. Returning upstairs for a much-needed glass of wine, I find a severed rabbit's head on the grass by the magnolia tree. I pick it up and its marble-cold eyes stare up at me in an accusatory fashion. Midgy insects swarm about it, buzzing and whirring as I collect up the decomposing flesh to deposit it in the dustbin. This has to be Bassett's doing.

These days, I go to bed exhausted, reading for a short while before falling into a heavy slumber or tossing restlessly for three-quarters of the night and waking too early. My hair is growing long and wild, blonded by the sun. I am becoming rustic and too solitary, but while Michel is elsewhere, I have decided to battle on here, continue the restoration of our farm, build it up, care for it, for the animals and Quashia, and await my husband's return. I don't want to abandon what matters here, what we have been creating together. The train of our dual journey . . . our *draille*, our dream.

And Quashia's shed seems to be taking vague shape. When the evening sun hits the big stones, coloured a rich honey by the red earth from which he has pulled and hewn them, it is a miracle to behold. He escorts me up the stoned path to admire what he has achieved and I begin to warm to this spot again. Late summer flies buzz in the air around us; flies following this high season and its delicious offerings. The fruits on the young trees are splitting, oozing, bursting with wasps. They need to be gathered but Quashia won't take them and there is only so many I can consume alone. The terrace needs major tidying up, of course, but not yet, and the shed, unwieldy and unaligned as it is, lends a crude, rough-cut nobility to the corner. 'We ought to create something special here,' I tell my loyal assistant. 'When your work is eventually completed.'

He roars with laughter, happy that his 'wretched shed' is making its mark. I snap photographs of him standing in front of it, posing like a soldier: stiff, obedient and unsmiling. The dogs fall over one another to be alongside him and he kicks them out of the way, but not cruelly. In his peasant way.

'You can send the pictures to your family,' I tell him. 'I could make you a little album. A gift for the Quashias of Constantine. Others, I'll send to Paris.'

He smiles proudly, loving the idea. 'It'll shut my wife up. Always moaning about why I'm not home. Why I stay so long here in between visits.' As soon as he has uttered this, he wants to bite his tongue off. 'But she's fine. She doesn't need me there; she can cope,' he adds, desperate to make amends.

'Monsieur Quashia, if your family need you, you must go. I can manage for a while.' Of course, I have no idea how I'd continue without him. We can barely operate as it is.

'They don't need me. She's surrounded by family; sons, daughters and more grandchildren than we can count.' Again I see the faux pas register in his rheumy eyes.

'Hey!' I cry, 'I have a great idea. When the work on your shed is finished, let's move the vegetable garden up here! You said yourself that the fence we've built is only temporary. We could plant it up together. And how about we buy an old greenhouse and reconstruct it here so that we have fruit and vegetables all year round? That'll keep all trespassers out. Or I'll ask Jacques if he can find us someone who might build the frame. There's a Mr Pear, I could try to contact him. I'll order glass panes and you can fit them.'

'Couscous,' he mumbles, dreaming of the vegetables he walks to the Arab market in Cannes once a week to buy for his meals.

'All-year-round couscous, yes!' I smile, happy that he's enthused, 'and tropical fruits!' Relieved that he is not angered by my refusal to purchase a weapon.

'But why doesn't Michel find us a blacksmith? When is he coming back?'

To temper poor Monsieur Q.'s frustrations and ease his fatigue, I suggest he takes the weekend off. It will be beneficial to him to spend some time in male company. Delighted, he zips off on the train early on Friday with companions to Marseille, leaving me alone. Alone and acutely aware of my aloneness.

I pass the tapering hours of the scorchingly hot Friday watering the wilting shrubs and flowerbeds. Hand saluted against my forehead to shield against the sun's rays, I stare skywards, beyond the biscuit-baked, stubbly-textured terraces, at the serrated-edged wings and lovely mottled markings on the underparts of two honey buzzards gliding in ever-decreasing circles. They could be scouting for rabbits, squirrels or shrews, though their principal food sources are wasps and bumblebees. This pair are nesting in our conifers, I am fairly convinced of it. I spot them quite regularly.

'Occasionally buzzards migrate all the way from South Africa to Siberia to breed, a phenomenal distance of thirteen thousand kilometres,' I might tell Michel if he were here to listen.

Water overflow soaks my feet. I shuffle back, lowering my gaze, and notice clumps of golden flowers in the dustbowl of our scarp. I would have sworn that nothing flourished here in this season of aridity save for our irrigated strips of trees and vines. The shrub that has drawn my attention has bright yellow flowers. I close the hose nozzle and pluck a stem which is sticky and perfumed like resin. I take it inside to my den, place it in water and search for it in my encyclopaedia of wild flowers. It is an aromatic inula, a member of the daisy family. In spite of the heat I shove on shoes and start touring the land. It takes me no distance to discover that the hillside is not barren at all. It abounds in blossoming flowers and shrubs, predominately yellows and blues. I gather an example from each and continue, scouting to the hill's vertex, where our grounds have no picketed demarcation. Here I come across fresh saucer-shaped tracks, indented circles of dried earth. I cannot be sure if these indicate boars or another predator. A curled, silver leaf on one of the tender olive trees takes flight as I approach. It puzzles me. A more thorough examination reveals a battery of tiny moths grazing on the stripling. I move along the plantation rows but do not detect these winged insects elsewhere. Lucky and Bassett are following at my heels. Intruder straggles behind, yapping and nagging, tormenting his companions until they snap and snarl and he slinks off to sulk behind a pine trunk. Suddenly Bassett streaks away, huzza-ing like a hunting horn, and disappears into the Hunter's land abutting our unfenced acres.

'Bassie!' I yell, but he pays no heed. I charge to the summit and hear a shot ring out. I ditch my bouquet and rush towards the jungle of growth. Another shot. I hold back; it is too dangerous to venture further. Bassett is howling. 'Bass!' I hear the whip and rustle of breaking branches as a creature, a wild pig, too heavy for Bassett's tread, recedes into the dense foliage.

I am about to enter when Monsieur le Chasseur appears from out of the brush, stony-faced. 'You are trespassing,' he snaps, hitching his rifle over his shoulder.

'My dog is in there.'

'Yes, and if he comes this way again, he'll be mincemeat.'

At that moment Bassett resurfaces, strutting on to home territory, tail erect, delighted with his foray, and I retreat, red-faced and furious. I glance skywards; the buzzards have disappeared. The shots would have scared them away. They are heavily hunted. Alone in the house, heart thumping, I arrange my flowers in a vase with the inula and then set about with trembling hands to locate the names of each. I have a field marigold, which flourishes abundantly in habitats such as ours and blooms from March to October. I pull out the flower – its stem is slightly hairy – and examine its petals, which are a lovely, rich golden orange. Tears are streaming down my face. What else have I retrieved? Bell heather. Silver ragwort. Chamomile. Yarrow. Verbascum sinuatum. Cupidone: this is delicate and gorgeous, a rich blue. Another with soft blue heads is chicory, a wild flower here. Love-in-a-mist and winged sea lavender heighten the poetry in the bouquet. Although sea lavender grows throughout the Mediterranean its preferred habitat is dry, sandy ground, usually near to the sea, but sometimes inland. It is cultivated for use as dried flowers.

My unexpected nosegay of discoveries cheers me, gives me a straw to cling to. Nothing is as bleak as it appears; when all about is ebbing, life continues. Growth is unfolding. I will dry and press these flowers and send the arrangement to Michel. 'Harvests from Appassionata, with love.' Each week, each season, I will find others. To remind us.

I spend Saturday alone. Flies hover by the magnolia tree, Michel's favourite spot. Their drowned bodies pepper the pool's silky surface. Jacques arrives to clean it, transporting in the rear of his truck the triangular wooden ladder. 'A gift from Alexandre,' he winks. 'I see the pigs have paid another visit. There are two walls on the lower western flank where the stones have fallen away.'

'I think they were here yesterday evening.'

'When the rains come, mudslides will destroy those terraces.'

'Please thank Alexandre. The ladder is a thoughtful gift but when I'm next at the *co-opérative* I'd prefer to pay for it.'

'Be warned, the fires are going to contribute further to your boar troubles.'

'Why?'

'Those that escaped with their lives have moved east, travelling out of the Var into the Alpes-Maritimes. You know, Carol, it's not my business but you are standing up for a principle while the work on your farm is going to rack and ruin. What does your husband say? Where is he? Alexandre can help you.'

When Quashia returns from his weekend I inform him that we must fence in the summit of the hill. He shakes his head. 'We are wasting our energies building fences that will be penetrated. Have you seen the lower groves? Wrecked during three days' absence. The boars have to be killed, Carol. I am going to buy my own shotgun, if you won't get me one.'

'You need a licence in this country for arms.' My words silence him temporarily, but I fear I am losing the support of the most essential man in my olive world, dear reliable Monsieur Q.

Convoys of cars and smiling faces arrive. The Irish first and then the Germans; day after day cries of greetings kick life into this silver-leafed hillside and I welcome the arrivals with open arms, bucked up by the company. Still I continue to work in my den or assist Quashia, while the newly installed guests and their offspring swim and laze or go off sightseeing. But when evening descends we assemble, gathering round the long wooden table in the garden for drinks before sunset and to enjoy dinner together *en famille*. Life as I cherish it at this old farm.

This renewed activity spurs me to call Michel. 'Your family is here and Irish relatives of mine. We miss you. Won't you come home?'

He's too busy, he says. He has no time. Business needs his attention. I replace the receiver, sending him love, disappointed and sad.

The children delight in helping me with the rabbits, cleaning out their hutch, picking lettuce leaves and feeding them to the hungry, nervous pair. We grate dishes of carrots but the furry twins turn up their quivering noses at them. They won't touch milk either, but they do drink copious amounts of water. I watch the Irish youngsters' eyes as they gaze upon these scruffy, clumsy brown balls of fear.

'How old are they?' demands my six-year-old niece.

'About two weeks, I'd say.'

'How old is that in human years?' her brother wants to know.

One morning I find the freckled little girl in the laundry room, face pressed up against the wire netting of the hutch, whispering to the rabbits, 'I'm from Dublin. Where are you from?'

I am grateful for the presence of these gleeful children with their bright, round-faced innocence, their never-ending questions and their imaginations spilling over with mystery and mischief.

Alas, the single hint of domestic disharmony is Intruder. Each day he grows more neurotic and when the children offer their palms to stroke and quieten him, he snaps at them and scurries into corners while the other dogs look on, moody and disconsolate. The truth is this stranger is not settling in. I christened him appropriately. I take to tying him up in the yard but his whining frays my already jangled nerves.

The baby rabbits, though, are a constant source of revelation and as they begin to grow, new distinct features cause me to suspect we are rearing hares. Now I understand why there was no burrow when we rescued them. Hares are born above ground and their mothers return at sunset to nourish them. Perhaps they hadn't been abandoned after all? They afford us great pleasure as we watch them develop and manifest their natures: their black and white bobbed tails, the black markings on the tips of their ears, their powerful hind legs and, when I pick them up, their frantic attempts at kick-boxing. The children are enchanted and so am I. Their enemy is Bassett, who arrives at the crack of dawn one morning outside my bedroom with a wild rabbit carcass, still warm, clutched between his teeth. He drops it at my feet. His message is clear as he lopes away.

'Don't be jealous, Bassie,' I call after him. To no avail.

Like the Old Woman who lived in a Shoe, I have a house bursting at the seams. My Irish cousin, Noel, with his family and Michel's German nephew, Hajo, who celebrated his fourteenth birthday with us here on the farm soon after we bought the place and who has come to visit this year with his mother, his adolescent sister and his strikingly good-looking young girlfriend are followed by Michel's sister, Angélique, husband Ralf and three sons. The men are calling for me to take heed of Quashia's words. They have made a tour of the grounds and return to report the extent of the boar damage. Noel warns that the wild pigs have begun to steal the apples and in reaching for them have stripped off leaves and branches, leaving them broken like fallen wings or withering on the ground. Further aloft, towards the hill's crown, the beasts are grubbing around the feet of the sapling *oliviers*, turning over the earth. Many of the small trees have been knocked sidewise, notes Ralf. Not yet uprooted but worryingly slanted. 'They will eventually die in this heat if their roots have been dislodged and they cannot reach subsoil water sources,' cautions Noel. I am glad that Quashia has gone off to his cottage and is not around to hear these warnings.

'Do you think I am being stubborn?' I direct my question to Noel, who is the closest I have to a brother, believing that he will guide me honestly.

'It's foolish, Carol, and short-sighted. Something has to be done.'

'You can't expect Quashia to work the way he does only to find that each morning the refurbishments he has already completed need to be repaired. Consider him, Carol, not the wild pigs,' chips in Hajo.

This evening we dine late and though it is after ten, the children eat with us. It is too hot to sleep. Noel, Hajo and Ralf have prepared a steaming barbecue. Our home-grown garlic is a huge success. The cloves take longer to peel – being small they are fiddly – but they are an extremely flavoursome bonus to our dishes. Unusually, the dogs grow restless as we squash together around the groaning table. They are pacing the terraces, barking and growling up into the darkness towards the stands of pines silhouetted on the hillside. Something is up there, spooking them. We hush our chatter to listen and a bloodcurdling high-pitched screech tears into the sultry, unstirring night.

'Jeez, what was what?'

I shake my head. I have never heard such a cry here before. Disturbed, everyone rises from the table. The children are terrified and cling fast to their mothers' hips. The screech rips forth again. Could it be a hooting eagle owl? A tree shrew? Or my honey buzzards? The hill returns to silence while we, shaken, return to the serving of supper, our conversation muted.

Suddenly Bassett bolts. Up and down the terrace, to and fro, back and forth, like a freaked horse. I call to him to be calm but due to my dedication to the hares and Intruder, I am not his best friend these days. He throws a backwards glance towards me and then sets off into the night, cantering and baying mournfully. On he goes, yowling and pacing, until he reaches the level below our little apple orchard where he pauses, eyeballing the upper reaches of the hill. I hurry from the table to bring him back but as I pass the bank of cedars, I am stopped in my tracks. There, gazing menacingly down upon our bristling little dog, looming in the exaggerated shadowed light as broad as a bison, is a wild sow. The beast holds its ground at the edge of the stone wall, glaring malevolently upon our hunting hound who, in return, is baring his teeth.

'*Viens ici*, Bassett,' I encourage breathlessly. But

without heed or warning the dog sprints forward, hurry-scurrying towards the wild pig.

'No!' I cry, rather too loudly, as the boar vaults through the air. For such a mammoth beast, she seems astoundingly agile. She lands with a reverberating thud directly in line with the dog and begins to charge, fit to kill.

'Bass!' I shriek. Everyone springs to their feet again. The children are wailing. Mothers are attempting to usher their young into the house while Bassett turns on his heels and flees, flashing out of the path of the fulminating mammal. He streaks past me as Hajo, who has had the foresight to run and fetch a torch from his car, arrives and levels the beam full on to the boar, who turns tail, retreating hastily to take refuge in the shadows between the stone ruin, the pines and the monumental Judas tree. Hajo steers the shaft of light upon the boar's pointed, tuskless face, locating its wild, angry eyes now fearful and uncertain, while Bass, safely ensconced between his two pals beneath the dining table, is shivering and traumatised.

I toss sleeplessly most of the night knowing that it is time to make choices.

The following morning, early, Angélique finds me bleary-eyed in the kitchen preparing coffee.

'Excuse for my English,' she says, 'and for my words, but I think you are not very fine in these days.' Angélique is a madonna of a woman, yielding yet powerful. We became close during the last days of her father, Robert's, life when we spent hours alone together at his hospital bedside. Although she is almost a decade younger than I am, I look up to her, admire and respect her. Falteringly, I broach my concerns about Michel, attempting to open up to her. 'I don't recognise him. I fear for his health, for our marriage.'

'You must go to him,' she counsels.

'Are you sure?'

'No,' she smiles, wrapping her arm around my shoulder. 'But once, when we were children, Papa was going through difficult days, it was Michel who lent the greatest shoulder. He spent hours with Robert, not talking much, creating small projects to give him back his confidence. It sounds to me as though Michel needs such support now.'

'He doesn't seem to want it from me.'

'Try.'

Before leaving for Paris, I telephone the refuge centre for lost dogs. Having explained my dilemma with Intruder, I am advised by the desk clerk that his breed of sheepdog can rarely cohabit. He is a loyal and faithful animal but an aggressive fighter if his top-dog position is threatened. 'Bring him here,' she advises. 'We will find him a good home with a master who has no others.'

Intruder must go.

I release him from the lead he has been attached to for the best part of the last three days, whistle him to the car and he pounces in buoyantly. He sits beside me on the passenger seat, mascot stance, tongue hanging loose, panting and dribbling, pleased as Punch with his jumped-up station. His eyes glitter like tinfoil because he thinks he has won my undivided attention; that he is selected and apart from the others who gaze up at the vehicle in forlorn bewilderment.

'I hate to do this, pal,' I tell him during the short journey.

When we arrive at the refuge and I read the accusation and desperate final plea in his expression it almost breaks my heart, but what choice do I have? I stand firm, kissing him on his wiry forelock and jumping away smartly as he takes a sharp-toothed swipe at my cheek.

From the refuge I turn inland, seeking out Alexandre who, I learn, is away for a week in the mountains with his family. I leave no message. When I arrive back at the farm without Intruder there is much canine jumping for joy and licking of my legs.

Two days later, I say *au revoir* to my house guests, leaving them to enjoy the farm while I absent myself to fly up to Michel, taking with me the dried and gathered flowers, bags of our garden herbs, figs, garlic and early-season grapes. I find him living a solitary and frugal existence. He has lost weight, but not shockingly so. What stuns me, though, is that he has painted all the woodwork in the studio where he lives and works the Matisse blue of Appassionata's shutters. A curving staircase which leads to the mezzanine where he sleeps is a rich azure; doors and window frames have received the same treatment, blue or turquoise. The two windowsills in the kitchen are ablaze with fire-red geraniums, placed in southern-baked terracotta pots. The stairs from street-level to *atelier* have been daubed a deep, brick red. No surface remains uncoated. It is a cave of intense colours.

Glass jars that once contained yoghurt, washed of all food traces, are filled with dark brown earth and seedlings or brightly coloured powders: yellows, purples, emerald green, white. Dozens of them, like a row of sentries, are marshalled against the walls. Since we first met, Michel has always expressed a deep appreciation of colour, of spectrums of light, of tone, palettes, shapes and forms. I have frequently thought that, aside from the love itself, it is one of the greatest gifts our relationship has offered me: the world unveiled and received through tinctures and textures of light. I had felt hopeful earlier in the summer that this was his pathway back to health, but now I am at a loss. My response to this space is that it is extreme, enveloping, suffocating. I suspect that I am in the company of a man who is in difficulty. Is this an identity crisis, an experimentation? A desperate bid for colour beyond a black depression triggered by shock?

Angélique's words were clear and simple but faced with the reality, I don't know how best to support him. I enquire after his health, his professional world, what films he might be preparing. He tells me that his affairs have suffered from his extended absence; contracts are slow; he has decided to bias his company exclusively towards the making of documentary films. Eventually, though, he wants to step back from business. He intends to travel less.

'What would you prefer to do instead?' Hoping that he might want to spend more time at the farm, I suggest that we reconstruct the ruin, build him a studio. He shakes his head. 'Thank you, but no. I cannot see yet what this new phase of life, the future, will bring but I need to face the present alone,' is his response.

'I hope it will include us,' I admit softly.

One Shot More or Less

The evening before we are due to set off on our hunting trip, Alexandre telephones to confirm with me what I will require: an extra T-shirt and a spare pair of natural-fibre socks and *no* perfume, he reiterates. 'You can wash, of course, but with unperfumed soap.' Hiking boots are indispensable. A heavy sweater is vital as is a mountain jacket – if I don't own one, he can supply this. 'Bring whatever food you fancy, not forgetting mineral water.' All to be transported in a rucksack, nothing carried by hand and I am not to wear white, anything bright or eye-catching. It will alert the *gibier*, the game.

'If you have khaki clothes, or a combat outfit all the better.'

'Combat? Me? I'm sorry, I haven't.'

He then informs me that we need to set off from his mother's house, a short drive from the foot of the mountain, by half-past four in the morning. 'Jacques will collect you. Arrange it with him. See you tomorrow.'

When I speak to Jacques we agree that pick-up will be at quarter-past two. It is now 9 pm. I only arrived back at the farm two hours ago. I stayed on in Paris for a few days to support Michel in whatever way I could, but he remained desirous of his space, and then I received a call summoning me to London. I have returned to an empty house, all guests gone and the cupboards bare. I have no bread and the *boulangerie* is now closed. Quashia, whose working day is back to its regular schedule now that the crushing heat has abated, offers to scoot to his local twenty-four-hour Arab *épicerie* and buy me a loaf. I gladly accept his kind offer and set about rummaging through the wardrobe and various drawers in search of sweaters, a rucksack and my hiking boots, which I have not worn for more than six months. I should have prepared for this, got used to them again.

At half-past one, after two and a half hours' sleep, I am out of bed again, running a bath, making sandwiches, feeling shivery from exhaustion. Outside it is the dead of night and Lucky stares at me with incomprehension.

Jacques arrives late, mumbling apologies. He managed only one hour's sleep, having spent the evening with his five-year-old daughter at the circus. 'The tigers were fantastic,' he mutters as we set off inland. Our journey is expected to take close to two hours. Aside from weekly conversations about swimming pool, fire or boar matters, Jacques and I barely know one another and, as this does not feel like the appropriate moment to get acquainted, I doze or stare out of the window. I can make out very little of the passing landscape because it is still pitch black. The alpine trees and mountain villages are little more than cut-out shadows but beyond, as we negotiate the hairpin bends, spiralling upwards in his Renault 4, the sky is navy clear with a corn-yellow half-moon and galaxies of stars to irradiate our route. At one point, I catch sight of a constellation that resembles the outline of a tree and because it is unknown to me I point it out to my new companion but, too tired to express interest, he merely grunts.

In the village of Belvédère, at an altitude of over 500 metres, within the chalet home of Simone, Alexandre's mother, who is upstairs sleeping, our arrival is greeted by a trio of men and Beethoven, a floppy black dog the size of a donkey. The television is on in the kitchen where the men are staring at a film about fishing as they drink coffee and kit themselves up in their hunting gear. The topic of conversation is fish. Aside from a nodded greeting, I am ignored. No one expresses surprise or disapproval that I, a woman, am to accompany them. I say nothing apart from a shy *bonjour* and then *merci* in response to an offer of coffee. They talk amongst themselves and I study the room. The kitchen shelves and cupboard tops are cluttered with a collection of ornate, brightly enamelled jugs. Everywhere is neat and frilly or wooden and pristine. Jacques, the fisherman, participates in the conversation principally to confirm the varieties of catch displayed on the screen. As well as Alexandre, who is dressed impressively in fitted khaki slacks with several large pockets and matching T-shirt, and looks from head to toe as handsome as a Greek god, there are two others. Jacky, an older man with a large strip of Elastoplast on his forehead, who is introduced as Alexandre's father but, I learn later, is actually his stepfather, and Didier, their lithe young companion and regular member of their hunt team, also dressed from head to foot in sharply pressed khaki.

Four yellow plastic bands, rather like hospital identity bracelets, are laid carefully on the table. They have lettering and numbers printed on them. The men discuss them – I cannot follow what they are saying – and then Alexandre packs them in his satchel.

'What are they?' I ask anyone who might be listening.

'*Les bracelets.*' Which leaves me none the wiser. My erroneous guess is that they are name tags, one for each man, required in case someone should be involved in an accident on the mountain or has to be left behind. A green quilted hunting gilet is tossed my way and we are given the signal to move. It is twenty to five. Outside in the yard, the men clamber into the rear of a white Transit van. I am about to follow but am redirected to the front cabin, to the central seat between Alexandre, who will be driving, and his father, who insists on referring to me as Madam and speaking about me as though I am invisible.

'Madam should be next to you.'

'Please call me Carol,' I ask of Jacky once the excessively playful Beethoven has been ushered back into the house, we are all in our places and the van is being reversed at breakneck speed down the steep driveway of Alexandre's childhood home. Jacky pays my request no attention. I doubt that he has heard me, chattering as he does incessantly and loudly. In spite of the hour the talk is ebullient and charged with expectation. A hunting trip is afoot, only the second of this season, and I am patently aware of myself both as female and as someone who has not comprehended the pleasure this sport affords them. As we drive along the high roads and narrow passes of the mountain village, Alexandre slows the vehicle to allow himself and his father, who leans right across me when looking to the left, the opportunity to peer up the serpentine entrances into others' homes.

'Ah, Louis has left then. He'll be at his post,' one remarks to the other, or 'Henri's car is there. He must have returned from his trip.'

'Your aunt's lights are on.'

'Impossible! She went to Nice.'

They seem to be acquainted with every single inhabitant and to know by heart the personal itineraries of the denizens of each and every dwelling, and they talk of the nearby coastal towns as though they were foreign domains a million miles from their picturesque alpine enclave.

Within no time we are parked on a stony slope at what appears to be the mouth of a mountain defile, and out we all tumble. It is ten to five, still night and, due to the altitude, exceedingly chilly. I hear a stream coursing from somewhere on high. It must be feeding the rather dramatic waterfall, Cascade du Ray, we passed a few minutes back. While the bags and rifles are unloaded I contemplate the magnificently clear, starlit sky and the dark silhouettes of eminent peaks encircling us. Four rifles are slung over four shoulders – their lethality disturbs me as the moon glints against the metal and creates a ghostly, coppery effect – my rucksack is tossed my way and I drag it on to my back. It is heavier than I had anticipated. I am handed a *baton*, a walking stick, by Jacky with the words, 'Madam might need this.' Alexandre takes the lead and we begin the ascent. The men set off at a lick and soon settle into a marching rhythm which is steady but rather too brisk for me. I am third in line as we snake our way in single file up a shingled, dusty and rock-strewn path. Behind me is Didier, the silent member of the quartet, and bringing up the rear, old Jacky.

Within minutes I am breathless and battling against the necessity to huff and puff. I am trying to avoid raspy inhalations which might draw the men's attention. I have slept for little more than two hours, I am out of condition, my backpack is already cutting into my shoulders and my boots feel like lead weights as I lift and tread. I am also hiking at a higher altitude than I am used to. Our farm sits at somewhere around 100 metres above sea-level. We are now close to 600, heading for a plateau, Cime Valette, which rises out of the clouds at 2,200 metres and has been described to me as a two-hour climb. I glance upwards trying to gauge the distance to our destination. However, in the blackness, beyond the stands of fir trees I cannot decipher anything. The sharp tilting of my head causes it to spin and I feel as though I might vomit. My breathing is growing constricted. I am gasping for air and, as I suck in, I hear a wheezing in my chest. This is soon followed by a shooting pain in my left arm while another attacks a nerve trapped in my neck and travels upwards into the left side of my head. I fear that I am on the verge of a heart attack. In fact, I am sure of it. I am suffering all the warning signs. We march on, scaling and talking. Or rather, the men, so fleet of foot, are joking and bantering, flicking their pencil-thin torches on and off as they, we, negotiate awkward roots or jagged rocks jutting dangerously out of the sharp bends. I remain silent. I am incapable of speech, concentrating as I am on my heavily plodding feet as well as my unwieldy, misfiring system. I am perspiring. Beneath many layers of clothing, my back is cold and damp yet I am hot and sticky. I am very aware that two men are directly behind me and that I am hindering their acceleration. Time is of the essence during these hunts and one of the fundamental rules is that the men must reach the summit and be stationed at their posts before daybreak. I am terrified that someone will notice my deteriorating condition. For their sakes, I cannot dawdle. I make a supreme effort and put on a spurt. On the other hand, if I keep going at this velocity, I might explode. My heart is hammering against my breastbone and my breathing is now so loud someone must have noticed. I stumble into what seems to be a small cairn at the pathside. It is dislodged by my clumsy footing and sends several rocks and stones rolling thunderously down the silent hillside. Suddenly Alexandre stops. He turns back and hands me his torch. 'Here, use this. How are you getting on?' he quizzes.

I haven't the breath to reply. All I know is that a quartet of strapping men are staring at me expectantly.

'Fine,' I manage eventually.

'The beginning is the toughest part. It gets easier. Let's keep going,' he concludes, and on we march and I have missed my opportunity to admit that perhaps I am not sufficiently fit for such an expedition.

Why am I here? I moan silently. It was Michel who

persuaded me after I recounted the episode of Bassett and the wild sow and acknowledged my sense of failure at resolving the dilemma.

'Accept Alexandre's offer,' he advised . 'Experience the hunt first-hand and then make a decision.' So here I am, labouring up a mountain face with four hulking men, two of whom I am scarcely acquainted with, the others complete strangers – and three of them are carrying weapons.

Ten minutes later, the going is no easier. In fact, from my point of view, it is considerably worse and the distance between me and the two men in front has lengthened. My heart and head are rattling. My saliva has a metallic, sanguineous taste to it and I am now convinced that I am going to die here on this mountain in the middle of the night, in the company of Provençal hunters. Eventually I reason that I must speak up. Pretending that I am going to achieve this hike is ludicrous. It will serve no one and is probably going to cause an accident – leaving me stranded on high with a yellow bracelet tagged around my wrist. I open my mouth to air my concerns and out spills a dislocated stream of semi-formed words, 'Can't . . . don't think . . . not managing to . . .'

The men draw to a halt again. I can tell from Alexandre's body language – his facial expressions are not clear in these wee hours – that he is growing impatient. They must keep moving if they are to be in position before the game comes out to feed.

'I think I will have to turn back. I am not up to this.' I finally admit.

Alexandre bends his entire body forwards as though

I have just taken a shot at him. I feel guilty and humiliated.

'You all go on,' I continue, attempting a lighter, less desperate note. 'I'll turn back and wait for you by the van. I can read a book, I'll be fine.'

The quartet group together and an intense debate begins.

'Madam won't make it,' I hear from the huddle of dimly lit bodies and I feel myself blush with shame. Finally it is decided that Alexandre, Jacques and Didier will continue on up to the post and Jacky, the seventy-two-year-old stepfather, who does not begin to look his years, will accompany me. This will not be the retreat to the vehicle I have suggested and had hoped for. We are to press on and continue the ascent to-gether, but at an achievable, less breakneck pace.

'Is that agreed?' Alexandre asks me.

I nod, head bent like a scolded child. Frankly, I would prefer to throw in the towel but I dare not argue the point and disrupt the schedule any further.

'If you still cannot make it, Jacky will see you back down.'

'That's fine with me, Madam,' the old man con-firms agreeably. 'I have been hunting for sixty years. What do I care about one shot more or less? We'll take it slowly and struggle up at your rhythm.'

I hand back the torch to Alexandre. He accepts it and the younger men regroup. Alexandre still leads, Didier goes second and then comes Jacques, who is more solid than his companions but a muscular, fit man all the same. Within seconds the nimble trio is out of sight and well beyond earshot.

I turn to Jacky. 'This is very kind of you.'

'Listen, we have all day, till nightfall if needs be. Let's take it nice and steady. In any case, feel the weight of this.' Jacky hands me his rifle, which is surprisingly heavy. 'And my backpack weighs forty-five kilos. All in all, I am carrying more than sixty-five kilos, and at my age, I am more than happy to stroll.'

Stroll!

Jacky now takes the lead and I stagger along behind him, mortified, still not convinced that I will ever see the plateau.

We rise for the better part of another hour and a half. Jacky halts regularly to point out beavers' lairs at the pathside and to bemoan the fact that there is so much less fauna these days. I learn that the water gushing from these mountain rocks feeds a river known as the Vésubie, which is an eastern tributary of the famous Var; that there are two rivers in the vicinity; and that the tall wild flowers all around us are *chardons*, or thistles, and are gathered and dried for bouquets.

And this small plant, what is that? I ask, desirous of a few to send to Michel. How I wish he were here. As far as I can make out it is a stunted version of the *chardon*, although none of these flowers resemble any thistles I would recognise from England. They have round, saucer-flat flower heads, rather like sunflowers except that they are white, furry and cupped by spiky bracts.

'*Chardons bas*,' Jacky confirms.

Later, when I search for the name of the dead blossoms I have collected, I identify them as milk thistle.

Jacky rests the butt of his rifle on the ground and leans into it and I find myself hoping it is not loaded. He looks about, sighing contentedly. He points to a distant peak. 'See the mountain beyond those two closer ones, beyond that widest aperture? That's Cime du Gelas. It's the highest summit in these southern Alps. There, to the west is Cime du Diable.' Devil's Peak. 'I have climbed and hunted every one of these *cimes*.' He patently knows this ancient terrain like the back of his hand. He was born in Andorra, I learn, and has been climbing mountains since he was a toddler.

Each of these pauses is a punctuation, intended to instruct me, to show me that beyond a certain distant cleft lies Italy, that close to where we are going to hunt there are five mountaintop lakes, that juniper grows well here, ravens breed in solitary pairs or even that the shining light to the east of us is not a star or planet but a television satellite – 'See how it turns!' These carefully calculated breaks are also respite, to allow me to catch my breath and diminish my heart-beat. This old hunter is a gentleman. I have no reason to feel ashamed. He seems perfectly content to lead me up the Alp face at my own speed and to share with me what is clearly the greatest passion of his life.

'Wait till the day breaks,' he repeats regularly. 'Wait till you see the beauty of all this. And these late dog days, *les jours caniculaires*, are the most splendid of all.'

'It is already beautiful,' I tell him honestly. My panic is subsiding. I am calmer, savouring all that is laid out before me, fusing with my environment. We have risen above the alpine forests now and the vegetation consists of little more than heathland, dried, spindly grasses and the tall thistles. This summer, I overheard the men say in the van, has been hardest on the big game, whose sources of food have withered to nothing in the sweltering temperatures.

Navy blue peaks, grooved like Pan's pipes, tower heavenwards to a dense lilac-aubergine sky. The stars shimmer like spilled handfuls of glitter. The day is beginning to rise with a faint mist. As I turn my head, ghostly halos, auras of light, appear and disappear and I cannot tell if they are caused by my light-headedness or are a freak of nature. The silence, aside from Jacky's chattering and the trickle of descending water, is truly awesome. Not a bird, not a whisper of wind, not a breath of life. Only the two of us, a most implausible pair, standing shoulder to shoulder, a rifle at one side, momentarily moored in the palm of these mountains, gazing upon the miracle of morning.

'Wait till we reach the summit, Madam, and you behold the valley of the Madone de Fenestre, in the Parc de la Mercantour. You cannot be closer to nature; you will never know such beauty.'

A tiny circular light flashes from on high, from the direction we are headed.

'See there, that's Alexandre! They've arrived at their look-out post and are signalling their position to us.'

'How much further?' I venture at this stage.

'About a thousand metres. Another hour or so of climbing.'

My heart sinks.

On we trudge, passing along the way two substantial wooden shacks.

'They belong to the shepherd,' I am told. There are

no signs of grazing beasts and the *cabanos* appear abandoned. In winter this must be a solitary and fearsome place to reside. Open to the winds of the world and prey to wolves, with only sheepskins and fires for warmth and comfort, these rough-stoned cots conjure up pictures of an earlier age when peasants wore wooden clogs and shepherds drank milk warm from their sheep.

Red ribbons of light hail the break of day. In the distance, I see a pinkish-grey blanket of pollution hanging above the sleeping metropolis of Nice while here the dawn is unfolding crisply, pure as the babbling brooks. A plane, then another, their underbellies shot with rouged sunlight, are approaching their seaside landing base.

It is a quarter to seven. Our marathon ascent is drawing to a close as, finally, I stagger, panting, up the last stretch of scree slope towards the lofty plateau, where there is a breeze and where the others, somewhere beyond view, are stationed, enjoying, no doubt, a well-earned breakfast. Within seconds of our arrival, as I rotate to imbibe the fawn and damson-dark colours, the velvet textures of nature, relishing the prospect of refreshment and rest, Jacky begins flapping his arms about. It takes me a moment to understand that he is frantically signalling to me to get down. I hover, confused, too tired to decide what to do, fearing that if I acquiesce my legs, trembling with the effort, will never find the strength to lift my aching body up again, but he is insistent and sets off at a run, gun at the ready, towards an abutting elevation, and then disappears. I cannot make out any sign of life or animal activity and confess that I dismiss his pantomime as macho posturing. Still, I am now obediently on my haunches, engaged in admiring the sweeping, khaki-coloured hills embosoming me, and I see why Alexandre suggested combat clothes. This, my first sighting of the national park, is stupendous, a patchwork tableland. Suddenly, a shot is discharged, sharply followed by another. The reverberations slicing through the peace and silence are utterly shocking. I half-rise to peek and hear the thud of agile hooves. In the distance, I spot three smallish brown animals bolting. They are climbing at a lick, making for a neighbouring crest while, at the same time, closer to us, a fourth beast has been projected skywards and is now tumbling down the upper slopes. The clattering bump and roll of its body echoing emptily round this mountainous amphitheatre sends a shiver through me. Clearly, the creature has been hit.

Jacky comes trotting back, full of beans and smiles. It is a chamois, a mountain antelope. They are the only species of antelope existing in the wild in Europe and survive happily in these elevated chains. One of the reasons Alexandre was so insistent that I did not wear perfume is because their sense of smell is very keen and even at this remove they would have picked up my scent.

'*Mamma mia*! You have brought me luck,' cries old Jacky. 'But I'm not convinced she's dead.' He has dug into his rucksack and pulled out his binoculars, *les jumelles*, and is peering through them in the direction of where his game has fallen. 'She's scrabbled in beneath that big rock. See her?' He passes me the glasses. I try to align them but I cannot pinpoint where the antelope has taken refuge. All I know is that the large grey-stoned crag where the chamois is hiding reminds me from my vantage point of a cindered chicken carcass.

'You go on,' he orders me excitedly, 'find the others, get them back here. I am going to try and shoot again but I don't want to frighten her, don't want her to run off, to escape into the park, because once she has made it there she is protected; it is illegal for me to take another pot at her and she'll die slowly.'

I am disturbed by this information. The possibility of the antelope bleeding to death within a hollow in the rock unsettles me and I cannot move. My instinct is towards the animal, not the man.

'Get going, Madam! Hurry, find the others, bring them back. I need back-up.'

I turn and begin to advance along the soaring path, but to where? I am dithering like a dope. I have no idea where I am supposed to be going, and I cannot stop picturing the injured creature holed up in the rock. The situation is resolved without my help when, within seconds, Alexandre ascends a nearby escarpment and strides fast in my direction.

'A chamois has been shot,' I call out to him.

'Yes, we saw it from our post.' He is followed by Jacques but there is no sign of Didier.

'*Putain!*' This literally means whore, but is a frequently used expletive in these parts to express surprise – the equivalent of 'bloody hell!' or 'dammit!'

'She's not dead,' I announce when the men reach me.

'I know. We must finish her off.'

Fifty or so metres below us, lying on their bellies behind another, smaller crag, guns cocked, two teenage boys have settled themselves.

'*Putain*! It is Tomas, the mayor's son, and that brainless pal of his.' Jacky and Alexandre hurry to speak with the youths and, it is my guess, to alert them to the fact that the game is ours, not theirs.

My attention is drawn back towards the valley of Madone de Fenestre in the Mercantour parkland, which stretches to the borders of Italy, my hearing attuned for the first time to the clunking of bells. This is not the pealing of the Madonna's church tower marking matins; it is a herd of tan cows grazing on the open flatlands, blithely unaware of the antelope stowed in cave-darkness high above them, shedding its life. Now that I train my eye, I can discern other herds of cattle, dotted here and there, ascending the sandy-coloured inclines. The Provençal word for those evocative-sounding cowbells is *picorns*. Their sedate, tinny rhythm strikes me as so at odds with the danger afoot here.

'Where's Didier?' Jacky asks of Jacques. I stare at Jacky, noticing that the Elastoplast on his forehead is curling like a telephone wire because he is perspiring.

'He thought he saw game over that way and took off.'

Jacky begins to wave frantically into the distance, in the vain hope of attracting Didier's attention. He grows impatient. This is the man who this morning told me that there are over two thousand species of wild flowers in this Mercantour park and that one shot more or less made no difference to him. 'We need him,' he grumbles to anyone who is listening, which is not Alexandre, because he has scooted down the hill-side to appraise the situation. Within seconds he is back. 'Your three antelopes who took flight have returned with another. Four of them! Take a look! See where they are feeding!'

'They are perilously close to the park,' is Jacky's résumé of the state of play.

'I'll get down beneath them and drive them back up. Don't worry, I won't take my gun. You and Didier make your way up that escarpment there. Didier can station himself at that lower bend, in the seat of it, while you, Jacky, you position yourself on the extreme left side, there, see the cusp of that high bluff? See where I mean?' Jacky nods excitedly. 'Train your rifles right in there.' Alexandre half-closes his eyes and circles with his extended arm to define with precision the dingle he is referring to. 'As soon as the game has settled in that basin of grass and I am out of range, you can open fire. But for God's sake wait until I am well clear of the dip. Don't jump the gun.'

'What about the wounded one? Where the hell is Didier?' Jacky is signalling like a madman into empty nature. 'We need him if we are going to pull this off. We have to get on with it, or the prey'll wander away.'

Alexandre swings about and fixes his gaze on me, decides against whatever was in his mind and settles on Jacques. Jacques understands instantly that he is to go and root out their missing soldier and speeds off along the track. 'Jacques, when you bring him back, you'll accompany me, won't you, and help drive the beasts up the incline and into the dip?'

Jacques nods placidly and continues on his mission.

All the while these two hunters are lifting their binoculars and peering at the chicken crag. 'You shot her in the side.' 'She's nearly done.' 'She's going quietly.' 'No, wait! *Attendez!* She's getting up again. *Putain*, she's moving!' 'She's going to attempt the park!' 'She'll never make it.' 'Where the hell are the other two?' 'Her head's cocked, resting now. She's fading.' 'Christ, Didier, where is he?'

And then the others are back. Now the men go over the tactics. Not once, but four, five, six times even, repeating the directions, the drill, as though it were a mantra, as though it were a mobilising force to energise them for the task in hand. Or an army manœuvre.

'After Jacques and I have driven the four beasts into the trap, I'll make my way along that upper shelf and approach the crag from behind and finish off the bleeding one with my knife.'

'It's like guerilla warfare,' I tease nervously, because what I am hearing is making me distressed.

'That's it, precisely, Carol! It's war.'

I wander back to the spot where all the rucksacks have been left, astounded that they have taken me seriously, that this hunt is so important to them, and open up my bag to retrieve mineral water and take a swig. It is hot and dry up on these upper ranges now that the sun has fully risen and I am feeling nauseous.

'I hope those bloody lads keep their guns quiet.' My

companions have approached and are raking through their luggage searching for chocolate.

'Don't worry, they've gone. Carol, you will wait here with the equipment.' I don't want to wait with the bags. Who's going to steal anything up here? Now they are loading their rifles with bronze cartridges the size of small fingers. Click, flick, click. Miniature missiles.

'I would prefer to observe from the look-out rock where the village boys were, if that is all right with you?' I direct my question to Alexandre because it is very evident to me that he is the commanding officer, and I feel I should ask permission; I have caused sufficient hitches for one day.

'All right, if you want to, but you are to stay down. Keep low even as you settle into position and you are not, in any circumstances, to move or shift about, understand?'

I nod.

'And no camera. It reflects in the light and the animals will spot it. Are my instructions clear?'

I nod again. Then take off, running, bent double as though with stomach ache, to my cache, which, when I reach it, is very much more cramped than it had appeared from above. I shove myself into the open hollow and wait. The men have disappeared off in their various directions. Jacky scales the vertical mountainside like a skater and I realise how much he must have held back earlier to accommodate me. I assume everyone is in position though I no longer have Jacques or Alexandre within vision. I wait, and wait, and nothing appears to be happening. I check my watch – half an hour has passed; the cold air of the early morning has long since evaporated. The sun is high in the sky; it's blisteringly hot. I try to rearrange my legs, which are growing numb beneath me, wriggling my calves under my buttocks without really moving. Three-quarters of an hour goes by. It is a long drawn-out wait. I concentrate on the shadows, the colours, the stillness. I wonder what Monsieur Q. is up to back at the farm, battling on with the wretched shed, no doubt, and Michel in Paris, how is he today? I am achingly aware how different my life has become without him and I still feel no certainty that I can help him through this crisis or, more crucially, that he wants me to.

Airliners, brilliantly silver and white in the warm daylight, cross the skyline noiselessly and then I lose them as they prepare for landing at sea-level, somewhere beyond the mountain ranges, at Nice Airport. Whenever I fly home, I see these southern Alps through the plane windows. This is the first time I have enjoyed the opposite aspect. I shall look out at them from the air with another eye now.

Very distant gunshots, nothing to do with Alexandre's band of men, explode into the silence of the late morning. Not many, but they are disturbing nonetheless in this zone of perfect tranquillity. Too remote, though, I assume, to alarm the unsuspecting antelopes we are trained upon. I have no idea what is going on. I cannot see the others, aside from Didier, who lies patiently on his belly with his weapon at the ready.

The sun beats down upon me. Wasp-like insects

buzz around my head, irritating me. I dare not wave them away. My eyes grow heavy. I try to remain attentive to what is happening. Which is nothing, as far as I can tell, besides cowbells jingling and insects zizzing.

I have fallen asleep in the heat. When I awake the men are returning, each from his separate direction. They are empty-handed, have thrown in the towel. I am secretly jubilant and then, as I squint to look more closely, I see that Alexandre has something slung over his left shoulder. It resembles a shaggy shawl.

The wounded chamois has finally been slaughtered and retrieved and Alexandre has humped it back to our plateau base. He lifts it from his neck and it unfolds on to the ground like an acrobat. What strikes me first is the blueness of the creature's sightless eyes, an arresting lapis lazuli and full of surprise. One of the metal-toned, hooked horns has been wrenched from the animal's brown furry head and I can see scarlet-red blood in the round hole where the horn had been growing.

The beast is almost the size of a fully grown goat. She has been tagged with one of the four yellow bracelets I saw hours ago on the kitchen table. Alexandre unleashes his knife from its black leather sheath and skilfully slits open the animal's stomach. His gesture has the ease of someone opening an envelope. Inside, at the base of the lifeless torso, are balls of chewed, damp grass; putting me in mind of generous helpings of tobacco. They have burst through the base of the stomach or were in the process of being excreted. The fetid stench of congealing blood and recently digested grass makes me want to throw up.

If she had lived, Jacky tells me, her horns would have grown to about six inches in length and would have been more curled. She, *la bête*, is a female and is less than two years old, so not yet fully grown. She has not coupled yet and would have had her first *chaleur*, her first menstrual bleeding, and also known her first mating, this autumn. The bullet has entered her right through her sex and exited through her right side. I cannot help comparing the shot with images of sexual entry, as well as dwelling on the fact that she has taken three hours to die. Her virgin self shot through with red-hot fire and pain. I watch on as the stomach bag is cut out of her and retrieved with its various poppy-black, saggy pouched parts attached. These I take to be her liver and kidneys but apparently they are not. Alexandre flings the jaundiced, balloon-like bag and its appendages behind him into the dry grass. Within minutes it is swarming with buzzing, beavering flies. The malodour of death is overwhelming.

The young antelope is splayed out on her back with her innards gone. She is a pretty little thing, even now, yet, strangely, I feel no disgust towards these men. I had expected to be sickened to my guts by what they have done, but I am not. I am heartbroken for the animal, for her missed opportunities, and I feel compassion as well as frustration for the pain she has suffered. Still, I watch on with dispassion. Could I do this? I ask myself, and the answer is no. Will I now be able to authorise the hunting of wild boar on our farm? And to that question, I also silently reply that I very much doubt it, but Michel was right. It was important to see this for myself before making a final decision and, in his words, 'to challenge my pre-conceived judgements'.

Suddenly one of our party spots a peregrine soaring overhead and the trio of hunters and Jacques pause to observe and discuss the falcon at its own chase. I wonder if the great bird is after the antelope's innards but the men tell me no. These peregrines usually track smaller birds, swooping on them in flight.

I mention that we have honey buzzards and, possibly, booted eagles nesting on our land. One evening, whilst swimming, I spotted an eagle circling overhead, I tell them. The men seem surprised and suggest that I might be mistaken, that it was probably also a buzzard. 'They're quite similar, you know.'

Jacky asks me if I have ever seen a *casseur d'os* at work. A bone-breaker? No, I shake my head. What is it?

'It's a bearded vulture, the largest of all alpine birds. Bloody enormous and a very curious sight. There are only half a dozen of them here in the park. They were reintroduced to the Alps about a decade ago after an absence of almost a century. If we were to leave this chamois here, it'd have it. It soars on high, patrolling the mountains for dead sheep or antelope, then it swoops down, picks up a large bone and carries it away, dropping it from a height on to a rock to splinter it, hence its nickname, bone-breaker. Extraordinary. When you watch it, it looks as though it is travelling in slow motion.'

'Why would it want to break the bones?'

'One of its richest food sources is the bone marrow. Once you've sighted one of those birds, you'll never forget it. They are pretty spectacular.'

Jacques remains silent and in the background, watching the sky. Like me, he listens and takes it all in but, unlike me, he does not ask questions. He films scenic moments with his video camera from time to time but he is not photographing this disgorgement. I wish Michel were here with his camera. I want to remember and share this nature reserve.

I am disappointed to learn that we will continue. Although it is only a little before noon I had been hoping that the slaughter of this creature would be a full-stop, that now the thirst of these red-blooded men would be slaked and we would turn back for home. But, no. The animal is bagged up into a green plastic bin-liner and stuffed into Alexandre's rucksack – everything he was carrying on the upward journey save for his precious gun, his *carabine* with its high-powered, detachable lens, has been transferred to Jacky's bag – and we set off. Alexandre strides forward to take up the lead. His trousers, neatly pressed when we left his mother's house, are stippled with blood around belt and pockets.

The mood is highly charged now, adrenaline is coursing. There are chamois about and although the quartet of antelopes grazing in the vicinity of this dying girl have smartly escaped for the second time today, they remain somewhere in the region and that creates excitement, offering the possibility of further scores later in the afternoon for these men. But then, all of a sudden, the conversation and plans seem to change. I am not sure why. Now they are considering making a descent of several hundred metres until we return to the wooded slopes where they can also track and hunt. Their talk now is of lunch and, after, pursuit of wild boars; it is unlikely chamois will be feeding at those lower levels. There are other species of deer there, though.

During our descent, which physically is as gruelling as the rise earlier, we encounter the shepherd, a toothless man with a navy beret. Probably in his mid-fifties, he looks to me more like a shopkeeper than a shepherd of the sierras. His opening gambit is 'Hunting with women now, eh?'

To which my best friend Jacky responds, 'And why not?' while I try to brush it off with 'I am not here to hunt.' But no one is listening to what I have to say, so I give up. They are wrapped up in the exchange of news. I smile to myself, remembering a story René recounted long ago of a farming family he had lived alongside in the mountains who nicknamed their shepherd 'Auntie'.

The *berger* tells us that he and his flock of 500 sheep and six dogs are ascending to the peak and from there crossing over to new pastures beyond this *cime* where, he hopes, remains an acre or two of edible grassland. 'The land is desiccated,' he moans. 'Even at this altitude. So we must climb higher.' During a long drawn-out conversation in the noonday sun – while we are entirely penned in by braying sheep and frisky, panting black or white dogs – I learn that he lives in the same village as Simone and Jacky and sleeps up here only from time to time. He shares his woeful tale of how an alpha male wolf sent thirty of his flock over the mountainside a few nights earlier. They had broken free of the pen and he lost the lot. Not one survived the fall.

I had not known until recently that grey wolves (*Canis lupus*) inhabit these southern French Alps. They are an endangered species everywhere and I had thought they were no longer in existence in western Europe. This is not, however, strictly true. 'The wolves crossed over into this national park from Abruzzi in central Italy during the last two decades of the twentieth century,' explains the shepherd when I ask him. 'There the cussed creatures are protected.'

Although wolves adapt to change better than almost any other mammal and their survival rate here, since their arrival, has been an ecological success story, they are still rare everywhere throughout their vast range of habitats. They continue to be hunted and persecuted by man as they have been for centuries because they have always been believed to be the predominant killer of valuable livestock. Farmers detest them and claim their presence to be the return of a bygone nightmare.

It has also been proven, and indeed this fact is borne out by the shepherd's losses, that wolves don't confine themselves to culling the old and sick animals in the herd, as was originally supposed. These canine predators will hit on young, strapping beasts, too, and very occasionally, they will slaughter more than they can immediately consume, though such surplus killing is unusual.

How can you be sure that it was a wolf? I ask.

'I can tell by their droppings; they contain fur.'

The resurgence of the wolves is a heated issue and not one in which I wish to engage this working shepherd. Fortunately, this morning, he has only one stray to worry about so, accompanied by his three fabulous Pyrenean sheepdogs, he descends alongside us, talking nineteen to the dozen, to salvage the lost lamb, leaving the rest of the flock in the protection of his other three herders, lean black collies whose coats are flecked grey with age. Jacky asks if we might lunch at his cote, which he warmly offers. It occurs to me that perhaps he is hanging on to our company because his existence is such a solitary one but when the track divides, we wave our farewells and part.

I desperately need to pee and pray that one of his two shacks will provide the necessary amenities, but as we arrive and I enquire, I am laughed at and teased. 'No, Madam, but why worry? All of nature awaits you. Make yourself at home.'

I drop my bag on the ground, secrete the loo paper I have brought with me up my jumper and disappear behind the two dwellings, hoping that none of the chaps will thoughtlessly follow in my direction with the same purpose in mind. Of course they leave me in peace and, when I return, they are already attacking their lunchboxes.

Jacky has unearthed a very wobbly wooden bench which he has placed facing the three other men, who are sitting on the ground, leaning against the cabin, legs akimbo, quaffing and munching. 'This is for Madam,' he explains, seating himself alongside me and, together, we settle like old chums to a robust, gamey picnic.

The men's lunches consist of *saucisson*, jars of game pâtés, rosé wine, entire loaves sliced on the spot with hunting knives, massive hunks of strong-smelling cheeses, slabs of chocolate and energy bars.

My own lunch is a far more modest, thrown-together affair. I unpack my tuna *pan bagnat*, which by this stage has grown soggy from the olive oil and the hours squashed in a plastic bag. Dressing the two wholemeal halves are rocket leaves from our salad patch; they look more like lifeless black caterpillars now, but I am too hungry to care. For dessert, I have two peaches given to me by Quashia, two bottles of mineral water and a bunch of delicious black grapes, also from our garden.

'Anybody fancy some grapes?' The men don't even bother to respond. They are still stuffing themselves. They talk and eat voraciously, slapping coatings of pâté on to doorstops of bread, chewing vigorously. Jacky pours me a glass of rosé – he has carted five glass tumblers along with him as well as an *isotherme* bag to keep the wine chilled. I decline; he insists so I acquiesce and sip it slowly. I am exhausted and fear the wine might cause me to keel over. He offers me a slice of *saucisson*. This I accept, which pleases him and he cuts me a helping as thick as a club sandwich. Jacques thrusts one of his banana energy bars my way. It tastes like no fruit I have encountered, is horrendously sweet and quite disgusting. Nonetheless our swimming-pool specialist consumes three on the trot, in between mouthfuls of bread with duck in green pepper pâté, swearing that they will allay his tiredness. His eyes are bloodshot with fatigue. He also polishes off the entire pot of pâté on two chunks of bread.

'*Qui veut un Boonty?*' I hear. Intrigued, I look up to see them offering one another milk chocolate Bounty bars.

Alexandre jumps to his feet, produces a leather gourd or wineskin containing red wine and proceeds to consume it in a manner that I have always believed was a northern Spanish tradition. That is to say raising the flagon and holding it some distance above your open mouth and pouring the wine in a steady, arched stream down the throat. The Provençal word for this wine container, he tells me as he struts to and fro in the sunshine, is *bachourle*, which he pronounces 'bat-choly'. When I look it up later in my Frédéric Mistral dictionaries, I find that the root of this word appears to come from *bacho*, a water trough or fountain basin. It also means drenched.

I ask if I might attempt a sip from his *bachourle*. My request causes much amusement which makes me a little awkward, but I do not soak myself in wine. In fact, I manage fairly successfully to train the flow directly in between my lips. Unfortunately, however, no one has explained to me that the draught is held in the mouth and not downed until the flask has been taken away, so I swallow the liquid straight away, explode in a fit of coughing and nearly choke. The wine is rough. My eyes are smarting and the men are falling about the ground with merriment.

When the remnants of lunch have finally been

packed away, and the shepherd's open-air dining room has been tidied up – while the man himself with his flock of 500 has scaled the very pinnacle of the mountain and is now disappearing from our sight, intent on a parallel escarpment – it is decided, much to the consternation of Alexandre, that our hunt, our *journée de chasse*, is to be terminated. As I stuff what is left of my two squashed bunches of grapes back into my sack, I overhear Jacky whisper to the others that Madam *'en a ras le bol'* which means Madam is fed up, has had it up to the back teeth or, literally, has overflowed the cup.

This is not precisely true, though I do not correct him. I am physically shattered and cannot face any more clambering about in the dusty heat or the thought of stalking another unsuspecting victim even within the cooler climate of the alpine forest. Still, the weather is exceptional, the locations stunning and I am having fun, relishing the adventure.

'Come on, let's get going!' Apparently, Jacky's wife, Simone, Alexandre's mother, has lunch waiting for us.

Lunch?

Back in the village of Belvédère in her manicured chalet garden, Simone, with Beethoven leaping and barking at her side, has been eagerly awaiting our return. She claps her hands with joy when she hears that Jacky has been the successful trapper of the day. Jacques helps himself to a bottle of water, installs himself on a flower-patterned garden swing placed in the shade beneath a spreading vine bower and instantly falls asleep. I go in search of the loo to wash and slap on some lipstick and mascara while Jacky embarks on a game of plastic bricks with two tiny children, nephews of his, who are toddling about in a capacious pen beneath a parasol on the terrace. Alexandre and Didier set off in the van with our antelope. They must go to the village to the office of their local branch of the Alpes-Maritimes Hunting Federation, to register the animal's death. Here, its tag number will be catalogued and the yellow bracelet handed in. The antelope will be weighed, date and time of death recorded, hunter responsible noted; all must be declared and indexed. These are legal requirements. It also means that their allowance has been reduced by one beast. The three remaining bracelets give this hunting party the right to hunt and kill three more chamois before the season is over. Each bracelet is equivalent to a licence to shoot. If a hunter is caught transporting an untagged pelleted creature, he will lose his permit and be exceedingly heavily fined, perhaps, in rare cases, even imprisoned. These men, this team of men, have three bracelets left for the season. *Sangliers*, wild boar, do not require bracelets. Hunters are free to shoot as many as they are capable of bagging just so long as they shoot in daylight and at a minimum of 500 metres' distance from habitation.

While the men are away, plates are being piled on to the table at a furious rate. It is now about half-past two, less than an hour since we enjoyed our al fresco feast. Simone refuses to allow me to lift a finger. I try to surreptitiously warn her, when I see what appears to be days of cooking and preparation being heated and served, that we will probably not be wanting very much.

'Why?' she cries out to Jacky, horrified.

'Don't listen. We're starving.'

The men return from the hunting association and the antelope is strung up in the garage ready for skinning after lunch. Their conversation debates the morning's missed opportunities.

A chilled local mountain beer is served and we all adjourn to the table. The food is laid out and waiting, hors d'oeuvres and main courses all at once, a smorgasbord of delights: mushrooms gathered from the hillside and marinated in Provençal goodies, ham from a pig slaughtered last winter by Jacky and cured in salt by Simone, a deliciously spicy chicken dish, steaming potatoes, cheeses, wines, beer, bread, cakes and then coffee and more cakes, every item homemade or home-cured. Beethoven is having a field day as everyone blithely hands him food while chattering animatedly. He is gobbling chunks of chicken, cake, ham, cheese, batting from one guest to the next, panting ecstatically, his thick-wedged tail wagging dangerously, jaws wide open with greedy glee. He'd eat the entire pig if it were on the table. No one seems to care or notice how much he is consuming. I cannot imagine what breed of dog this enormous slobbering brute might be and when I ask I learn that he is a cross between a golden retriever and a Newfoundland.

'Was he named after the film?' I ask Simone.

She furrows her brow. 'What film?'

While I narrate stories of our own dogs to Simone and discuss the finer points of olive-oil pressing, the male talk still centres on the hunt. Our morning's escapade is recounted and analysed over and over again, each man chipping in his tuppence-worth on why or how we bagged only one creature, how we lost four others by a hair's breadth and of the extraordinary good fortune Madam brought to Jacky. Simone, who has not laid up a place for herself, does not partake of the meal and has placed her chair on the periphery of the feeding group, remarks to me that this is the pattern of life until the close of the season. Every Wednesday, Saturday and Sunday, the men will be up and out before dawn and for the rest of the week they will talk of what has passed or what is to come. They breathe, eat and sleep *la chasse*. Their lives are consecrated to the hunt.

'And you?' I ask.

'I was born in this village. My first husband, Alexandre's father, was a hunter, Jacky is and now so too is my handsome son.' She throws a mother's doting glance towards Alexandre. 'What can I do? I only have the one child and he is the apple of my eye. Just so long as he and Jacky are happy, then I am.' She brings out photographs of her granddaughters, both of whom are teenagers and exquisitely elegant.

I compliment Alexandre who grows visibly peeved when his mother returns to the table with yet another photo. This example is a family portrait of Alexandre with his wife and the girls.

'I have a lovely daughter-in-law, don't you agree?'

I nod.

Alexandre rises briskly, giving his mother a withering look. 'Let's skin that beast!' he snaps. Evidently there is a chapter here I have missed, an underlying tension that I am not party to and cannot read. Simone retreats. The rest of the party congregates by the garage doors.

In the skilled hands of Alexandre, the antelope's pelt falls from its flesh like a dancer shedding a costume. Simone arrives with notepad and pen. She has been designated the role of recording the apportionment of the parts of the beast. The meat is carved into six cuts. Each member of the six-man hunting team, whether or not they participated in today's hunt, is assigned a morsel. Today, they were three so meat will be kept refrigerated for the second trio. The joint each member of the team has been allocated is catalogued in Simone's book. Apparently, after each successful trip, the choice of meat rotates. Jacky offers me the succulent *gigot* earmarked for him which I refuse, but he insists. 'Even if you do not want to eat it, Madam, perhaps your husband would enjoy it.'

I think of Michel alone in Paris, struggling to keep his company afloat and I accept. Simone's aunt, Tata, arrives accompanied by her husband, Tonton Auguste, who hunts with the others. He is eighty, the oldest member of the party and positively glowing with health. The couple have presumably popped in to collect Tonton Auguste's share of the chamois, though I do not see him receive it.

Everybody finds a seat out on the terrace. Yet more home-made cakes are served along with a pitcher of freshly brewed coffee. Tonton Auguste settles at a corner of the table in the shade and proceeds to read the *Nice Matin*. The women call me to join them.

Their talk is of cooking. Simone describes at great length what she served us for lunch and how she prepared it. Tata responds with her variations on the same recipes and when they catch me smiling, they question my amusement.

'The French and their cooking, their obsession with discussing every mouthful,' I rejoin.

The women sigh. 'Ah, but, we can't help ourselves. Here, taste this cake. Do you know these plums? Which liqueur have you used?' . . . And so the day creeps towards its conclusion. Jacques tries once more to sleep; the hunters are wrapping up the meat, washing their knives, making all ready for the next outing, which will be the following Saturday. Jacky is crawling about on the ground playing with the babies. Beethoven is crashed out in a cool corner, farting in his sleep, dreaming, no doubt, of another hunt, another celebration. It is a convivial and very French scene and could last into the late hours when dinner might be served, but here in this mountain village the sun sets early, disappearing behind a neighbouring peak and this signals the moment to bid *bonne nuit*. Everyone offers farewells, throwing arms around one another, embracing and kissing and embracing again, after promises of olive oil in return for cured hams and cakes and another meal, another gathering somewhere at some point in the future, and then Jacques and I begin to wend our way home.

Driving coastwards, dusk at our windows, in the company of this handsome pool man who is somewhere between stranger, fellow hunter and friend, I feel a keen sadness that Michel has not shared this curiously original day with me, both its beauty and brutality; that he was not there with me on the plateau to witness the glorious break of morning and to feel the beat of the sun from on high. How I wish that I could deliver these rare experiences to him; how I wish I could dispel his present crisis. But lost as I am, I also feel a certain peace. The mountains have offered me that.

Jacques and I are both silent, lost in our individual worlds, dead tired and reflective. Our thoughts trailing behind us, floating in and out of the day we have lived through. Laconic though he is, I suspect that he, like me, is facing difficulties and challenges he never alludes to.

Eventually I ask him whether, in the light of this outing, he might consider adopting the sport. He considers the question and decides no, but he stresses that what his friends are doing is essential work. 'As you saw, Carol, the hunts are strictly controlled and if the packs are not culled they grow too large, the grazing grounds prove insufficient and there are greater risks of disease and sickness.'

I suggest to him that the wolves are the antelope's natural predators and argue that they might be a more eco-friendly solution to the problem. He frowns, not understanding my drift.

'In the United States, during the eighteenth and nineteenth centuries, the early settlers hunted bison, elk and deer without regulation, which caused the slaughter of over sixty million wild beasts. In those days there were numerous grey wolves but, as their food sources diminished, because man was hunting their prey, the wolves began to stalk and kill the only other meat available to them: the settlers' livestock. This created a fierce war between settler and wolf that raged for well over two centuries, until the wolf was all but driven to extinction. In those days, it was not unusual for government agencies to pay hefty sums for the carcass of a wolf. This encouraged private bounty-hunters who ranged the mountains and plains in search of wolves to trap. Many men made a healthy living hunting wolves for the cash pickings. Bounty-hunting was only outlawed in the United States in 1965. By the end of the sixties, fewer than 700 grey wolves survived in the wild. Of course, today the grey wolf is a protected species there.'

'I don't get your point,' yawns Jacques.

'If the wild game and the wolves were left to their own devices, nature would be its own regulator of numbers. Hunting would be unnecessary.'

'Mmm,' he mutters, switching on the headlights. 'I think I'll stick to fishing.'

Counting Sheep

The weather is gloriously warm; burnished and autumnal. The leaves on the deciduous trees are variations of oxblood, citrus and flecked apricot. Day after gloriously beneficent day, the temperatures average 25 degrees with sunsets synchronising the season's colours. Unfortunately this delivers us no rain, which for the farmers is worrisome. The ground soil has turned to powder and without irrigation nothing is surviving. It is the first time that we have been obliged to water so late into September.

Michaelmas has passed. Now begins October and Michel has flown south for the autumn television festival, Mipcom. It is a joy, a relief to have him home, though I barely see him during the five-day market. He is up and out by seven in the morning and does not return until after midnight. He has agreed to stay on for the weekend after the event but intends to spend those free days writing his 'follow-up' e-mails. He talks of transforming his favourite spot beneath the magnolia tree into an exterior weekend office, if the weather stays fine. I entreat him to donate Sunday to us, in the hope that we can dedicate it to more relaxing activities and spend precious time together. 'Let's play hookey and take off on an unlikely escapade,' is my plea.

While Michel is running to and fro, attempting to open new business deals, meeting with executives, lunching network personnel at one or other of the beachside restaurants, Quashia renews his attack on his never-ending shed in the light of structural comments from Michel and the garage delivers my restored car, spick and span and good as new. It must require a gentle spin, surely? The perfect excuse, I claim, for our outing. Well, an excuse. The question is to what destination? The Camargue is marginally too far for a day out.

Jacques has been recounting stories to me of the *transhumance*, the shepherds' custom of transporting their flocks to winter grasslands. Not dissimilar to bees, the sheep must be installed in pastures closer to sea-level where there is little likelihood of snow and where there will be plenty of grazing. Already, over the past three weeks shepherds everywhere have been on the move. If we took a helicopter up into the Alps, he says, we would look down upon dozens and dozens of flocks, each five or six hundred strong, descending the mountainsides, intent on the lowlands. It must be quite a sight.

On Sunday, two shepherds with their flocks are expected to converge upon the village of Roubion, where the public have been invited, for a couple of hours only, to participate in this fabled tradition, to accompany the beasts as they are steered from one village to the next, a distance of no more than four or five kilometres.

'Why don't we join them?' I suggest to Michel, though I am not altogether convinced that spending the better part of a day walking with sheep will appeal to him. Surprisingly, he seems enthused by the plan. He will take his movie camera along, he says. 'It might make an interesting inset in a magazine programme. Yes, let's make the trip.'

We wake to Sunday, warm and sunny, and breakfast in the garden. While I swim, Michel picks grapes and prepares our *petit déjeuner*. I arrive at the table outside, dripping wet, to find a fruit face smiling up at me from a bowl of plain yoghurt: one grape divided into two for the eyes, a sliver of apple for the upturned mouth, a triangle of pear as the nose and eyebrows of pollen crumbs. With the sun drying the water slipping from my wet hair and this simple but delicious meal in front of me, I am reminded, as I pour us both coffee, of our early, stony-broke days here. I used to laugh then when I remarked that we would never be so happy, so carefree again. I turn my attention to the sea, to a fleet of sailboats that signal a regatta departing from the old harbour in Cannes. So much has changed. The years have marched on and this one has served us a shocking blow but the man at my side seems less damaged this morning, less withdrawn, and he remains, at least partially, in my life in spite of his words in the summer, and for that I am profoundly grateful.

We throw our hiking boots into the car and off we go, to encounter the autumn shepherd trail as the beasts plunge seawards to their winter pasturage. If nothing else it will be a healthy and vigorous tour in the beautiful meridional Alps, an opportunity for us to be together and for Michel to de-stress after the tensions of the television market. We leave the motorway at the last exit west of Nice and begin our cruise inland, entering an industrialised zone where empty parking lots, full of curled and withering shrubs, seem eerily abandoned in this robust Indian summer sunshine. Beyond the blocks, we pass through a valley bordered on one side by a desert-dry, pebbled river and, opposite, a parade of lushly decked-out garden centres, each one open for business and teeming with weekend shoppers. Here we say *au revoir* to the urbanised, serviced coastland, progressing towards the lower gradients of the most southerly of the Alpes-Maritimes mountains.

Now we commence our ascent into nature.

At somewhere close to 700 metres, at a steep and perilous fork, we swing to the left, following the signs for La Route des Grandes Alpes. Here the road narrows and my recently installed engine begins to whine rather than purr as we continue to gain vertiginous height. The circuit is no longer consistently tarred. Long stretches remain what they always were: shingled, dusty, spiralling goat tracks. To the left, hundreds of metres below, water courses through a wooded ravine. I am beginning to silently panic about the car. It seems sturdy, but the replaced engine is a stranger to me and what of the tyre grip and the brakes? This is not quite the gentle test drive I had envisaged. Thoughtlessly – we are in the Alps, after all – I had not counted on the vehicle's trajectory being quite so dramatically dangerous. While my imagination conjures up possible variations on 'lunging over the shelf at breakneck speed', reality brings forth from out of the zig-zag of now-you-see-me, now-you-don't bends an imposing Renault, appearing from nowhere, descending in the opposite direction. I am at the wheel, as I was that drizzly night outside Monte Carlo, and my memory flips me back to that nightmare encounter.

Both the other driver and I brake surefootedly on the central curve of the bend, and my car slows to a halt without a hitch. Fortunately we had both been progressing at a snail's pace but, even so, we narrowly avoid a head-on collision. Both vehicles are now eyeball to eyeball, precariously perched within centimetres of the drop. We are 1,000 metres above sea-level. Keeping my sights firmly fixed on the cliff wall, not daring to acknowledge the yawning abyss, I reverse, inching backwards, while the other car creeps forward, eager to hit the road again. Breathing deeply, calming my tremor, I shut out the vivid replay of our accident. When we are stationary I glance at Michel, wondering if he is reliving the same horror, but his thoughts seem locked off elsewhere. I stretch my right arm across the gearbox and lightly rest my hand against the back of his. His fingers are surprisingly cold again and, for a moment, I am freaked, but I don't remark on it. We are together, having time off in one another's company. Still, this fluctuating distance of mind really unnerves me.

We continue our journey.

The autumn colours are staggering. Alpine evergreen interspersed with a deep honey red, which, I hazard a guess, are the leaves of a variety of maple. The plane trees are elf green fading to soft yellow, like the flesh of unripened melons. Dotted here, there and everywhere within this canvas are thickets of stumpy russet bushes, which I cannot identify. Casting our eyes down the giddying cleft, ahead or to the left of us, depending on the swing of the path, is the rushing river, crystal grey with slippery-wet stepping stones that put me in mind of otters plunging through metallic jelly. It is a theatrical panorama, and as if this were not sufficient, an extraordinary, unexpected card is then casually tossed our way. We are plunged into darkness, entering a tunnel of blasted rock, and emerge out the other side into blinding daylight, where a most astounding geological transformation has taken place. The mountain itself has changed colour. No longer the limestone beige so common in this neighbourhood, it reveals itself now as aubergine. Yes, aubergine. Every cliff, every rock as far as the eye can see is resolutely, resonantly, aubergine. As a backdrop to the palette of autumnal vegetation it is breathtaking and, above it, reigns a serene sky, blue as a laundry rinse.

'What stone is that?' I ask Michel. 'I have never seen such a rock hue before.'

He shakes his head. He, too, has been taken by surprise.

On we climb, turning on sixpences, wondering if somewhere way back we might have taken a wrong turn, until we see a sign, followed soon after by a sighting, far ahead in the distance, of the village of Roubion. It is gliding high in the mountains, seemingly attached by a bootlace, flying in the face of gravity at 1,310 metres. A fairy tale, rising up out of nowhere like a lost city of grottos.

'This is not going to be a touristy event,' I say to Michel. 'We have barely encountered a soul so we may be the only outsiders.'

How I am to eat my words!

When we eventually approach the village we are forced to a halt by a vanguard of cars and a mountain lass waving and sprinting from one vehicle to the next. Flushed and excited, she explains that the village is jammed solid and there are motors parked all along the kerbs. 'The only solution available is to keep travelling, until you reach Roubion le Buisse. There are heaps of places there,' she assures us with her peaches-and-cream smile and clear-as-running-brook eyes. 'And there will be a *navette* to bring you back down.'

I cannot imagine what kind of shuttle will be able to negotiate this chaos. In any case, if it is not too far, we would prefer to return on foot. It will be a pleasant stroll and surely swifter. The question is, how to get to the next village? This hive of surcharged activity is the only passage through. Because we are in France, *bien sûr*, several of the cars that were queuing behind us have grown impatient and attempted to overtake, thus cleverly blocking infiltration from every angle and leaving not so much as a patch of dried grass on which to turn or reverse. Angry words ensue from all directions. Arms are spinning like windmills. Cigarettes are carelessly tossed on to the ground as drivers and their passengers, swearing and huffing, march impatiently alongside their transport. We stand aside, contemplating this incongruous corridor of traffic. Where have all these vehicles appeared from?

Peacefully, side by side, we take in the view and bask in the sunshine, while around us folk are getting themselves extraordinarily twisted and knotted. Our patience is soon rewarded. Within a quarter of an hour we are on our way, bypassing Roubion and moving on to the higher station.

Hélas, because every other car has been given the same instructions, the parking up here is also *complet*. In fact, there are cars spilling out from everywhere. So much for fresh mountain air. Eventually, we find ourselves a steepish ridge of tufted bank and, with a fierce hit on the Merc's throttle, or, as the French would say, a determined 'crush of the mushroom', I manage to get it parked.

The *navette* turns out to be a clunky old pick-up truck. Departing now, with a load of twenty-five people aboard, all standing like cattle in its open rear. The passengers are to be deposited at the village entrance before the truck swings back for the next swarm. Evidently there are no traffic restrictions or police on duty or, perhaps, because today is a *fête*, all heads are turned towards the scenery. Whichever, it is no distance back to Roubion and we choose to stroll.

Entering the village, we meet countless visitors milling to and fro and it is difficult to negotiate a path through the throng, but the buzz of expectation all about and the Sunday-afternoon bonhomie jolly the crush. Cherry trees and chestnuts adorn the squares and cobbled streets. Villagers mingle with and pass through this unexpected onslaught, bleating at one another, 'Baa, baa, baa,' and giggling senselessly as though they are keepers of a secret language. Hundreds of children are skipping and sliding like urchins in the dusty lanes. A loudspeaker blares out foggy incomprehensible messages. The air smells warm, of juniper, cooking and dung.

We see nowhere for lunch. Signs point to a pizzeria but the likelihood of a table can only be a dream.

'Ann! Ann!' shriek the schools of kids in thick mountain accents, running in front of Michel's camera, waving. Their cries bemuse us. Who is Ann, to cause such an uproar? It is only a little while later that we realise what they are actually yelling is '*Âne!*', the French for 'donkey'.

And, as if on cue, a pantomimically attired donkey is led out of a barriered mountain pass at the rear of the village by a very commanding fellow. Broad-shouldered and tall, he is a hirsute chappie with a large black beard and a rug of frizzy chest hair. He walks his docile ass, a bunch of plastic pink flowers adorning its forelock, from one set of excited youngsters to the next, smiling and engaging in chat with them, allowing them to stroke the beast's muzzle as he answers their questions. At first I take him to be a gypsy, here to profit from the crowds by selling donkey rides, as is the custom at chilly seaside resorts in England, but it soon becomes clear that this fellow is the master shepherd and the donkey is part of his retinue. Further back, beyond the tunnelled rock, is the muster point where the sheep are assembled, waiting to get on the move. 'Thierry!' we hear someone call to the shepherd. Thierry's skin is a very dark shade of plum and has the texture associated with living days and nights in the open, exposed to the extremes of high-altitude elements. His eyes are kindly, compassionate and a piercing shade of russet which makes a startling combination with his plummy complexion; the colours are as remarkable as the rock set against the autumn hues we have just driven through. He wears a brilliant red checked shirt with the sleeves rolled up, similar to that of the wine expert, Guillaume Laplaige, and a navy-blue knitted waistcoat. His clothes look as though he might have been rolling down the valleys in them. They are not dirty but crumpled, vaguely dusty and laced with grass stalks. He herds with his son-in-law, who is also a shepherd. Both sport flat, chocolate-brown velvety hats, scruffy and beaten. I ask the younger man if there is a name for this style of head-dress and he stares at me uncomprehendingly. 'Hat,' he says.

When the high-altitude days grow cold and frosty, before the snows arrive, Thierry drives his sheep south for *l'hivernage*, the wintering. The journey lands them, eventually, at his birthplace close by the old Roman encampment at Castellane, where the animals are housed in a *serre d'hiver*. This, in the olden days, would have been a capacious barn but today is much more likely to be a larger version of a plastic-covered greenhouse. Here the beasts are given health checks by the authorities, injections against diseases such as brucellosis and then, in the springtime, before setting off to their summer pastures once more, they are shorn. Thierry has never ventured further afield, never even visited the coast, he tells us. His only expeditions are into the high Alps, to watch over his flocks.

'I own no property, no longer have a wife. I have no fixtures or responsibilities save for my sheep, my *brebis*. I have worked with them all my life because I love them. I love the look of them, too, and if I couldn't travel to spend my summers with them it would break my heart.'

Approximately five hundred people have converged on this isolated upland locale to participate in the *transhumance*. A bemused, red-faced man standing at his doorway tells us that this crowd is far bigger than they had been expecting or can realistically accommodate. The hordes are now queuing, in the usual French scrum manner, for the plastic tumblers of sangria offered free by the local council to all visitors. Every attempt Michel or I make to secure a couple of tumblers results in body blows, so we give up and decide to pay a visit to the church. Inside it is sombre and unadorned but what peace in comparison to the racket outside. Although it is Sunday, this house of God is deserted and not a candle burns anywhere. While Michel films the interior, I search about for one to light but see none. There are no signs of any recently celebrated service and I wonder how regularly it is used as a place of worship. In the olden days, shepherds frequently stabled their ewes in mountain churches and I ask Michel if he thinks this old stone building with its painted walls might ever have served such a purpose.

'Possibly. The ewes might well have been milked in here, out of the harsh winds. A pottery or wooden vessel known as a *piau* would have served the purpose.'

I am shivering. The stone façade keeps the nave chilly. We return outside into the startling sunlight, to find the crowds massed in the square in preparation for the transfer. The loudspeaker is relaying garbled instructions. We have the choice of preceding the troupe or holding back and walking astern. Most choose to forge ahead. Michel suggests we bring up the rear.

'Come with me.' He offers his hand. I take it; it is icy. He guides me through the tunnel in the rock and out of its far exit. We have stepped beyond even minimal civilisation out into the vastness of pure mountains. A strip of a path leads away from the village and, here are penned possibly a thousand sheep. Watching over them are several dogs and the young flat-hatted shepherd. Because the creatures are bunched up tight together and cannot move forwards or backwards they have begun to scale the cliff face. Thirty or forty goats and sheep have strayed and congregated high above our heads, cleaving to the rock at right angles like geckos to walls. Bells are clunking as they negotiate the scraggy terrain.

Thierry returns with his clip-clopping donkey. He and the younger man patiently contemplate their stock. A surprising number of goats litter these flocks. Several dozen would be my estimation. I ask Thierry, who is now waiting close by us, how many sheep he has in total and his answer momentarily confuses me: 'Well, more than a good or so dozen thousand.' It is his young relative who translates this as 'nigh on fifteen hundred'.

240

The two men wait in silence, speaking only when a tourist shoots them a question. Otherwise they stand surveying their beasts, shooing away flies with their handkerchieves or with a fan-like wave of their hats. Between them is the donkey, a docile, people-loving mule with its tail flicking at the flies on its rump and its upright ears twitching against the pink flowers. Strapped within its backpack this beast of burden is transporting metres of rolled orange netting, attached to slender iron pickets used, no doubt, for penning the sheep wherever the entourage chooses to bed down for the night. Do the men sleep in the open air? Or in stone huts similar to the *cabanos* seen on my recent hunting trip? I peer into the mule's luggage but see no sleeping bags or tents.

The mule's name is Zamzong. Thierry repeats it twice, nodding his head proudly.

'From the Bible.'

'Zamzong? Ah, Samson.'

'*Oui*, Zamzong.' Thierry tells us that these days with good roads and even the possibility, in extreme cases, of helicopter patrol, the role of the donkey in the *troupeau* is more or less defunct but, he says, patting the ass, he wouldn't travel without her. 'Her strength is less necessary, but she's my girl and my best friend. I'd hate to summer in the mountains without her.' So Zamzong is a girl!

We learn that the younger *berger* and his wife, Thierry's daughter, have two small boys. During the mid-year school break mother and children travel to the shepherds' camp to holiday with him. The hardest weeks of the year are 'come September when the new term begins' and the family returns without him to Castellane. Then he has six or seven weeks of work ahead before he can join his wife and little 'uns again.

Aside from the sheep, goats and solitary Zamzong, there are two Pyrenean sheepdogs and one Doberman whose collar is also decorated with flowers; these complete the *troupeau*, which is now receiving its marching orders.

'It's time to get going!' 'Let's head out!' 'Move on out!'

I smile. It reminds me of *Rawhide*.

'Hold back!' *'Attendez!'* 'Nobody budges until the animals have been rounded up!'

The lean, black and tan Doberman is set to the task. Up he goes, scaling the almost sheer cliff face with poise, barking at the fat fluffy sheep, nudging them into action. They scamper and two-step but then drop to the road, one after another, a snowstorm of clumsiness, while the goats clop down with haughty grace.

The procession gets underway. Bells are jangling, hooves are trotting, sheep are bleating; a descant of livestock on the move.

'Folks, stay back behind the last beast!'

'Don't mingle with the *bêtes*.'

We are ordered, we are herded.

Since most of the onlookers have chosen to head the column we find ourselves in the fortunate position of walking directly behind the last of the flock with only a handful of others. I smile at Michel. 'Good idea to hang back.' He squeezes my hand as we trail a battery of furry, swaying backsides, and I am delighted we have this day.

Children from the lines behind us begin to worm their way through the ranks of grown-ups, eager to pat and slap the animals. As we pass through the tunnel, returning to the church square, hosts of new arrivals push and shove to pinch our places. Their assertiveness panics the beasts at the rear of the herd who, before we know it, begin to bolt. They are soon galloping at racing speed; the crowd behind matches their pace, thundering through the streets, out of the village, towards the mountain road. Everyone is desperate to keep abreast and in pursuit of the squad. Looked at from on high, we must be a hugely comical sight. Five hundred people pursuing fifteen hundred sheep, several dogs, a few dozen goats and a donkey decked in flowers, all dodging and bucking, bells clunking, clattering along at full tilt, charging as though from an avalanche through echoing cobbled streets, out to the mountain pass, in and around parked cars, whooping and giving chase. The sheep, of course, are completely mystified.

Tinée, the Doberman, is barking manically, while the flocks are scurrying up the high banks and tumbling like skittles on to their fleeing, fleecy comrades. I cannot see beyond these muddy buttocks of mutton to the leaders of the procession, who surely must be Thierry with Zamzong and the two sheepdogs, but here at the rear all hell has broken loose. How must it feel to have this Light Brigade of humanity and stampeding wool bearing down upon them?

The assistant shepherds, *bergers bénévoles*, unpaid helpers brought in from as far afield as Grenoble, are predominantly women. They each tote a long-haired switch with which they thwack the ground when the sheep begin to stray. Now they are shouting to the crowds to keep back, rein in their children; to the kids to keep their distance; yelling at black and tan Tinée, named after the river fed from these mountain springs, who is haring up and down the banks like a yo-yo. All the while the shepherdesses are thwacking and whipping at the ground, but we never see them hit the animals.

Eventually, all is back under control; the pace calms and we walk and chatter in the afternoon sunshine. The air is perfumed by the smell of untreated wool. I lean down and stroke several of the beasts' backs and my hand sinks into their warm, fibrous coats. The walking is hot going and our rhythm is constantly interrupted because we are obliged to halt while the strays are gathered up, and there are plenty of them. The shepherds are yelling repeatedly, 'Slow down! Keep behind the beasts!' While the sheep romp up the steep banks and gorge themselves on the *maquis*, Tinée rushes after them, tongue lolling, barking and chivvying until the sheep leap and dodge and fall back to the road, tripping over themselves and their fellow travellers. Looking ahead towards the massed animals weaving in and around the cars, within this scenery of sky-high landscape, I am reminded of a flying carpet.

'Why do you do this?' I ask one of the young female helpers. The locals are French-speaking. No one converses in Provençal.

'There are wolves in these hills,' she tells us. 'It partly accounts for the foundation of the association that brought me in. It was formed to create a bond between owners of livestock and those interested in pastoral life and willing to lend a hand. I am an agriculturalist – I studied at the University of Grenoble – but anyone can put their name forward if they fancy helping out. I take my vacations during the two seasons of *transhumance*. It is tough and tiring work for one shepherd alone or, if they are lucky, two to guard travelling flocks for weeks on end, throughout long nights, always on the lookout for wolves.'

'What is the organisation?' I ask. 'Where is it based?' But the blonde-haired shepherdess has been called back to duty and off she strides, elegantly swinging her whip.

During this uphill passage – curiously, the village we are approaching is marginally higher than the one we are relocating from – the young shepherd is caring for a lamb that has been falling behind. It was growing anxious, unable to keep pace, and found itself trapped within hundreds of pairs of marching feet. Now the shepherd is carrying junior on his shoulders, little black hooves slung round his neck, as though this tired, unhappy lambkin were a collar.

My boots are growing heavier. The soles are gunged up with the freshly fallen turds that are decking the lane. The sheep project their pellets into the air out of brown furry bottoms, whilst on the move, whilst falling over one another, bumping up against each other. It is as though they have no sense of direction or sight, yet when they lift their incurious heads, this dirty-cream sea exposes glimmering blue-black eyes.

I love the sound of their bells. Everywhere, bells.

Picorns. Some are extraordinarily resonant because they are worryingly large. A number of the goats' *picorns* in particular are so enormous they brush the ground. Bearing the weight of these hefty metal instruments around their stalk-like necks cannot be comfortable.

Roubion le Buisse: journey's end. For today, this will be the shepherds' resting place. The sheep are to be grazed here for a week. In winter, this higher Roubion is a skiing resort. How it copes with the influx of sporting addicts is beyond Michel and me because it is hardly more than a hamlet. We see no hotel. There is a prettyish *auberge* looking out across the street to the green-swathed Alps directly *en face*. Here drinks and plates of *charcuterie* and salad are served, rather in the style of bar snacks in an olde-worlde English pub, but there is precious little else on offer in this hinterland parish aside from clean nature and tranquillity. Today, however, the throngs are eddying and flowing up and down the hillsides, more multitudinous and disorderly than the sheep who are munching peacefully within their makeshift folds. A dozen or so wooden chalets dot the inclines but these appear to be privately owned. We stop for a noggin at the *auberge*, where they are advertising *vin chaud*, though we decide, because it is so warm outside, to order glasses of Côte de Provence red and settle ourselves crosslegged outside on the grass in the autumn sunshine to quaff them. Whiffs of the sheep droppings squashed into the grooves of my boot soles drift our way, but they are not unpleasant. It is all part of the excursion.

'It was a good idea, this day out,' smiles Michel. 'Fresh air frees the mind.'

I take this opportunity to suggest that I accompany him when he returns to Paris. He goes silent, sips his wine, shakes his head. 'Your visit was nice but I must be alone.'

I bite back my disappointment. 'How can I support you, then?'

'By what you're doing.' And he leaves it at that.

Afterwards we stroll the main street where stalls are lining the roadsides and the shallows of the grassy slopes. All are selling locally produced goodies. There are nobbly walking sticks carved from cherry wood and holm-oak, intricately patterned socks spun from sheep's wool, deliciously tempting goat's cheeses from a female farmer in Clans. We pause and buy several, more than we can reasonably consume. 'You can take some to Paris,' I murmur as I stuff them into my bag, fighting not to give way to the turbulence that is building in the wake of Michel's imminent departure. 'And Quashia might like one.'

We pause at a stall selling dark and golden pots of honey and, lo and behold, there on display are large jars of rhododendron honey and the *apiculteur*'s label is our very own M. Huilier's.

'Are they here?' I ask excitedly.

'No,' replies the young stallholder who, with his dark, curling locks and soft pale voice, reminds me of a country hippy, a survivor from Woodstock, or a knight from bygone days.

'Send our good wishes,' we cry. 'They are bringing their bees to us.'

Yes, the next *transhumance* we will participate in will end directly at our door.

The following morning, I pack up Jacky's donated leg of venison and most of the purchases from Roubion's market stalls and Michel flies off laden with them to Paris. A lull, a breath of calm, after the to-ings and fro-ings of the Mipcom television market returns to the coast and in another, far less pleasing sense, to the farm and my daily life.

As we kiss goodbye I see in his eyes that he has already left. I miss him from the instant he disappears through the Departures gate, more so because we have made no plans for our next meeting and nothing has been resolved.

'Why don't I come and visit you soon?' I offer again.

'We'll see,' is his minimal response.

Checking my watch on the drive home, I am thinking, 'Take-off time.' 'Now he is in the skies.' Doubts haunt me. Will we find a way to rescue our marriage, to realign our common life, which seems to have taken a turn as oblique and as incomprehensible to me as the wall of Quashia's shed?

Since Michel's arrival and departure, there has been a flurry of dismantling and reconstruction of 'the hangar', which is what both men have now decided Quashia is creating. Everywhere are pegs and string, a cat's cradle of intricate skeins to assist him to make level the tilts and bevels Michel has corrected, and the responsibility rests once again with me. I traipse the hill from time to time to encourage, to keep an eye and follow as closely as I am able the instructions Michel has left with me, but I am ignorant of all building skills and feel helpless in the face of the exercise. The lower structure is in place, after a fashion, and Quashia is now occupied with the installation of the timbers that will support the corrugated base of the tiled roof, but they look worryingly insecure to me.

'Carol, can you pop to the builders' merchants and pick up some glue? It's for these roof tiles. You know the one?'

I nod. 'How many tubes do you want?'

'Twenty,' he calls after me.

Twenty! 'Monsieur Q., you cannot possibly need so many.'

'Twenty,' he insists, and off I go, as obedient as the mason's votary.

'I've left you a cheese in the garage, Monsieur Quashia.'

'Thanks,' he calls between bouts of hammering.

And so our life continues, returning to the struggle of keeping everything afloat: Appassionata Without Michel. Once again he has retreated into his tunnel of silence. It is as though he has walked out of my life.

The Fortunes of Saints

The first draft of the script I was contracted to write is winging its way to Los Angeles by Chronopost, leaving me at a loose end. There is barely an olive harvest to give my attention to; there has been no feedback for months from the various oil bodies regarding our AOC, not since the letter I ignored; the wild boars have, mercifully, taken to driving others to distraction; Quashia hammers constantly at his shed, laying tiles now, and there is little input I can make to improve the situation so, turning my attention to my rather moribund life as an actress, I call my theatrical agent in London. 'Is there any work?' I ask him.

'Darling, it's difficult all round but you have been away so long. I could probably find you a theatre tour. I had a conversation with one of the managements this morning. They're casting for a thriller. It's a bit of a pot-boiler. It won't be coming to town, of course, and you'd need to sign for six months . . .'

'Six months! I couldn't. I have responsibilities here.'

'Well, there's nothing else right now.'

'No television?'

'Soaps, police series and game shows, darling. That's what British television has been reduced to, I'm sorry to say. I'll try to find you something, though, a nice little cash cow is what you need. Still, if I were you I'd stay where you are, laze by the pool and drink champagne.'

So here I am casting about for opportunities, ways to stay focused, to reassure myself that battling on with the farm is my best option. My husband is adamant that he needs time alone and the truth is I am floundering. My life feels rather as though the roof has blown off it.

At the beginning of our summer, in those few days before our accident, when I had pressed Michel for our outing to the Camargue, I found no festivals for us to participate in. Now approaches a renowned autumn weekend, a religious celebration and a gypsy pilgrimage held at the twelfth-century church in the Camarguais fishing port of Saintes-Maries-de-la-Mer. On the Friday morning I decide on a whim to attend it alone, to trace the journey we had intended to make. One call secures me a cheap hotel. I throw a few ill-assorted clothes into a travel bag and take off, leaving behind me our land of sloping hills and villages perched in mid-air where patriarchs in berets pass their *après-midis* playing pétanque in the squares, passing through conifer forests in the Var blackened by the summer's atrocities, red-earthed vineyards and plains of silvery olive trees. Grove after grove of silvery olive trees. Simply driving alongside them lifts my spirits.

Van Gogh, who spent miserable days of sadness and sickness in Arles, the capital of the Camargue, discovered that the olive tree was a source of wellbeing and an inspiration to him. He wrote to his brother: 'Ah, my dear Theo, if you could see the olives at this moment. The old silver foliage and the silver-green

251

against the blue . . . The murmur of an olive grove has something very intimate, immensely old. It is too beautiful for me to try to conceive of it or dare to paint it.' Eventually he dared: Van Gogh managed eighteen canvasses of olive trees.

I flash by the distant Alpilles range, north-east of Arles, where Frédéric Mistral was born, lived and wrote his poetry, swing left off Autoroute 7, with its convoys of articulated lorries hurtling to and from Barcelona, and whisper a brief *au revoir* to all those ancient murmuring trees, to the clefts and gullies, the escarpments and precipices. I am now bent on a meridional line. South, seawards from Arles with its magnificent classical and mediaeval structures, into a delta where the Romans and Greeks have not left their imprints, to a territory where the influences arise from other, I suspect, more pagan sources.

On my approach to the coastal town of Saintes-Maries-de-la-Mer I pass through windswept, alluvial marshlands. Gone is all greenery. Winding through terrain flat as a pancake I find myself in a reedy wetland where little grows besides rice and a vine cultivated in sand. Birds overhead wheel and whistle. The landscape and vegetation are so different here that it is hard to believe I am a mere two hours from our stone-terraced olive farm. There is not a knoll, hillock, cairn or midden to break the horizon in any direction, not unless I turn my head back, northwards. The physical features of this Provence are quite new to me. Marshland, grassland, swamps. Golden-hued; wet, caney and reflective. A primitive topography enclosed by two estuaries reaching to the sea like yearning arms, flowing and forked from their mother source, the Rhône. These lesser waters are known as Grand Rhône and Petit Rhône. In between them lies this mysterious, croissant-shaped, alluvial delta: the Camargue, where native white horses and solid black bulls roam freely as they have done since prehistoric times. I soon begin to sight them, grazing on marram grass at the borders of the swamps. Herds of them. White horses, black cattle. *Manado* is Provençal for herd. The finest of these wild white horses were selected from the Camarguais herds, the *manades*, for games involving the bulls. Animals are never killed in a *course Camarguaise*. In that sense it is dissimilar to Spanish bullfighting, the *corrida*. I appreciate that. I stop the car to observe them. The bulls return my interest. They raise their bovine heads, Houri-eyed, with stupendous lyre-shaped horns, and outstare me. Unlike the horses who feed on, oblivious. White herons, known as cattle egrets, perch on the bulls' thick-set necks and on the haunches of the stallions.

Not only are there no olives here, there are precious few shrubs or trees of any description in these sodden plains. It is due to the excessively saline atmosphere. I notice a few random figs, gnarled, knock-kneed and mottled by the winds, but there is little else in the way of arboreal cover. I drive by a pine. Its towering height in this lowland is a luscious originality, almost an affront. Its brilliant greenness brushing the deep blue sky bowls me over. A bold placement and unexpected.

Everywhere I turn my head there are birds: harriers overhead, songbirds, wading birds plodding about, their beaks dipping in and out of the mud like shoppers rummaging through stalls at a market. I slow the car so that I can better observe them. The songbirds are the most numerous of all. On a telephone line, within minutes of one another, I spot two raptors, still as stuffed toys, but I am not able to identify them. The afternoon is warm, not clammy as I had expected, but clear and sunny, though the air is brackish. On I motor, chasing the setting sun, not disappointed by my stolen day, cruising through the vast plains, deserted save for the abundant wildlife, on my solitary journey to the sea.

Several images, one directly after another, make me whoop with delight. They begin with my first-ever sighting of a huge flock of the region's renowned rose flamingos wading and strutting in the shallow water. And a party take flight! What a spectacle! White and lipstick pink with black underwings. The wings beat silently over an orange-pink sun reflected in the flat wetland water. I sit gazing by the roadside, losing all sense of time, wishing Michel were with me, wondering how this year might have turned out if we had left for this trip when we had planned to.

On the move again, I begin to notice examples of the traditional *mas*, the farmhouses; each one is pure white. They date back to days long ago when the region's mounted herdsmen, who tended the bull stock, lived in *cabanes de gardians*, whitewashed cottages with thatched roofs. Set back from the roads beyond corrals of white horses, they are very lovely.

Saintes-Maries-de-la-Mer was the first place in Provence to adopt the Christian faith. Once a thriving fishing port, now a tourist hangout, it received its name in the nineteenth century. In earlier days, I don't know how far back, it had been called Ra after the Egyptian sun god. Its present appellation honours two saints: Mary Salome, mother of the apostles James and John, and Mary Jacob, the sister of the Virgin Mother of Christ. Legend has it that this pair of Marys, in the company of Mary Magdalene, Lazarus, his sister Martha, along with their dark-skinned Ethiopian servant, Sarah, fled Palestine and beached up on this littoral, having beaten their way across the Mediterranean sea from its distant eastern shores. This boatload of washed-up saints, servants and Christian evangelists was on the run from persecution by the Middle Eastern Jews and Romans who feared the recently baptised, apostolising Christians. In those days, of course, this village was nothing but a windy wasteland of sand dunes and salt marshes. The story goes that all the disciples aboard the boat continued on by foot, venturing deeper into the heart of Provence, to preach their gospels and bring faith to the Gauls, save for the two, more elderly Marys, Salome and Jacob, who, judging their travelling days at an end, remained behind and built an altar in Saintes-de-la-Mer on the spot where the present-day church stands. (I love the idea of the 'elderly women' staying put – they were probably somewhere in their mid- to late thirties, poor devils!)

What happened to their Ethiopian servant is not clear. There is even a question as to whether this Sarah figure really did accompany the refugees on their seafaring odyssey or whether she simply happened to be on the beach and gave them safe harbour in this remote and primitive place after what must have been a traumatic voyage. Imagine their condition when they docked. They had fled Palestine in terror of their lives, had been at sea for weeks, months? Surely this shipload of faithfuls, predominantly women, must count as some of the earliest boat people or asylum-seekers?

I find it a fascinating tale, particularly the inclusion of Sarah. There is no documented information about how or why the black-skinned woman, who has not been canonised by the Catholic Church, should have been promoted to the role she holds today. Nevertheless, she is venerated by gypsies worldwide and christened by them Saint Sarah, patron saint of gypsies and travellers.

It is close to midnight when I reach the seafront and, in spite of the well-advertised *pèlerinage*, pilgrimage, which is due to commence the following afternoon, the place is as deserted as any out-of-season resort. I park my car on the front and walk in the direction of the water to stretch my limbs and inhale the saline air. My hair whips against my face. Beyond a low stone wall, the waves are rolling against the breakstones, hard and battle-grey. The sky is covered with louring clouds and streaky patches of silver light where the moon is trying to break through. It threatens bad weather.

Standing by myself, no one at my side, a mere speck in the middle of the night, looking out across the moving sheet of metal that is the Mediterranean towards its eastern shores, its north African coastline, too distant to see and only imaginable, I ask myself what has impelled me to make this solitary journey from one side of the Provence coast to the other. I cannot fully formulate an answer but healing is certainly one of the words that springs to mind. I am alone, uncertain about how best to move forward or what to hang on to and I fear the disintegration of my marriage.

I return to the car, pull out my bag, cross the street to my two-star hotel and bang hard on the door. Without greeting, a po-faced woman leads me up one flight of stairs to a bleak, sea-facing room where I fall into bed exhausted and sink into a deep but dream-infested sleep.

Yesterday I left our south-eastern corner of Provence, where the equinox days were golden and delicious, and I awake this Saturday morning to brooding, stormy weather. Sombre and impenetrable is the horizon. A windswept hike along the beach beneath a troubled, pewter sky finds me in conversation with a stick-insect of a woman dressed entirely in white out walking a brown and white shaggy dog. Like a wraith she appears from nowhere, staggering over dunes wreathed in misty sea air with her panting, inquisitive companion at her side.

I mention the pilgrimage. Her wrinkled eyes are weepy from the wind and whorling sands and as pale green as celery. 'Is it this weekend?' she asks sniffing, staring inland towards dead-level, boggy infinity.

I find her question strange. How can someone

live in this secluded billet and not be aware of the event?

'I've never been. Some say it's worth seeing, but watch your bag and jewellery because the pilgrims are gypsies and even gypsies at worship won't pass up an opportunity to rob you.'

I wish her good day and wend my way back towards the town.

En route I run across half a dozen caravans parked at the shoreline by men on fold-up stools, sipping hot drinks and fishing in the rough waves, and then, further along, dark-skinned families lolling about on the rocks, wrapped up warm, doing nothing by the choppy sea. I head for the church, popping into the tourist office along the way, keen to confirm the weekend's sequence of events. It is lunchtime. Still, they are open and an obliging young man hands me the programme, affirming the procession, but it is tomorrow, not today, and no gypsies will be in attendance. 'They only grace the May festival when the relics of their Saint Sarah are brought out. For that occasion gypsies make the pilgrimage from the four corners of the world. During ten days in late May our fishing port is journey's end for them and a colourful gypsy party it is, too; an opportunity to baptise their children in a holy place and to perform certain secret rites which are associated with giving their daughters' hands in marriage. But this October weekend, the celebration is in honour of the Marys and is strictly a local observance. You won't see any gypsies – *boumians* is our Provençal word for them – today.'

I thank him and, disappointed, cross the street towards the church, deciding that I must eat something before the opening service at three o'clock. As I enter the labyrinthine lanes of the old town, two weathered, brown-faced women in full-length skirts, boots and shawls approach me, rubbing flat cuts of shiny cobalt-blue glass between their thumbs and forefingers.

'Give me your left hand, sweetie,' demands one.

I tell her no thank you.

'Are you afraid of us? Afraid of gypsies?' she challenges.

'Not at all,' I reply, 'but I prefer not to have my fortune told.'

'Today is a holy day, a saint's day,' the other calls after me.

'Which is why I am pressed for time.'

As I reach the side entrance to the church a small band of female *manouches*, as tattered and colourful as the first pair, descend upon me. Each holds the same blue charm between her dirt-encrusted thumb and finger and offers to bless me, read my fortune, sell me good luck, whatever will earn them a franc or two. All of which I decline.

'It's a saint's day,' they holler mournfully as I enter a restaurant that looks welcoming and bears the name Le Félibre – the Provençal word for a writer or poet working in the local language. Within, the *resto* is deserted. Evidently I am too late. Then, almost out of sight, in a darkened corner near an oblong fish tank, I spy an occupied table, cluttered with steaming dishes, where three women and a man are heartily engaged in lunch. They are the family who run the place and, yes, officially they are closed – it's gone two o'clock – but they offer their home-made vegetable soup, which I accept gratefully.

I left my dismal hotel almost as soon as I was out of bed without so much as a cup of coffee and now, after my lengthy promenade down by the sea, straining my body across the windswept dunes, I realise that I am ravenous and, with a gannet's manners, gobble down everything brought to me.

Afterwards, I ask the young woman who has served the soup, following it with a delicious dish of sliced aubergines lightly cooked in olive oil, dressed with warm garlic and freshly pulped tomatoes, if the name of the establishment was chosen to honour Provençal writers.

'Yes, indeed.'

'Do you speak it?'

'No one does. Some of us get the drift when we hear it or see it written, but that's not often. I don't know a word of it really.'

'Is it taught in the schools hereabouts?'

She shakes her head.

'Any programme afoot to initiate it?'

Not that she is aware of.

'A pity, *non*, after all the sterling work achieved by Frédéric Mistral and his colleagues?'

She shrugs.

Outside in the square elegant women in long dresses and men in dark velvet jackets and hats are gathering. The costumes are traditional Arlesian; yeoman farmers and wives. Another initiative of Mistral's: to encourage the people of Arles to celebrate their authentic traditional culture, including their clothes.

My hostess hands me my change. I thank her and she returns to the family table. I hurry across to the church and install myself on a bench at the front of the nave, but there was no need to rush: the place is almost deserted. Given that there is time and no jostling for places, I slip to the crypt, where the relics of Saint Sarah reside. It is illumined by hundreds of flickering candles; the flames' heat has contorted many of them. On the far side is an imposing statue of the black-hued saint, dressed to kill in a dozen spangly cloaks: gypsy clothes. I place coins in a box, light a candle, add it to the forest of wax, cross myself, say a brief prayer – my Irish Catholic upbringing never resists these moments – and then return to my seat.

Standing in a pew behind me is a man who, apart from bizarrely bleached hair, looks like a Camarguais cowboy – as the highly skilled horsemen, the *gardians*, who manage the bull herds are known. I find that I have two hymn sheets and he has none, so I hand him my spare. He frowns, nods his thanks and accepts it.

To the left of the altar, a red-faced organist with crinkly curls leads the hymn-singing. Those present are already engaged in this scratchy prelude, but the church remains half-empty. Middle-aged women occupy the front three rows; each clutches an elongated candle. The opening of the service is signalled by a bell. From the rear doors a white-robed priest approaches, preceded by a one-armed altar boy holding aloft a large bronze cross. What is about to take place, the Cérémonie de la Descente des Châsses, the Descent of the Relics, is celebrated nowhere else in the world but in this single church.

High above the altar in the bell tower is the chapel of Saint Michael Archangel, where the relics of the two saints, Mary Salome and Mary Jacob, are stored. (Frédéric Mistral set the very last scene of his famous poem, 'Mireille', in this upper chapel.) The bones of the two exiled saints were uncovered in the church's vault in the fifteenth century and on 4 December 1448 were put on display for the first time. To this day they are kept in the attic chapel, in what is known as *la châsse*, the reliquary or shrine. Today's service is about bringing the shrine out of storage, down to altar-level, and blessing it. The hymns and prayers are spoken and sung in French and, occasionally, to my delight, in Provençal.

On high, where the *châsse* is stored, a trapdoor has opened and a wooden chest, painted sea-green with images of the female saints adorning either side of it, is sliding forward in fits and starts. Two men lean out from behind it and attach the chest to a hook on a pulley. The chest hangs in mid-air, swaying rather alarmingly to and fro, metres above the altar and the priest's pate.

The instant the chest appears, the congregation begins to shout: *'Vive les Saintes Maries!'* repeating their chant over and over. More hymns are sung, more shouting takes place and at some point, while my attention is elsewhere, a woman steps from behind the altar, where there are several other rows of pews, and lights the candles of the front-bench supplicants. They, in turn, pass the flame to the row behind and so on until the church is aglow with lighted candles.

I am fascinated by what is going on above. The

chest has tipped sideways. It looks precarious. The priest beneath continues his sermon, 'From the shores of Palestine gifted to us were the Olive Tree and the Marys.' Then he sings and chants, 'Long live the Saint Marys!', blithely unaware of the danger that could befall him. I suspect that only myself and the two men leaning far out beyond the trapdoor, looking mighty anxious, have foreseen the potential accident.

The fervour in the church is mounting to a pitch not far short of hysteria. A woman across the aisle breaks down and begins sobbing loudly. Another trots forward from alongside the altar to embrace and comfort her. The supplicant sisters cling to one another, still clutching their burning candles.

A squeaking from above draws my attention back to the marshalling of the relics. The chest, swinging in small circles and still perilously tilted, has begun its jerky descent. Slowly, as it inches and lurches downwards, the two men attach bunches of flowers to the chains of the pulley. These, I learn later, are prayers, votives, supplications. Everyone is shouting. A forest of arms is raised in invocation towards the sea chest bearing the bones of the Saint Marys, candles held aloft. A bunch of flowers not properly secured plummets from overhead and lands on the priest. The workmen stare altarward with expressions of cartoon horror, but the man of God continues as though nothing has happened. Another woman seated by the altar flashes forward and snatches away the offending bouquet.

Behind me, a couple of rows back, a gravelly female voice shrieks for Sarah. '*Vive Sainte Sarah! Vive Sainte*

Sarah!' Heads turn and an aged, plump gypsy grins and winks mischievously, but no one seems offended. The sobbing woman is now on her knees, forehead pressed against the stone floor, wailing, but still managing to keep her candle upright.

'*Provençau e catouli,*' the churchgoers sing in rousing voice. '*Nosto fe, nosto fe n'a pas fali . . .*'

'Provencaux and Catholics, our faith, our faith has not faltered . . .'

When the hymns are sung in Provençal, as this one is, and the sermon spoken in the native language, it does all seem to fit together. The passion is quite contagious and I really do have the impression that I am experiencing something unique. Beyond that, however, I cannot get to grips with what the woman at my side might be howling about, or what the contents of this sea chest, which has now reached the altar, evokes in these faithful that it can ignite such displays of emotion. The parishioners begin to swarm the altar, extinguishing their candles against the chest and then kissing it. The priest holds up a silver hand with a photograph set into it, of whom I don't know, and the congregation queues to kiss it.

I lift my head. The men have gone, the trapdoor has been closed. The sea chest will remain where it is until tomorrow morning, when it will be transported to the beach and carried into the Mediterranean, and I will return to participate.

After this curious service, in the lane outside, the green-shirted, bleach-haired cowboy, whose jawline is as square as a street lamp, catches my eye. He is brandishing the hymn sheet. 'What made you give me this?'

'I had two and I thought you might like to take part in the service,' I reply, moving on. He accompanies me, intent on striking up a conversation. I learn that he was born on a farm on the outskirts of this fishing village and that his mother and sisters are still residing in the same *mas*, but he himself is living in Bethlehem. I am fascinated to know what he is doing in Israel, but there is a disturbing aura about this man and so I bite back my curiosity. I make my excuses and he bows a stiff farewell.

The day has turned horribly cold and I wonder how I will pass the rest of it. Another walk or back to my hotel to scribble down my impressions of the service? I wander through the lanes, feeling lonely, trying not to notice families out shopping together. Black-skinned dolls are on sale in many of the *boutiques*. The trinketed streets are narrow and winding, medina-like, and many return me to this *place*, set back from the beach, where the church is situated.

I take the sea route to the hotel and stop at the only open café on the front to order tea. While I await its arrival, I browse the hymn sheet, trying to find familiar roots that will help me penetrate the Provençal words and then, lost, I dig out of my pocket the various leaflets that were given to me earlier at the tourist office. One explains the history of this unusual weekend. As I open it up, another falls to the ground and I bend to retrieve it. It is advertising a gypsy flamenco evening, this very evening, to be held at a privately owned *mas*. I read on and see that it involves a dinner and so I dismiss the idea as surely prohibitively expensive and possibly unsuitable for a woman travelling alone, though such considerations have rarely held me back in the past. I drink my tea and make my way back to my hotel, which is as lively as a graveyard. The room is freezing. I try to keep warm by burying myself deep beneath the bedclothes, but fail. I get up and pace to and fro, wrapping myself in yet more pullovers. I lean against the window, wondering how Michel is spending his Saturday, and ask myself, 'What am I doing here?'

During the tail end of the afternoon, while I am still idle at the window, it begins to rain. The wind sheets and lashes against a tormented ocean and the weather shows no sign of letting up. Should I call him? I don't want to disturb him. Does he miss our life together at the farm? Eventually, I return to the bedside table, pick up the phone, hesitate and then dial the number of the *mas*.

'I want to enquire about the flamenco fête . . .'

After a brief conversation with a friendly young woman, during which I discover that the ranch has rooms to let and one is still available, I am packing my bag, checking out of this disgruntled place and streaking across the street in the pelting rain.

'Where are you? Is it difficult to find?' I had had the presence of mind to ask before replacing the receiver.

'We're out of town. Drive past the port and head for the swamp areas towards Aigue-Morte.'

The wind is whipping along the seafront, the waves spray the street and there is not a soul in sight, but I am on my way to see flamenco dancing out amongst the mosquito-infested reedbeds.

The roads throw up muck which obliterates my

visibility. I am driving slowly, wipers slapping to and fro but achieving little besides shunting the slushy grime back and forth. I am lost somewhere in the marshes where there is no street lighting, headlights on, making little progress. I should have requested more precise directions. It is by chance and good fortune that I spot a sign signalling the ranch and I turn off the road on to a narrow lane which leads me past two small white cabined homes. Both face out across the potholed track to the waterlogged pastures where, in the distance, I make out the spherical silhouettes of a small troupe of grazing black bulls, *les taureaux*, their curling horns aloft. I slow the car to standstill and open the window. A blast of cold wet air, rich with wood smoke, slaps my eager senses. The image of these bulls in this murky October dusk is quite spooky, Hallowe'enish. Humpbacked hags with billowing cloaks.

In the far distance I hear the blunt ring of rifle shots. The ring of death. One, two and then a third. *Gibier à plume*, they'll be gunning here. Feathered game. Migrating birds are also at risk. It is late; the hunters will have been buried in the mire of the reedbeds for a couple of hours, rifles cocked on their forearms, retriever dogs panting at their haunches, hungrily anticipating the evening flight, *la passée*. It is at this hour that the birds leave the protected areas and bird sanctuaries and make for open pastures. Little do they know that lead pellets, not supper, await them. During strong weather, such as tonight's, the fowl are forced to fly lower, which gives their predators the advantage.

Another shot blasts the damp night sky, followed by a short, sharp volley. I picture the descent of half a dozen teal, floundering, plummeting into the ice-cold water, and the hounds, following their master's bidding *'Va chercher! Apporte!'*, splashing through the mudbanks to retrieve the dying or dead prey.

Here in the Camargue there is a great debate raging between ecologists and animal protection organisations on the one hand and, across these swampy waters, as it were, the long-established hunting societies who claim that this is their territory and who do not accept that they are duty-bound to adhere to the recent changes in hunting protocol served on them by Marseille, Paris and the European Union. 'This is our home,' they retort, *'chez nous,* and we'll do what we bloody well like.'

I close my window and move on. Thank heavens the wild boar have found other tracts of land to hunt and are no longer on our farm.

I have no idea what to expect as I swing through the open gate of the ranch into a very puddled car park sheltered by wooden poles roofed over with dried reeds. The *mas* is painted white in the traditional Camarguais fashion. I splash through the rain to the front door. A tug at the bellrope brings a shuffling manservant who must be eighty if he's a day. With scarcely more than a nod, he takes my sodden jacket and leads me through to a fashionably decorated, low-ceilinged salon. It is enormous with a full picture window at the far end looking out across the dismally opaque countryside.

A log fire crackles its welcome in the wide hearth.

Apéritifs – it is now almost half-past seven – are being served by the octogenarian retainer, Hermès, assisted by a very ample Arab woman. A gathering of people, sixteen in total, all French but probably not locals, are sitting hugged up by the fireside conversing by candle-light. A bald-headed fellow is cross-legged on the rug sipping champagne with the smile of the cat who has got the cream. Suddenly, I spot the stranger from the church, seated apart and further into the room. He is wearing a dark suit with collar and tie and is the only guest so formally attired. A livid green drink in a crystal flute rests on the round coffee table in front of him. He waves me over. I hesitate, preferring not to settle in his company. Mercifully, the arrival of our hostess, Annette, rescues me. She is an attractive, slender young woman with fashionably highlighted, shoulder-length hair, sporting Armani jeans, to-die-for cowboy boots and a white rollneck sweater. Lumbering along at her side is a hefty, alabaster-blond Labrador whose name, I learn later, is Ghost. I introduce myself and explain that I telephoned earlier to request a place at the party. She waves such niceties aside. I am here, and that is good enough. 'I instructed the girls to make up the downstairs suite for you in the main house. No one's using it. You might as well be deliciously comfortable,' she smiles. I try to protest but she won't hear a word of it. I am offered a *coupe* of champagne, which I gladly accept.

'Ah, you've met someone,' says Annette as the cowboy waves eagerly to us both. 'I find him a little strange, don't you?' she whispers, smiling an acknow-ledgement at the man. 'He has attended several of these soirées but I haven't quite worked out who he is. It can be worrying sometimes because my husband is away frequently and so I am often alone here.'

A coloured photograph of a thirty-something, dark-haired man is standing in a frame on the coffee table near the fireplace. A cursory glance had led me to assume that he was Annette's husband, master of this establishment, but a closer inspection reveals the lead singer of the gypsy group, strikingly handsome with eyes that burn into the viewer and a guitar pressed proudly against his breast.

Dinner is announced and Annette disappears.

I make my way through to the dining room which opens, via sliding glass doors, out on to a tiled terrace where a swimming pool is lit by underwater spot-lamps. This evening, of course, the terrace has been closed off. A dance-floor beyond the pool, raised on bricks or wooden blocks and facing out over the marshy flatlands, is hung with white muslin curtains which are whipping furiously in the wind. All around the terrace, bunting has been slung between the trees and from it hang swirling, soft-hued Chinese lanterns.

'It's a pity,' says Annette, who has arrived at my side. 'You should see the marshes from out there on a fine evening. They are spectacular. The illuminated rose in the lanterns reflects the light of the sun setting across the swamp waters, which in turn reflects the rose-pink feathers of the flamingos.'

'One spectrum of the Camargue, pure white tinged with rose,' I say. 'You are not Camarguaise, are you?'

She shakes her head. 'But, alas, our patio is not in use this evening.' My hostess calls to a young man to run outside and take down the drapes before they are blown away in the storm, which is growing more violent.

I am placed at a table with the bald-headed gentleman and his family. It is his birthday and they have come from Toulouse for this party. I discover that his father was a great friend of Claude, our water-diviner. This is not as remarkable as it might seem, given that our man is a very celebrated figure in the south of France, and it creates an amiable point of conversation between us.

The meal on offer is positively sumptuous and way more than I can manage.

The gypsies arrive. Annette is deep in discussion with them about what is clearly a change of programme, an interior performance instead of the garden show. The singer scans the room, clocking his audience but catching no one's eye. He is no longer the young stud in the photograph. He struts proudly into the dining room in black, stack-heeled boots and discreetly checked cream waistcoat, guitar hanging at his side, but he is fifteen years the senior of the image by the fireplace and a chubbier version of his younger self. His hair is still collar-length and curly but now it is streaked with grey. Still, this gypsy, Ricao, remains devastatingly handsome.

'He is a relative of Manitas de Plata,' a fellow diner informs me. 'Manitas is in his eighties now. He lives in the Languedoc.'

The Languedoc is the neighbouring region to this western outpost of Provence. Manitas de Plata – the name means 'little silver fingers' – is a legend in France as well as a hero to his own people, the *Gitans*, who are Spanish gypsies. He preceded the Gypsy Kings in gaining worldwide recognition for his popular guitar music and was also renowned for a much-publicised affair in the 1960s with the sex kitten of those hip Saint-Tropez years, Brigitte Bardot. To boast kinship to such a godfather would give this performer a certain royal lineage. I study the gypsy singer and speculate on the truth of the claim.

Three chairs are placed up against a wall near the door. Our entertainer considers them and wanders back out of the dining room. Another course is served. Hermès, who is originally from Paris, refills my wine glass. 'This is your first time here, madame?'

'Yes. I suppose you have seen these performers on many occasions?'

He nods, 'Many times, madame. They have talent but they are gypsies.'

'Meaning?'

'They would steal rather than work. A franc stolen is more cherished than ten earned. They come here without a cigarette or coin in their pockets and expect us to supply them.'

I am disappointed by the prejudice in this remark and do not pursue it. The singer returns, settles himself in the central chair and waits. His gaze alights on no one. He is not of our universe; he is contained in his own. We are tourists and, for a brief moment, I wish that I hadn't attended. Seconds later, two other guitarists appear, one whose face is as lined as a stone carving, the other a younger man. With them arrive two women in long blue dresses laced with frills, their hair tied tightly back in severe buns in the flamenco tradition. Inaccurately, I take them to be mother and daughter. The women are the dancers. They stand shyly to the side, pressed against the wall, like young girls at a high-school dance. The singer strums one chord and then begins to sing unaccompanied, letting out an extraordinary, chilling ululation. His voice is higher-pitched than I had expected from one so earthy and the sound is almost oriental, the melody Moorish. I have given up on my meal but others are still eating, and further courses are still appearing. I am transfixed by the voice of this gypsy, now partnered by his own guitar and that of his fellow musicians. He is mesmeric.

The younger woman orbits to centre stage, unfurling herself as though being released from a fishing net. Semi-bent with arms outstretched, she dances, weaving and spinning like a seducing spider. Two arms seem to become ten as she twists and reels. The older woman clack-clacks her feet. To this she adds handclaps like castanets, and moves to centre stage where she, too, begins to dance. The image of Michel's gyrating body on that hospital trolley in Monte Carlo flashes into my head and, shocked, I push it forcefully away. This woman's style is quite the opposite of the younger female's. She barely moves her torso but her stillness is electric. It brings to mind two other images. The first is the late Nina Simone in performance at the Juan-les-Pins summer jazz festival shortly after we moved here. Centre stage, alone, beneath a diorama of stars, umbrella pines her amphitheatre, she sang the blues without accompaniment, bewitching an audience of over two thousand.

The second is from my days at drama school, where the professors spoke to us of Lorca's essay 'In Search of Duende'. I had never heard this Andalucian-Spanish word before. *Duende*. Its meaning is ghost or goblin, but what it actually describes is a quality equivalent to 'soul'. Lorca depicted it as an inner force, a black sound. 'A mysterious power that everyone senses and no philosopher can explain.' There is no true synonym in English. Some might suggest charisma, but I would debate that. Charisma can exist without the emotional depth, sensibility or 'soul' that is at the root of the energy known as *duende*.

I had feared that I had fallen upon a tourist show, but not at all. I excuse myself from the table and move to a seat alongside the players. Here I can better focus on the interaction between them and the subtleties of their art. For, indubitably, they are artists. They perform for almost an hour and then, without taking a bow or curtain call, without applause, they exit the room. Their departure goes unremarked.

The meal continues. I drift through to the empty salon and sit alone by the fireside, my thoughts running deep. The music replays in my head, the dancing, clapping women, and the memory of Michel lying on that hospital table, his figure clattering in spasm. How I dreaded the extinguishing of his life that night and how I grieve alone now for other losses, less comprehensible wounds and emptiness.

After dinner, coffee is served in the salon, and the guests begin to wander in, ordering brandies or another bottle of wine, or disappearing out into the night or, in the case of those who are staying over, to their beds. The cowboy, I notice, has left the party. A short while later, one of Annette's young waitresses appears with a bucket of water and starts chucking handfuls on to the log fire. It hisses and smokes and guests begin to complain.

'It is too hot for the women to dance here otherwise,' explains the nymphet. I had not expected that the musicians would return – only five diners remain – but, within no time, the quintet reappears, gathering between us and the fireplace. Backs to the hearth, they face us. Loosely speaking, we are an untidy circle. I wonder if it conjures up for them the time-worn tradition of sitting by camp fires, singing together or narrating their stories. They talk amongst themselves as though we, the onlookers, were not present. I am trying to identify the language they are using when, without warning, our star, Ricao, breaks into song. His wringing note, in this smoky candlelight, evokes a wolf howling into the shadowed night. The women clap in syncopated volleys while the men strum and the dying embers crackle. We sit by the fading firelight bewitched by their music. The women dance again and when they are not dancing they tap-tap their hands, led by the guitars, and my heart wants to burst.

Annette appears with a glass of wine in her hand and settles herself on the back of one of the sofas. Her Labrador follows, bumping against her legs, knocking into chairs, until he eventually slumps heavily at her feet. I am surprised by his clumsiness, his lack of grace.

Outside, the storm is raging. I hear a branch snap and thud heavily to the ground. Poolside chairs clatter and roll. Angry goblins are about, making mischief.

The power of the *duende* is at large in the windswept night, and then the music fades to silence. We who are within applaud. Ricao bows his head; that is all. Silence rules until the bald-pated birthday man calls for champagne nightcaps and the gypsies are each served a flute. I, too, am included in this celebratory moment. Now the gypsies, sitting with us by firelight, seem amenable to conversation. They answer a question or two and then they break into song. And after, we return to silence. They ask nothing. They express no interest in us or our lives.

'Manouche gypsies are Provençal gypsies, they tell me. We are Gitans, Spanish gypsies. Our mother tongue is Catalan.' Though tonight they speak to us in heavily accented French. The international language of the gypsies is Caló, but it is slowly dying out.

'Are you fluent?'

Ricao shakes his head. 'Not at all. None of us speak it. Few do, these days.'

Their songs are sung in Catalan and others in Spanish. They live near Montpellier, in flats, not caravans. Slowly they are being forced to give up their itinerant lifestyles. It is a choice they must make if they want health care and education for their children. It is one of the reasons why Caló is falling into disuse. In olden times, when they were always on the move, they would meet up with other caravans from far-off places and share their stories and experiences, communicating in their international tongue. That happens less and less now. Their lives are more insular, more chained to the system of the countries where they reside.

One of the women, the elder, mentions Lorca.

'Do you know his work?' I ask her. 'His Gypsy Ballads?'

'A little, not intimately, but I know he spoke of *duende*. It is the soul in our music.'

And then, mid-conversation, they rise to leave, bowing reservedly. It will be a long drive back on a night such as this. The rest of us wander off to our rooms. I fall asleep to the sound of doors closing everywhere within the ranch house, then silence. The gypsy's voice slowly returns, breaking into song. Ricao's howl, like a lone wolf yowling in the steppes, like the sorrow tearing at my heart.

The following morning, I rise early and return to town for the mass. As yesterday, it is a bilingual service. Afterwards we leave the packed-to-the-rafters church to make the procession to the sea. This is the highlight of the weekend's pilgrimage. The crocodile is headed by those in Arlesian costume, the women in lovely long dresses with lace shawls accompanied by menfolk in black velvet jackets and flat hats. In their footsteps come the priests and celebrants and then the *châsse*, the sea-chest reliquary containing the relics of the Saint Marys. Outside the portal, proud riders on horseback await us. Every horse is white; an authentic Camarguais stallion. These men are *gardians*, the dexterous horsemen who tend the herds. Each carries his *trident*, a three-pronged metal fork attached to a long wooden pole instrumental in the rounding-up and herding of the yearling bulls. When the horsemen are singling out the young *taureaux* for branding on the ranches in the spring, they prod the beasts' buttocks with these sharp forks to drive them to the branding sites.

The reliquary is ferried on the shoulders of four young men with the solemnity accorded to a coffin. It appears to be extremely heavy and the procession is slow-moving. To share the burden, two teams of four bear it through the streets, passing it back and forth between them every three hundred metres or so. I wonder how the bones of two thousand-year-old women could weigh so much. During this procession to the sea, the chant of 'Vive les Saintes Maries' is non-stop.

On arrival at the beach, the chestful of relics carried aloft by the men is borne into the water. The *gardians* head the column, cantering forth on their stallions, wading way out into the wavy sea. When the horses are thigh-deep, the riders sodden to their breeches, and the men carrying the *châsse* waist-high in water, the train turns to face the beach. It is a theatrical moment.

The crowd has been asked to hold back. Aside from a pushy journalist or two, even the most zealous of the pietists obeys. The priest has forgone the pleasure of a salty bath and is seated on high in an upturned fishing vessel. He puts me in mind of Neptune, waving his arms and chanting blessings in French and then Provençal. The instant the sea-based line-up turns, cameras begin flashing from every direction. Photographers are shouting to the parade to face this way, now that, 'horses to the left!' and so on, and I cannot dispel the idea that I am attending a miniature-scale

Cannes film festival with its posing and its paparazzi. I turn from the beach and leave them to it, hiking back across the sand and along the high street, milling with onlookers, to find my car. On my way out of town, I stop at a wooden shack by the roadside to ask directions for Pont de Gau, which I have read about in the leaflets I was given at the tourist office. A handsome, muscular man comes out to greet me, proffering slices of *'saucisson de toto'*.

'What is *toto*?' I ask.

'Taureau.'

'Ah, it's beef sausage then?'

'You could say that,' he sighs, dismayed by this foreigner's lack of poetry.

I am offered a small plastic cup of chilled muscat. The wine is too sweet for my palate so he swiftly moves on to a *vin du sable* rosé.

'It will make delicious drinking for you next summer, this *gris de gris* rosé,' he enthuses.

Though I have no notion of what life between now and next summer might bring, I end up buying an example of half the produce in his wooden shack, which is the point, of course, of all this hospitality. This tradesman, Renato, lives about five kilometres' distance from here, on the far side of one of the lakes, the *étangs*. His uncle owned a farmhouse across the street, which is why he is pitched here. This was his uncle's shack, he explains, until he died. While I am busy admiring his enticing stock display, a pretty, dark-haired, olive-skinned woman arrives in a weather-beaten car. She bears a basket full of provisions. Lunch. This is Renato's lady. There is no electricity and no water in the shack. He slices her *toto* sausage and pours her a thimbleful of the rosé. Another car, sporting a Dutch number plate, pulls up and out climbs a skinny, worried-looking fellow with a map. Even as he is making his way towards Renato's shack, its proprietor is cutting another *saucisson* and preparing more wine – how does he keep it chilled in here without electricity, I wonder? The conversation has turned to an American the couple are acquainted with, whose name they cannot recall, who owns a restaurant in Mougins. 'That's your side of Provence,' says Renato. He refers to our region as though it were the far corner of the world. I pay for my shopping and leave him to the seduction of his next customer. The sun has broken through. My skin and hair are encrusted with breezes off the sea, off the marshlands. I lick my lips and taste fresh raw salt.

The Camargue gives refuge to an extraordinary wealth of plumed fauna, a notice at the Pont de Gau Ornithological Park informs me. This bird sanctuary was founded by a naturalist, Jacques Lamouroux, in 1949. Since his death, it has been run by his son, René, who I ask if I might meet. Alas, he is absent.

Reading one of the brochures I find on sale at the ticket office I see they have a care centre which rescues injured birds, tends them and then, if they are capable of surviving back out in the wild, releases and tags them. I sadly recall our little warbler, Orpheus, the debut to our summer. Apparently, in these parts almost 6 per cent of all injuries to birds are caused by lead shot in hunting 'accidents'.

I stride out purposefully. The paths are clearly sign-posted so I can choose my direction with ease. Rafts of ducks and the magnificent pink flamingos are every-where. Their reflections rainbow the water. *Roubines*, narrow water courses, flow close to the paths' peri-meters, like old-fashioned drainage systems; they criss-cross the land all over the Camargue. This sudden parenthesis of heat is a treat and most unexpected. Still, I decide to be energetic and cover the entire circuit.

I breathe deeply. I am growing to appreciate the stink of these swamps. Close to, they have a high, pikey smell, with midges and insects that look like water boatmen skimming their surface. As I march briskly, circling the marsh lakes, I hear gurglings and bubblings in the water. It could be a diving pond tor-toise scared by my footfall, or an aquatic snake. The viperines in these wetlands are not dangerous – they prey on tadpoles and small fish – but I would much prefer not to encounter them. The otters, though, *les loutres*, with their surprisingly long tails and shiny wet bodies, gobbling the grass at the bank's edge and then cleaning themselves with precision, are enchanting. I tarry to watch them. Lifting their shiny otter heads, with impossibly extended whiskers, they groom them-selves and, though constantly alert, take not a blind bit of notice of me. I love it when they cock their hind legs and diligently scrub their backsides and under-bellies. They are really quite comical. I laugh yet I am downhearted that there is no Michel to share this with.

It is too late in the year for mosquitos. Although it

is dry and warmish, the wind, which even in summer would keep all but the most persistent at bay, has not entirely died down. Male mozzies are not harmful to us; they feed off plants. It is the females that suck our blood, I read on a sign at the entrance to the park. They need blood from mammals and fowl to succour the superabundance of eggs they lay in these stagnant waters. Grey herons and magnificent purple herons take flight before my eyes. The purple ones are a spectacular sight. There are eight heron species frequenting the Camargue marshlands. Scarlet darters are in evidence everywhere. In fact, there are several species of dragonfly landing on and taking off from my stepping feet, in and out of the bushes and the stubby tamarisk trees. Hundreds of them. I recognise the blue-tailed damselfly, for we have these on our land, but the marmalade-toned ones I have never encountered before. The sight of all these dragonflies brings back Michel again. I slow, remembering the dozens of waterlilies he bought for our pond at the farm, all of which the dogs ate. So much brings back Michel. I strike onwards, determined to stay in the present. Signs hammered into the earth at the waters' banks clearly warn visitors: *Chasse Interdite* – hunting forbidden.

I smile. I am not entirely alone.

When I arrive back at the ranch, exhausted, Annette is nowhere to be found. She has gone riding. The place is deserted; all the other guests have departed. Young waiters flit to and fro, tidying up. I pack up my bag in my room and then settle with a book in the salon, by the fire, waiting to say *au revoir* to my hostess. The pretty waitress who extinguished last night's fire comes to enquire what I would like for dinner. Annette has left instructions for the chef to prepare my preferred choice.

'You will eat together,' she announces.

'I had been intending to leave,' I protest genially.

Beyond the picture window the day is falling fast and the light is fading to luminous grey. It has that special quality that flat land gives off: nothing lies beyond the darkness except misty impenetrable infinity. It has begun to rain again. I hear the drops drumming against the leaves in the garden. A heavy percussion. Autumn leaves swirl and bunch and get trapped in corners of the yard and around the legs of garden furniture. The hulking Labrador, Ghost, comes lumbering in through the door, rambling to and fro as though lost, and then drops like a brick by the heat of the fire. I hear Annette's excited voice from somewhere out in the hall. When she enters, dressed from head to foot in brown riding leather, she is flushed and exhilarated, full of the charge of the ride. '*Ah, bonjour*, Carol.' She throws off her jacket and falls back into one of the chesterfields. Ghost struggles to his feet and draws close to her, to us. I notice then for the first time his quartz-white eyes.

'He's blind?'

'Yes, one hundred per cent blind, and it is inoperable. I have tried everything, spent thousands but there is nothing to be done. Poor Ghost will never see again.'

'What happened?'

Annette confides that her neighbour was responsible.

I am horrified.

'Ghost was trespassing. He got into the habit of
scooting over on to the man's land and chasing his
geese. The fellow warned me and I tried to keep the
dog away but he was frisky, full-blooded and dis-
obedient. One afternoon when I was occupied with
business here, Ghost slipped his lead and shot off. I
found him later in the evening, wandering aimlessly
down in the lane in the dark, eyes gouged. The farmer
had pierced the dog's eyes with a horseman's trident.'

While Annette goes off to shower, I ponder the
barbarism of such an act.

My hostess and I meet again at seven for drinks and to
dine together. Aside from the staff, we are quite alone.
I learn that her husband lives and works in Paris.
There are complications: a former wife, a child from
that first marriage. 'We came down here to begin
again but he has been drawn back.'

'And you run this place alone?'

'More or less.'

'I admire you. I find Provence a very male land,
earthy and virile, but also an enigma; romantic, poetic
at heart but racist and brutal too. Are you afraid?'

'I keep a gun beneath my bed. And I have Ghost.'
Annette catches my look. 'He can still hear and he can
bark. Only the immediate neighbours know of his
affliction. And you?'

'I have three dogs, no gun.' I admit that I too am
struggling with an isolated farm and a long-distance

husband, but I disclose nothing of our accident and Michel's estrangement. I am not ready to own up to it, or to face the dawning reality that Michel has gone.

We smile. Two women washed up from other shores, other lives, now woven into the fabric of Provence. For better or worse.

280,000 *Bees for Breakfast*

With renewed resolve I return to the farm. All the same, our dearth of crop refuels my heightening sense of displacement, of purposelessness. In silvery olive groves all along the Nice uplands, the time of reaping approaches. My little agricultural magazine is predicting vintage harvests in superabundance for *oléiculteurs* growing the *cailletier* variety. Alas, not at Appassionata. The work involved in the gathering of olives, delivering the mounds to the mill and reuniting with those weathered farmers fussing over the quality of freshly pressed oil; all of these have been braided into the tempo of my seasons. This year, more than ever, I yearn for this *raison d'être* and for the fatiguing physical demands of bringing in a crop.

Due to the summer's phenomenal heat, the smattering of olives we have produced are ripening early. Hearteningly, many of those fat, dark oleiferous drupes are springing forth on the saplings. If this is a teaser of yields to come we can look forward to oodles of oil in our dotage. This autumn, however, the sad reality is that the slender output will not meet the mill's requirement of 100 kilos of fruit that entitle Appassionata to a single-estate pressing. I prefer not to throw in our lot with others because the quality cannot be guaranteed and many will have been treated with pesticides. Yet I would hate to see the few kilos we do have shrivel and rot on the ground. So I telephone the mill for advice.

'Bottle them for table olives,' suggests the miller's wife.

Michel talked of us experimenting with table olives and René has promoted the idea on several occasions. He swears it is more lucrative than flogging oil. Even so, because I relish the oil-pressing process, I have never really been attracted to marinating the fruit. Still, circumstances suggest that this is the year to try. The miller's wife instructs me over the telephone. 'For every kilo of drupes – and remember, they do need to be of the finest quality – you use ninety grammes of sea salt. Place the olives in a glass jar, cover them with water, add a few twigs of thyme, home-grown is preferable, and leave them tightly sealed for several months.'

It sounds simple enough, I decide to give it a go. I will harvest alone. I won't net the trees; the fruit is too scarce to bother. I have no need of ladders; the junior trees are barely my height. This frees Quashia to crack on with the 'hangar' and complete the wretched thing before winter sets in. I work in my den until the afternoons and then I pick a few olives until sunset, storing them in a crate in the summer kitchen ready for bottling.

Mid-October brings with it a fleeting snap of cool weather which presages the first signs of deep autumn and we are grateful for it. The monstrous heat has left us. The skies are quiet. All tourists have departed. In the Var, the clearance of thousands of tons of charcoaled debris before the spring reafforestation is underway. Quashia shifts to his winter schedule. He begins at eight, breaks for lunch, then labours till six. Soon, when Ramadan comes round, he will slog through without a meal. I no longer walk out of the house every morning to a blanket of blinding heat. We are more energetic. Today, we have released our fostered hares. Quashia carried them, kicking and boxing, down to the stream in the valley beyond our property, when he set off for his lunch. He has returned with all but a tear in his eye. He swears the little fellows turned back to thank him before hopping off. 'I'd grown fond of them,' he moans.

'But they had to go. They are ferals, not pets.' Gérard, our vet, who came to inspect them to reassure me that they were not infected with myxomatosis, warned that they could never be tamed. 'Soon, Monsieur Q., there will be bees to look forward to,' I console. I e-mail our apiarists to reaffirm how much we are looking forward to the arrival of the hives. I receive a response which perturbs me.

'We have been hearing on the radio about the exodus of *sangliers* from the burned-out forests. Troupes of them are hunting down your way, we understand. As a rule, the only beast that will approach or disturb a beehive is a cow but, no doubt, you know that autumn is the boars' mating season and a pregnant sow can be extremely aggressive. Imagine if a hive were knocked over, or damaged. Please confirm by return that our little girls will not be in danger. Otherwise, we must find ourselves an alternative *placement* as soon as possible.'

I reply assuring M. Huilier that their girls will be untroubled by *sangliers*. There have been no sightings of wild boar on our land for almost two months. Quashia is convinced that they have found new grazing lands. Alexandre warns me they will be back. If they do return, I tell him, I will call him in. I am praying it will not come to that.

While I am completing my *cueillette*, the gathering of my few ripened drupes, I telephone René – I miss him and his anecdotes – to confirm the advice I have been given on the preparation of table olives as well as to learn what news there is of Claude, the water-diviner.

'How much thyme should I add to each litre jar?'

'None,' is his response.

'None? But I rang the mill and was told to soak a few sprigs in the infusion.'

'Once the olives are ready to eat you can spice them with whatever you fancy but it is best at this stage to prepare them *au naturel*. Leave your options open as far as flavour goes.' Claude is working again, René says, and determined to keep occupied. 'I have been at his place almost every day. He's extending his groves; we're planting another hundred and thirty trees. Ten-year-olds, bigger than yours. Back-breaking. Fortunately, he has all the necessary machinery and the land is flattish, unlike the grind at your place.'

'Do you think he's too busy to see me?'

'Not at all – he's been asking after you. He said he was pleased to hear from you when his wife died. I'll talk to him in the morning and call you back.'

Our olive guru so rarely makes contact when he

promises that I am quite taken aback to hear from him the following morning. 'What are you doing later? Claude is inviting you up here to visit his groves and stay for an *apéro*.'

Before I am given the opportunity to react Claude is on the phone, his manner as gracious as ever. And so it is agreed that René will collect and deliver me to this multimillionaire's estate at the close of their working day. I am delighted. We haven't seen one another in a long while.

'I won't bring you tomatoes because I know how loaded you are.' René is back on the line.

'Actually, René, if you have some to spare . . .'

'I thought you were laden. Let me guess, they're all blighted. You didn't treat them.'

'You are right, we didn't treat them, but they were not blighted. Wild boars . . . I'll tell you when I see you.'

Claude's olive farm lies about a hundred metres higher inland than ours. I am not quite sure what to expect. René has eulogised the plantation so often, and never loses an opportunity to remind me that the small boy who sat beside him in class at the local village school is today one of the most successful business merchants in the south of France. My one and only encounter with Monsieur, the water-diviner, impressed me greatly. I had been expecting a charlatan, a sharp-talking Provençal trickster, but my fears could not have been more unfounded.

We arrive at his gates, which open with a key card, unlike ours, which bear an old-fashioned padlock. The immersion into his plateau valley property is gentle and meandering. Everywhere there are white wooden picket fences, which I have never come across in this part of the world before. It feels like a ranch in the United States. 'These were originally the horse paddocks.' René is pointing out generous flats of land which flank our approach. He pulls up behind Claude's navy blue four-wheel-drive. I recognise it from the visit he and his late wife made to our home. Three more cars are stationed in front of a tractor, a plough and several other pieces of rather impressive farming machinery. Two black guard dogs come bounding and barking towards us, followed by a white husky.

'These were the stables,' said René, ignoring the animals, who are jumping up on me, knocking me backwards and scrapping amongst themselves. I leave them to their high jinks. Aside from the elegant building René has described as the stables, there are two impressive Provençal-styled bungalows, at some distance from one another, but no sign of human activity.

Our olive guru escorts me to the upper paddocks where row upon row of olive saplings have been recently planted. All are visibly irregular; they remind me of Quashia's wonky shed. Loamy earth, freshly turned, lies higgledy-piggledy in miniature hillocks, as though a mole has gone mad. To the left and right, on the incline above us and beyond the main house, there are statuesque *oliviers*, all with forked or three-pronged trunks. Unlike these specimens, ours are almost entirely solid, circular, single-trunked, thicker than cartwheels. Here, at this marginally higher altitude, farms sport the scars of centuries of cooler climes, decades before the frost of 1956, and it is easy to see how the trees have fought back, grown anew, multiple-limbed. Claude's holding is a celebration of olive trees. There is no other vegetation here. The odd Barbary fig cactus scattered about but otherwise, nothing: after our long hot summer, even the ground scrub has withered. To irrigate his trees Claude has installed a complex watering system which snakes its way through the magisterial groves.

A cry from somewhere above hails the arrival of the man himself. Stepping across the fields, waving, is a figure I would have barely recognised. Stooped now, with grief etched on his face, he does not immediately meet my gaze. Still, he shakes my hand, assures me of a warm welcome and signals our path. 'Shall we begin?'

Off we go, inspecting every tree, admiring their handsome offerings. It cannot be denied that Claude is in for a bumper crop. Scads of fruit. Interestingly, the difference in altitude means that his fruits are a month less ripe than those on our smallholding. As a rule, we would gather mid- to late November. This is sooner than some farmers, but we prefer our fruits to be pressed before they are too ripe because we are partial to that tangy, peppery flavour an early *récolte* delivers. This year, due to the heatwave and scarcity, I will be done by the beginning of the month. Claude will commence picking in three weeks, the time we would normally be harvesting.

All his trees except four, bunched together in a re-mote corner, are *cailletiers*. He does not know the variety of this quartet. Their fruits are considerably smaller.

'I wonder why they are here?' I muse.

'Why to pollinate the others, of course!'

This explanation surprises me. I have never heard it before and it reminds me yet again that there are myriad myths about the olive tree and at least a dozen different systems of farming.

'Ours are all *cailletier* except six smaller trees I planted by mistake soon after we arrived here. They are *tanche* olives but, if we are to gain an AOC ticket, they cannot be pressed with the rest of the crop.'

'Perhaps not, but they are useful for pollination,' rejoins Claude.

I do not argue with him. Our hill has produced olive trees for somewhere in the region of four hundred years, well before the French Revolution. As far as I am aware, mixing varieties to pollinate has never been essential. I suspect Claude is operating a method of olive farming that I have not come across. René says nothing to correct either of us, so I drop the subject and we drift on to inspect his two *forages*, drilled wells. He indicates at what junctures on his hand he 'felt' water, where the underground rivers converge, what the drilling processes involved and how the water is discharged. Of course, as this man is a diviner, water and the sleuthing of it is a passion of his. His equipment strikes me as complicated and extremely expensive, but, due to the prohibitive cost, we have failed to drill to any source at all, so who am I to comment? Claude inventories, in minute detail, the function of every machine and then the system by which water arrives here from the mountains. All water used externally on the estate is from clear alpine streams. My technical and engineering skills are non-existent and he soon loses me. I apologise. He shrugs. We hike up to his pump house. It has been constructed with eight valves. These enable him to irrigate selected areas of the grounds or to boost the pool level without wasting the precious fluid willy-nilly, all at once.

'I need to repair this step and paint that door again. See how it's flaking. And I must refill this cracked cement patch here. As you see, there is a great deal of work to do. Let's tour the rest of the grounds, shall we, and then we'll have a glass of champagne. You drink champagne?'

I nod, asking myself why at seventy-nine he is creating such a workload for himself and the answer is clear to me. He is mapping an inheritance for his offspring, protecting this fecund valley that has been his life and, perhaps most important of all, giving himself reasons to look to that future, albeit without his mate. During the remainder of our tour he recalls how he constructed the main house from recovered stones which had originally belonged to the drystone walls enclosing the land.

'It was in poor condition. Sections had subsided and the expense of re-erecting it would have been astronomical. *Mon épouse* suggested we gathered the stones together to see what we had.' He frequently makes reference to '*mon épouse*,' my spouse, when pointing out a structural addition or a stone configuration designed by her, and I sense how present she remains in his daily life.

Olive farming offers this man meaning and purpose,

as it does me. Claude's crop will be a windfall this season; he has only René to assist him. Two near-octogenarians. I could offer my additional pair of hands. If they accept, it will allow me to participate in the cycle of harvesting and pressing, a process that I have come to count on, to look forward to. And, without saying a word to either man, perhaps keeping company with another who is pining for his partner will help me through my solitary and uncertain days. Even if it doesn't, the olive gathering and oil-pressing certainly will.

Once we are settled at the table on his terrace, looking towards his trees and a church tower on a faraway hill, full champagne flutes before us, Claude recalls the Liberation. He, like René, takes delight in recounting his war stories. Neither knew the Great War but both their fathers did and these two were strapping young men during the Second World War.

'On 24 August 1944, four hundred US Dakota planes flying in from Corsica zoomed across this valley. From this very spot my father and I watched their arrival. I was a naïve fellow but keen as mustard. It was a thrilling moment. We were liberated the same day as Paris. Interpreters were needed for all the American soldiers arriving in those planes. I had been learning English, studying religiously, craving the day when the Allies would land. During the ten days they were based here before they moved on to Italy I served as interpreter, and a very proud one. I love Americans.' The sorrow I read in Claude's face when we arrived has softened. 'We had such fun. Many of the Yankee soldiers were my age. We taught one another street talk that made us laugh.'

'For example?'

'They thought it hilarious when I referred to their commanding officer as Big Vegetable. To us, that means a VIP. And we describe a man who is drunk as being round as a shovel. The Yankees would call him oiled. I loved that! Oiled!' Everyone at the table – including Claude's two daughters, who have joined us – giggles at the image. 'Ah yes, even today, I swear they were the best days of my life. Only my family has given me such a sense of purpose and fulfilment. And now my olive farm, of course, is seeing me through these days of loss.'

I smile and shyly offer my olive-picking fingers. The response is overwhelming. I will join them here whenever I am able and lunch will always be part of the deal. We raise our glasses and drink to it. So I will be a participant in this year's harvest after all, even if it is only on loan.

'Carol, I am so delighted that you will assist us. René, please, serve our *chère* guest more champagne. Carol, please, get yourself well and truly oiled and go home round as a shovel.'

The days are sunny and warm. I dedicate Saturday to catching up with the profusion of boring housework I haven't attended to. The barking of the dogs does not alarm me – they can be set off by the passing of any stranger in the lane below us, so I take no notice unless it becomes insistent, which is why it is only an hour or so later, when I am carrying a load of sheets down the stone steps alongside the stable, that I see anything amiss. There is a rabbit sitting in the *parking*. Rabbits never venture this close to the house: the dogs would nab them in a second. I hurry to the little creature, who doesn't hop away. Something is wrong. Or might it be one of our fostered hares returned? Quashia swears one comes by the cottage regularly to see him. The dastardly hounds, led by Bassett, are skulking by the swimming pool, fifteen metres away.

'Shoo!' I order, but they don't budge. I approach the rabbit. It hops off, but there is something odd about its gait. It smacks into the stone wall that surrounds the shallow end of the pool. I hasten to retrieve it before Bassett beats me to it. The stunned creature attempts another feeble escape, but struggles as though drunk. With minimal agility I trap it between my hands. It bucks a little but not too much. It is then that I realise the rabbit is blind. Worse, it has an open, jaggedy wound in its neck, which looks recent but is not bleeding.

I throw a glance at Bassett, who lurks and gloats with mean eyes. I love Bass. As dogs go he is a softy, in some ways more girly than the two bitches, but his nature is that of a hunting dog and I have captured his prey. He stalks towards me and I fear for a second that he might make a snatch for the blind animal squirming in my grip. It's Monsieur Q.'s day off. If he were around he would know what to do – wring the rabbit's neck, most likely, and put it out of its misery, but I am incapable of that. I determine to protect it from further harm though I doubt that I can save its life. We have no hutch. Quashia broke it up when we released the hares.

I run around, Bassett shadowing my heels, searching for a solution. Eventually, I choose the wooden cabin in Michel's palm grove. It is spacious and it locks; the place is used only for storing the tiles and balustrades left over after the restoration of the upper terrace, and there are precious few of those. I settle the rabbit on the floor and the second it hits the wooden deck it hops to the glass wall and – bang! – stuns itself again. In spite of all my efforts to shift it, it remains pressed up against the glass, straining for what? Sunlight? Bizarre, when it has no sight. Heat, perhaps. I have the dickens of a job sliding the door to. I don't think the cabin has been closed in years. I go back to my work, quiet in the knowledge that the maimed thing will die peacefully and not at the teeth of my black and white hound.

When I return later, I find its blind and wounded corpse. The ants, even in this short space of time, have already set to work. Seeing it there, in its helplessness, reduces me to tears and I sit on the cabin floor howling, or perhaps it's myself I am crying for. I cannot leave the rabbit for carrion so I rummage about in the garage for Quashia's shovel, dig a hole and bury it beneath a lush palm. What astounds me as I carry it to its resting place is how much heavier it is in death than in those last minutes of life. It is a warm, furry lead weight that I, still sobbing, lay in the ground and cover with red soil. Preoccupied by the dead animal, I cannot decide whether Bassett blinded it or simply bit its throat, or whether this little mammal was a victim of the myxomatosis virus, which, according to Jacques, is on the increase down here. If the latter is the case, should I have burned its carcass? Are the dogs in danger of contracting the disease?

Myxomatosis was deliberately circulated by man to curtail the rapid escalation of wild rabbit populations that destroy farmers' crops. Rabbits breed fast and can be pests. I cannot argue against that, I have seen the damage perpetrated here. It was the Australians who originally imported the flea, *Spilopsyllus cuniculi*, that transmits myxomatosis, purchasing it from Brazil, where it was first identified. They used it to devastating effect in the outback, where more than half the rabbit population was decimated by the virus. From there a French physician brought it to the environs of Paris. He wanted to control rabbit increase on his private estate, but the flea spread and is now at large everywhere in France. In 1953 it reached England. It is not known whether its channel crossing occurred by chance or was contrived.

The rabbit's blindness puts me in mind of Ghost and the Camarguais landowner who deliberately extinguished the dog's sight because he feared for his geese.

'The law of the jungle,' Michel might argue if he were here, but Michel is not here to listen to my thoughts on this or any other variation of man's inhumanity to man or beast. He is elsewhere, hacking his way through his own jungle, a dark place, it seems, where my love is futile.

To cheer myself later, I telephone our beekeepers to establish the arrival date of the hives.

'Oh, madame,' cries Madame, 'how splendid to hear from you!' Her effusiveness continually amazes and delights me, particularly down here where, as a foreigner, it is not uncommon to be greeted by surliness, suspicion or financial trickery. 'Everything is on track. We have begun our *transhumance*. Yours will be the last delivery of the season and we expect to be with you by the end of next week or Monday of the following. But we'll phone to confirm the date.'

I thank her for this consideration.

'We had counted on delivering by six in the morning' – *six in the morning!* – 'but works have closed off our mountain road during darkness hours so we can't set off till six.'

I have to say that I am mighty grateful for these nocturnal roadworks. The prospect of crawling out of bed to greet the dawn approach of 600,000 bees might have panicked me.

'Our estimated time of arrival is nine, but the late hour won't agitate the bees because the *bache* will protect them. We are so looking forward to seeing you and your husband again and, if by chance you are not home, we'll install the girls and return later to greet you, bringing honey, of course.' And on she trills and I find no opportunity to enquire what the *bache*, the plastic sheeting, guards the bees against or to tell her that my husband is absent.

I telephone Michel to pass on this news to him; an excuse to be in touch.

'Bees are usually transported by night because they never leave their hives after dark. Hence the *bache*.'

I still don't follow. He explains that as soon as the sun goes down and the last of the foragers have returned to their queen, Monsieur and Madame lift the hives on to the trailer. They must be on the road and have the hives installed at their new address before sunrise. When day breaks and the bees see light, they set out from the hives in search of nectar. If there were no plastic sheeting to cover them and the sun rose while the van was in motion, the bees would fly off and return to the same location, expecting to find their home which, of course, would not be there, and they would have no means of locating their new address. The sheeting creates darkness and fools them into believing that it is still night. It keeps them indoors, as it were, and even if a clever little girl exited the hive, she could fly no farther than the plastic.

'So, finally, beehives. Congratulations. You have worked hard to put this arrangement in place and the honey will be all the sweeter for it.'

'Thank you,' I whisper. Several years it has taken us to welcome hives to our estate. I am sad that Michel will not be here to participate in this propitious olive farm moment, but he does not offer to fly down.

After the weekend, searching everywhere for Quashia to assist with cleaning up the lower terraces in preparation for the arrival of our bee stock, I discover him on hands and knees rooting out potatoes and leeks within our recently re-rigged enclosure, beneath the cradles of olive netting haltered there to protect the vegetables against rabbits.

'We have work to do.'

'But I'm collecting my supper.' He emerges grinning, carrying a small swag of onions. 'I'll have my *marmite* to begin with, followed by these onions in salad, olives and a chunk of bread.' The *marmite* he is referring to is actually the pot used to cook his stew. It is bound to be already bubbling on the gas stove in the cottage. Ramadan has just commenced and food is uppermost in his thoughts. He last ate at half-past four this morning. It is getting chilly and he has worked all day without sustenance.

'Next year's honey,' I tempt. 'It's on your way home.'

'Honey?' His eyes light up.

I lead him to the lower terraces and point out the placing for the thirty hives. Due to the hot dry summer, there is no new growth in the grass so no scything or strimming is necessary, but the ground is scattered with big stones forgotten since last year's olive harvest. We use them to pin the nets in place at the foot of the trees and Quashia never gets round to tidying them up.

'Plenty of room,' he walks to and fro, considering the layout and the distances between the young and old olive trees. 'When I worked in the mountains, years back, erecting electricity poles, there were hives everywhere, all standing in straight lines. One row here. Another there. That's how they'll do them.' Then he stops and spins round. 'Why down here? Why not up behind the house where it's warmer and lighter? It's a bit damp here, not enough sun.'

'Because the beekeepers use a small crane to convey the hives to their winter grounds and we have no access for it elsewhere. It's the same problem we came across when we wanted to drill for water and, later, we'll have to face it when we begin to fertilise the olive striplings up the hill. We lack wide tracks. There are only footpaths.'

'I'll carry the hives myself,' he exclaims. 'They can't be that heavy. Tell the beekeepers to leave the boxes here and, when they've gone, I'll transport the whole lot up in the wheelbarrow.'

'No!' I cry. 'You are not to touch them, not in any circumstances. They are full of bees, Monsieur Q. Six hundred thousand honey bees.' Quashia raises his eyebrows, impressed. 'And the owners will be back and forth to keep an eye on them. In any case, it could be risky having them too close to the house. Sometimes, even in winter, they come out and, as I said, there are six hundred thousand of them.'

Quashia looks at me in amazement. His rheumy old eyes wrinkle. 'Mmm, pots and pots of honey.'

'You are just like Pooh,' I tease.

His face creases into a frown. 'What's Pooh?'

'Never mind. The bees will be safe here and out of harm's way and, if they do fly out, there is no one to be troubled by the swarm.'

'Except the postman,' retorts Quashia with a kindly but mischievous nudge.

I turn with a look of horror. So keen have we been to nail down this arrangement, it has entirely escaped our attention that over the laurel hedge, no more than a dozen metres from this spot, is our letterbox.

The calendar shifts to November and, after a week of capricious storms, delivers a heartening rise in the barometer. It is early Saturday when Michel calls, informing me that he is on his way home. 'You'll be here for the arrival of the bees!' In high spirits I rush to the airport but I am shaken by his overtired and un-shaven appearance.

I prepare him lunch and once our al fresco meal on the terrace has been cleared away, I hose down one of the sunbeds and drag one of the mattresses out of storage, encouraging him to get some air, sleep the afternoon away while I work. I am glad to see him relax, but I am worried.

Later, he confides that he is here to give me news. He is closing his business. The time lost in the sum-mer broke the back of what was already a tough operation to keep afloat. I am devastated for him. I know how hard he has worked and what his modest production company means to him, but the fact is that few independent producers make any kind of living in France these days. The market is too restricted. Even if one project succeeds, the next may not, and the investments, financial and emotional, are heavy.

'Can I help? What are you going to do?'

'Return to Paris and begin again.'

'What can I do?'

He stares hard at the table. 'I don't want to put you through this any more.'

I rest my hand on his. 'We're a team,' I assure him.

On the Monday morning after our brief weekend together, the beekeepers telephone during breakfast to announce their imminent arrival. They will be at our gate in five minutes, an hour early. We bolt our coffee and scuttle down the drive, dogs leaping and playing at our heels, to find *les apiculteurs*. Their truck and trailer with hives aboard are already parked on our grassy lower terrace. Madame is at work with an *enfumoir*, a cylindrical metal jug attached to a small pair of bellows. It is fuelled by pine needles or the dried paste left over after all oils have been extracted from olive drupes. Madame is burning pine needles. The function of the *enfumoir* is to release smoke clouds that calm the colonies after their journey. I have never seen one in action but our bee-mistress explains that since the time of the ancient Greeks such appliances have served to counter any risk of aggression or stings. Once the plastic sheeting has been removed the bees will start to emerge; it is a tricky moment for the keepers. Their girls could become disoriented, panic and start stinging. The resin-scented smoke relaxes them, and it certainly perfumes the morning air.

The commute from trailer to our lower grove is underway. Wooden pallets are being laid out in two rows as bases for the hives and to stabilise them. We lend a hand carrying the populous boxes. No bees emerge. But there are only fourteen hives.

'Ah yes,' sighs Monsieur. 'We found a valley with hundreds of wild roses. Winter rose honey was too tempting to resist.'

'But we did not want to let you down,' Madame butts in. 'So we have brought you two hundred and eighty thousand bees. I hope that will suffice.'

We are grateful for those entrusted to our care.

Each hive has a coloured spot on it in one of five colours, each signalling the age of the queen residing within. The queen herself has also been daubed, rather like a miniature branding, with her colour. It is an international code recognised by apiarists worldwide.

A queen is expected to live a maximum of five years, so a three-year-old is judged a pretty old girl. The hives are lightweight now but in the spring, when they are chock-a-block with honey, each tips in at 60 to 80 kilos.

They all have a *trou de vol*, literally a 'hole of flight'. It is their exit route, their front door. 'Watch this space,' laughs Madame, 'You'll see bees in profusion.'

'Take heed,' cautions Monsieur, dawdling alongside his metal and wooden boxes. 'They are a drug. We'll miss them, but we'll pop down once a fortnight to make sure they're happy.'

After a swift coffee with us, because they have another rendezvous, Madame nudges her husband with the words, '*On y va, mon cœur.*' Let's get going, my heart. Michel has missed this affectionate remark but he has noted the tenderness and professional symmetry at work between Mr Beekeeper, a mincing, slightly desiccated man, and his warm, voluptuous wife. Since his retirement, with their bee farming and the building of their new chalet giving stupendous views south from the high Alps, their lives, they declare, are just beginning.

Once we have waved the couple off, Michel and I return to the hives. Watching the swarms hovering in clouds above their homes is quite, quite beautiful. We sit together, hand in hand, crouched at the foot of the driveway, observing them. Their movements are circular and graceful and oh so silent in the wintery sunlight. It is a form of poetry to me. I am certainly beginning to understand Monsieur's caution. These furry hexapods could become addictive.

'It's not so different to those first dribbles of the new season's olive oil, is it?' I say, pressing my head against Michel's shoulder, squeezing him close, pained that I cannot be his talisman, that I am unable to wave away his defencelessness, his fatigue in the face of misfortune.

'Look at them! I am *so* tempted to draw closer, to raise the roof off a hive and expose their world within, to sneak a peek at their day-to-day living, their relationship to their queen and perhaps, who knows, catch them dancing.'

'Don't you dare,' he mumbles. And, of course, I resist.

After a brief meeting between Michel and Monsieur Q., during which the final stages of the hangar are discussed, I deliver him back to the airport. From there he departs for Paris giving no promise of a return for the upcoming Christmas holidays. Empty and apprehensive, I throw my energies into olive harvesting at Claude's, but his fruit is not ripening and he is taken ill. He swears it is nothing serious, 'just not up to scratch, a flu of some sort', but a doctor friend advises rest and he retires to his bed. I roll up anyway to help René with the crop.

The days are cooler than at Appassionata. I pick by hand because that is my preference, scaling ladders and the lower branches. The olives are plentiful but green and way too hard. Because Claude's plantation is sprawling I toil alone for hours without a sight of my silver-haired friend. Hours passed in amongst the willowy foliage help to sooth my deepening anxieties and the work is satisfying, even if it does not have the same thrill as cramming our own baskets. We make a trip to the mill, just the two of us in René's old Renault. He is depressed by the load and fears the return will be minimal. It all takes me back to our earliest days, to the excitement and gamble of a new pressing, and my heart feels heavy at the thought of what lies ahead for Michel and me.

'Where have you been?' cries the mill-owner, Christophe, when we walk through the door. 'I thought you'd abandoned us, chosen another establishment. It is happening more and more.'

Evidently his daughter-in-law hasn't mentioned my call bemoaning our dearth of olives.

'We have no fruit this year,' I explain.

'No olives? Have mercy! What about your AOC?'

'Still no news.'

He huffs and smacks his head dramatically with the palm of his hand. 'It'll all come good,' he assures me with uncharacteristic optimism. 'But no olives, *mon Dieu!*'

While René oversees Claude's pressing, I zip upstairs to the shop to buy soaps and pots of green and black *tapénade* home-made by the miller's wife. Inside the door a display of *santons* greets me. These are the small Provençal figurines made out of clay or wood that people Nativity cribs. Christmas is round the corner! Here, in the south, every home displays its own crib and most families include a selection of *santons* from the numerous local characters on offer: the miller with his donkey, the fisherman, knife-grinder, tambour player and many others. The figures stand outside the stable, waiting to pay homage to the infant Jesus. Within, of course, are the shepherds, the Three Kings – the usual cast of players.

'Want to buy a set?' asks the miller's wife. I shake my head. I can hardly bear to contemplate Christmas. But I am fascinated to know where the tradition sprang from. She happily explains. The idea was conceived in 1789, during the Revolution, when the churches were closed and there was nowhere for Catholics to honour and celebrate the Nativity. It was a church statue-maker from Marseille, Jean-Louis Lagnel, who came up with the idea of making figurines that ordinary families could buy inexpensively and keep tucked away in their homes. They proved an enormous success. *Santon* in French, or *santoun* in Provençal, means little saint. To this day there is a *santons* fair in Marseille.

When René has completed Claude's pressing – a shocking result, he whispers, shaking his luxurious grey head, more than 7 kilos for a litre – he coughs up for the mill charges, we offer our good wishes and everyone embraces, crying, 'Merry Christmas!' Back at Claude's farm, the mood is less jolly. The oil is not exceptional and his health is deteriorating so the men decide to postpone the remainder of the *récolte* until after the New Year. Claude wishes me the best for the coming season and presents me with a magnum of champagne, a *petit* acknowledgement of my contribution.

At Appassionata's altitude, along the verdurous lowlands, the harvests have been gathered, the copper-red earth is at rest and I, like the majority in the occidental world, turn my thoughts to Yuletide. Michel remains noncommittal about the holidays. His reasoning is that he must rebuild, must use the quiet period to catch up on so much lost time. Otherwise he doubts he will ever ride the wave.

'Why not bring the work with you, I'll leave you in peace,' I promise. And so, thankfully, a few days before the event, I extract a positive response from him.

Delighted, I gallop round the shops, stocking up the trolley, spending way more than I can afford, gathering up yards and yards of flashing lights at giveaway prices from a shop announcing imminent liquidation, determined that the farm will flag a bright and celebratory air and not smack of the turmoil I have been living through. I have few do-it-yourself skills but I set about garlanding the salon with my recently purchased illuminations. Nails go everywhere except in the walls and I hammer fingers when the fiddly things shoot from my grasp. I stand back to admire the final effect. It looks like nothing more than a sparkly, shapelessly knitted cardigan sleeve. Oh well, it's the best I can achieve. Outside I sling a necklace of coloured lights above the stables and am rather chuffed with the result until I close the upper doors and crush three bulbs in the attempt; my decorations have been hung too low. Next stop Cannes, the old port, where we have always bought our blue pine Christmas tree. Because the season is upon us and business is slowing, I find a towering bushy example and barter ruthlessly for it until eventually our regular vendor, who is an antique-dealer by trade and does not remember me from Eve, nods his head wearily and hands it over for a third of its astronomical asking price. He binds the tree tightly with string, pinioning its spreading boughs, and straps it to the roof of my car. Even so, its angel tip juts forward and shadows my vision like a stormy sky. I scale the hills gingerly, arrive home safely and cut the tree loose. An error. Its fronds spring forth like a dancer in flight, which creates difficulty in unloading it. I shove and push and heave. Flushed and pricked by its needles, I finally manage to roll it to the roof's edge and it spins to the ground, thudding on the tarmac, snapping several of its stems in the process and sending the dogs scurrying away. I am whacked. And how will I ever get it up the stairs and into the house, let alone dress it and have it in place before Michel's arrival? Somehow I manage.

In amongst the hustle and bustle of fur-clad Parisian trippers laden with elegantly parcelled gifts, I find my husband at the baggage carousel. 'Sorry I'm late,' I pant. He looks misplaced within this arriving world of voluble Christmas spirit, and his vulnerability breaks my heart. People all about us hug and clasp and screech with holiday cheer. He greets me with a brief kiss and a tender brush of my cheek but I can already tell that he is frozen still. His gaze is fixed in a caught-off-guard expression and reminds me of a teddy bear's button-eyes sewn on too tightly. The wound on his forehead is slowly healing, but what inner scars remain, what internal derangement might the accident, so swiftly followed by the closure of his company, have precipitated? Michel has always been such an elegant man. The way he moves, lays a table, his sense of arrangement and colour, his manners and social graces, and although all those qualities remain, I cannot help feeling that I am in the company of someone who does not fit himself – who is not, as the French say, *bien dans sa peau*, good in his skin – someone who cannot find a way through the channels of his body, as though the signals from his brain have been stunned. His hands dangle loosely, operating like empty gloves. He is not clumsy, far from it, but he appears to flounder in the face of things. Lost.

Come. Come home. I take him by the hand and lead him to the car.

Back at the house we go scouting in the garden for a yule log: it's my excuse for us to tramp about the shabby acres together in our wellies in the crisp, falling light. Rooting and exploring, we are re-encountering the surfaces in one another's company. Robins abound. Berries, too, the colours of the robins' breasts, and narcissi pushing up through the apertures in the stone walls. Hands on grainy bark, we stand before sky-scraping pines in indecision. Which to choose? 'According to Provençal lore it needs to be cut from a fruit tree,' I say, but in that case our choice is limited. Most of the fruit trees are way too young to start having bits lopped off them. Eventually we settle on a smooth, otter-grey, S-bend from our elephantine fig alongside the pool. He won't miss it, will he? And we stagger with it up the rock-hard slopes, sliding over mulchy fallen leaves into the house to throw it on the open fire to join other red-hot logs of pine and oak. Afterwards, crouched on cushions on the worn rug by the flames, I slip on a Helen Merrill CD and serve us a welcome home glass of Claude's champagne. It's an upbeat beginning.

'Remember when we slept on that horrid lumpy old mattress in here?' I say. 'There were five geckos on the chimney breast. "They are the guardians of the house," you said. "They are watching over us." ' I glance about the sitting room. It is less shabby these days, pristine white, and the geckos rarely enter any more. They hide away behind the blue shutters hooked back against the exterior façade, keeping their distance. Only when they are disturbed and scurry every which way at once do we see them indoors.

'We'll have to find ourselves other guardians. Any suggestions?'

Michel shakes his head.

The following day is tranquil and sunny and we are easy in one another's company if not noticeably chatty or intimate. We lunch outside together on the terrace, but when the sun begins its descent behind the hills and the afternoon grows chilly we return into the house to curl up by the log fire, to work, read or watch films. I potter a bit in my den and suggest driving to the market to buy oysters, which are traditional here at Christmas and oh so cheap, but Michel shakes his head saying he doesn't fancy them. 'Well, we have turkey. What else might you like?'

Nothing special, he tells me. He takes handfuls of cash and off he goes to the hardware supermarket, returning with rainbows of paint and a job lot of brushes of all sizes. He seems delighted by his purchases and I am, too, for him, and enquire, encouragingly, I pray, what he intends to do with them.

'Paint,' he replies absentmindedly.

He sets himself up an outdoor *atelier* beneath the magnolia tree where in the summer we are tucked up in the shade. He lays out a transparent plastic ground-sheet, places his paints and white spirits, his tools, in orderly rows and disappears in search of something else.

I go inside to throw another log on to the fire blazing away in the hearth, wanting to leave him free so that he does not feel watched over. Standing in the kitchen, by the sink, staring out of the back window up the hill towards the pine forest, I catch sight of a rabbit poised on hind legs beneath one of the palm trees. There is very little food about at this time of year and we have wire-netted almost every plant on the estate to keep these and other scavengers at bay, but we forgot Michel's flourishing palm grove. The creature drops down on all fours and draws close to a serrated trunk; back up on its hind legs, head lifted, it begins to nibble hungrily at one of the lower fronds and I marvel at how, when the tips of the leaves are as sharp as needles, it doesn't cut its mouth. It feeds on regardless. Well, I'll leave it be. It's Christmas, after all, and the rabbits are less harmful than the boars.

I think of Michel occupied elsewhere on the land and resist the temptation to cry. At least we are both still here, I tell myself. We can rebuild.

I will not give up.

When Michel returns from a tour of the grounds he

tells me that there are wild boar tracks all over the summit of the hill.

It is Christmas Eve. Jacques is coming to clean the pool later and I want to leave a gift of champagne for him but the pool-house doors are jammed shut. They are made of iron and I haven't the strength to lever them open unaided. Quashia tells me that he will handle it. When I am next in the garden, I find him and Michel together. Quashia is laughing, happy to have his friend and *patron* home. They have oiled the lock, to no avail. Michel is now bent to it with his ear pressed against the door. He reminds me of a safe-breaker as he listens for the clicks that might release the mechanism. He rises and shakes his head. Quashia asks to have a go and before anyone can stop him he steps forward and smashes a long crowbar against the lock. Now it is well and truly jammed.

I am gobsmacked. 'What did you do that for?'

'Sometimes the shock releases the problem.'

I continue on my way to gather herbs for the turkey I have stuffed for this evening's meal, our Christmas dinner.

The next thing I hear is the whirring of the drill. I decide it is better not to know what the pair of them are up to. They are worse than Laurel and Hardy. I am now engaged in the grimy business of emptying out last night's ashes from the grate. Opening the front door, I am assailed by the thundering ring of a mallet hitting metal. I sigh. Glancing back into the sitting room, I see a trail of cinders marking my route. My pail, I now notice, has holes in the bottom. Michel joins me outside on the upper terrace. He looks shiny from exertion and downcast.

'How did it go?'

He shakes his head. 'We did our best but we couldn't save it. We had to remove the lock.'

'It's no big deal. Knowing Quashia, there's probably another one in the garage.'

'Unfortunately, the drilling buckled the door and, while we were removing that, the concrete frame which held the double doors in place cracked apart.'

'How?'

'It was very old.'

When I pass the pool house on my way to swim I find one lone blue door hanging by a prayer and a stray upper bolt. It is all that remains of the pool house frontage. This is so unlike Michel.

Jacques arrives, bearing a gift-wrapped poinsettia for us and we give him the champagne. He joins us for an apéritif and we sit looking out over the sea. 'Alexandre says there have been reports near the lake park of wild-boar damage. It seems they are back and wreaking serious damage hereabouts,' he warns.

'They've been here, too,' I admit.

We talk until the sun goes down about the old vineyard, his passion for fishing and our hunting trip and then his wife calls wanting to know why he's still working.

'I'd better be off.' He kisses us both and wishes us happy holidays. 'Did the boars break the pool door?'

I shake my head.

He looks puzzled. 'What happened?'

'Best not to ask. Have a splendid Christmas.'

★

The weather is glorious, a true Côte d'Azur Christmas Day.

I catch sight of Michel climbing the hill, carting a plastic bucket containing some of Quashia's bits and pieces and the larger of the two chainsaws. I deduce that he is going to embark on a spot of much-needed pruning. It's a touch early in the season, perhaps, but that's fine. When I take coffee to him later I find him cutting back the branches of a tree that has been dead for some time. I am baffled. He must mistakenly believe the deciduous oak is in hibernation.

'How's it going?' I lay the tray on the ground. Michel switches off the chainsaw and deposits it by the sawn logs. He is sticky with perspiration and sawdust.

He looks admiringly upon his work. 'Fine. Nearly finished.'

I am anxious not to negate his efforts. 'It could be dead, that one. Difficult to say.'

Michel turns with an expression of surprise. 'Of course it's dead. It has been since the spring.'

'So you're chopping it down?'

'No, I am going to paint it blue. First, I am structuring it, then I will buff it and, before I leave, I will paint it blue.' He bends to retrieve his coffee. 'Imagine. You will stand on the terraces and look up at the young olive groves, every day growing taller and stronger, and in the midst of them will be a beautifully sculpted blue tree and, as a backdrop, the equally cobalt sky.' He falls silent.

'We'll paint the shutters the colours of Matisse's chapel.'

He peers at me quizzically as though trying to recall.

'Remember? Azure blue. Côte d'Azur. The blue coast. It is what you said to me the second time we came to visit Appassionata, after an outing to Matisse's chapel in Vence.'

He drops his gaze and shuffles his boot against the stony earth. 'Did I?'

'You don't remember?'

Gaze remaining earthwards, he nods. 'So I did. A long time ago now. I'm sorry.'

'For what?'

'For the way it worked out.'

For the way it worked out.

I lean in, kiss him on the cheek. 'It was an excellent choice, and so is your blue tree.'

I descend the hill to the flowerbeds where I rummage about the borders until I unearth the Fijian shells and for the second time this year they are laid out along the wall. I recall what Angélique said to me about how Michel created achievable projects for his father. Christmas birds are chirruping in the winter sun and my spirits are lifted. I like the idea of a blue tree and perhaps, after the tree, I will suggest the restoration of the ruin. I'll find a way to finance it. *For the way it worked out.* Michel could begin again here, start a new company from home, cut down the expenses. It will work out. Yes, my spirits are lifted. His wellbeing will be the finest of Christmas gifts.

Later, as we are sitting together by the fire, I cite

Picasso. When the artist lived in Mougins there was an electricity pylon that had been erected within sight of his villa. Picasso fought to have it removed but, getting no joy from the blank wall of officialdom that reigns in these parts, he set about painting it and transformed it into an object of delight. We have one of those ugly poles. It rises up out of the lower garden, smack bang alongside our pool and fig tree and divides our view of the sea in half. Ours remains not because we tolerate its unsightliness but because we have not had the spare cash to pay for its removal. To take it away and feed the electricity underground from lane to farmhouse would cost us, according to an out-of-date quote from the EDF, France's electricity board, somewhere in the region of 50,000 francs or £5,000. At that price we decided a while back to live with it until there is little else to spend our hard-earned dosh on.

'When you've finished your tree, wouldn't it be terrific if you painted our concrete monstrosity?'

Michel does not answer. He stares into the crackling flames, deep in thought.

I persist. 'Tree blue, perhaps? A marriage of wood and concrete, how about that? Or, what else, fig-leaf green?' Still he makes no response. 'You're very silent. What are you thinking about?'

'The roof.'

'Why, is there a problem with it?'

'No, not this roof. The idea of roof, the concept of it. I think we should get divorced.'

I close my eyes, aware of my quickening heartbeat, of the flutter of panic and the icy fear within me. I want not to have heard him, to be mistaken.

'Please don't say that, Michel. We can get through this, I know we can. We'll rally, whatever the problems are. But, please, don't let's talk of divorce. Not yet. I am here for you. I'll be a bridge, or if you need more time alone then we can refigure our marriage. However you want it to be.'

He remains silent.

'There have been many occasions when I was down or facing difficulties and you offered masses of love and support and I would say "How can I ever thank you for all that you give me?" and you answered, "The day will come, I'm sure, when I will need you." This could be that day. Please let me be there for you,' I whisper. 'Please.'

'This is different,' he answers flatly.

'What about the olive groves, and your blue tree?'

'You will take care of them and cherish them, I have no doubt of that.'

And so, after the holidays, Michel leaves me, returning to Paris, packing possessions, clothes, articles that he has never taken away from here before. It is January. I stay on alone.

A Beast's Love

The days have tipped over the winter solstice and are lengthening again. Even so, the nights are endless and black. I do not sleep well. I cannot sleep at all some nights. Winds rage and the trees bend and howl like this bereft farmhouse woman might. Down comes Michel's blue tree, ruptured at the base. I salvage what segments are salvageable and arrange them like fantastical Pompidou Centre piping beneath the covered porch by the pool. Ella goes missing in one of these terrible storms. She can barely walk but even so she seems to have taken flight. For three days we see no sign of her and I fear the worst. Out in the darkness I tramp the terraces before bedtime, trying to exhaust myself, calling for her beneath the misty stars.

By day, I traipse the damp lanes in the rain, searching. Quashia suggests that in the past she has headed for the stream. With her weak limbs and her aged bones, if she has slipped in the mud or got herself tangled and trapped in amongst the biomass, she will never lever herself free, and even if she did, she hasn't the strength to negotiate the hill to home.

When the storm abates, wellingtons donned, we descend to the rivulet, thwacking the dripping bushes with sticks as we track, to where Quashia released the hares late last autumn. Each of us takes a bank, calling and beating at the undergrowth, but she is nowhere.

In this sodden wintry weather, at her age and with arthritis, I fear she has no hope of surviving the night-time temperatures and days without nourishment; she must have perished. I return to the house, desolate. The worst is not knowing. Quashia heads off to his cottage for lunch. I begin the ascent to the farm. In the lane I bump into our portly bearded postman. He draws his scooter to a halt, nods a restrained greeting and rummages in his satchel for our letters. A quick glance shows me there is nothing from Michel.

'You look upset.' His remark takes me by surprise. He is usually sullen and shares nothing bar complaints.

'Ella is missing.' I doubt that this will raise much sympathy.

'Now, which one is Ella?'

'The golden retriever.'

'Ah, the old girl? The redhead?'

I nod, puzzled by this cheerful change of heart.

'How long has she been gone?'

'Three days.'

'Well, good news for you. I saw her a couple of mornings back. I was delivering the letters at the *foyer* and had to brake fast because she came out of the brush and went staggering across the lane in front of me. She looked pretty dirty, I must say, and it did surprise me at the time. I thought she was off hunting in your neighbour's jungle. Go down and enquire of the Arabs. One of them is bound to have seen her. She's probably there now, being spoiled and overfed.'

'Thank you.'

'Good luck.' And with that he tips his cap and shoots off on his bike. I stare after him, flabbergasted.

What has happened to our grumpy postman? Has he fallen in love? I hurry along the lane to the labour settlement, the *foyer*, asking everyone I encounter whether they have run across Ella but, to a man, they shake their grizzled Arab heads. Eventually I come across one toothless old geezer, squatting by a mossy boulder, sucking at a twig, sporting a frayed towel wrapped as a turban round his skull. 'The rickety red-head?' he mumbles. 'She was here.'

'When?'

His menhir features crease with concentration. ' 'Bout a week ago.'

No, that cannot have been her. She hasn't been missing that long. I trudge back to the house. After lunch I update Quashia. 'Perhaps you'd visit the settlement and enquire. They may not have understood my French but you speak their language.'

'I was down there an hour before you and I went looking this morning. No one has seen her. I think we must face facts, Carol.' His words dry in his mouth. Quashia loves the dogs as much as we do and I can see how upset he is.

I nod. 'Well, thanks for trying, Monsieur Quashia. I'm going into that plot next door. If I can wade my way through it.'

'Carol, I've looked, and called and called her. In any case, it's dangerous. If the bossman is hunting, he can't see through the thickets. One bullet and you'd be a goner. It's the season, he's been in there every day this week.'

'And Ella?'

Quashia lowers his eyes.

We have eagles on the land, I'm sure of it. Sometimes I hear them in the wee small hours, or rather, I hear extraordinary cries echoing from the summit of the hill. Similar to the calls we heard last summer, the night the she-boar flew at Bassett. These calls travel down the slopes in long notes, as pure and resonant as a soprano or the Arabs' muezzin. A creature from on high. I know it's not Ella. It must be a bird. I close my eyes and imagine a mighty eagle standing atop its lofty nest, its alpine minaret, conversing with the wind. I lie awake, tossing, listening to other noises of the night, wondering where our retriever has got to. Beyond the shutters I hear the paws of a smallish creature padding through the dead, damp leaves, thumping its tail over the dark-soiled, well-trodden passages. Could it be Ella, cold and hungry, resurfacing out of the earth's bleak winter? Just in case, I am up and out of bed. I draw a dressing gown about me, slip on shoes and go outside into the black but starry night.

Snufflings. Please God, don't let it be the wild boar, not this close to the house.

'Ella?' I call softly.

The noises of the night retreat into watchful silence. I circuit the house by the back garden and make for the stables, where the other two hounds are bemused by my arrival, bleary-eyed as I switch on the light. 'Where is she?' They stare at me, yawning, huddled against one another, curled up like a pair of furry snakes. Outside, I hear an owl hooting from the high hillside. These calls I recognise, though it is rare to sight owls. I stare upwards for so long my head goes dizzy and the blackness seems to dissolve into light. The night is busy and mysterious, but I am cold and bereft. I pull the dressing gown tighter about me and trudge back into the house.

The next morning, very early, I am at work in my den when I hear Quashia rummaging about in the garage beneath me. I open the window, lean over the casement and shout good morning. He appears with a grin from one side of his face to the other. Ella has returned.

'I can't believe it. I thought she had died on the Hunter's ground.'

Her fur is snarled, tangled and tousled. Twigs are caught up in the hairier, coarser patches of coat around her buttocks and she has a bad cut on her left hind leg, but she is home more or less in one piece and I couldn't be more glad or astonished to see her.

'Between you and me, Carol, I was sure she'd died in there. It was one of the reasons I didn't want you going in.'

I call in Gérard, who gives her vitamins, injections, a dressing and caresses. 'She is suffering from shock and muscular exhaustion. Looks as though she's been caught in a trap, judging by this incision. Remarkable how she's freed herself, remarkable how she's battled her way back. An exceptional tenacity, this retriever possesses.'

I hug her tightly and wonder what she has fought her way back from. Her eyes gaze at me wearily. I see a haunting there.

'I hope your bees prove equally robust,' our vet says, packing away his medicine bag.

Worrying about Ella, I have ignored them for a couple of days. He reads my question. 'Walk down and see for yourself. Something has been feeding around the hives.'

Try as I might to deny the facts, I cannot. The earth in every direction round the fourteen hives has been thoroughly ploughed, and within inches of the bees' flight path. 'It's the boars.' Quashia shakes his head sadly. 'It was still dark when I came up this morning so I didn't notice this mayhem, but at the top of the land five olive trees have been broken. We'll save them. Even so. There must have been an army of the blighters here last night.'

I gaze upon the destruction and, as I do so, a cloud of bees rises and circles in the New Year sun.

'Monsieur Huilier told me that only cows dare to approach the nests. The *sangliers* won't touch them.'

'Not on purpose, perhaps, but it only takes one great pig to take a clumsy step and these three hives, for example, stacked on top of one another, would go over in a second.' I close my eyes at the thought of it. 'You promised me, Carol, gave your word, that if they came back—'

'Let me think about it, Monsieur Quashia.' I snap because I am tired – not a decent night's sleep in a week – and because I have been praying it wouldn't come to this, and I dearly wish Michel were here to make this awful decision for me.

I return to the house. The elation I was feeling at Ella's return has deserted me. In my den, I lift the receiver and then replace it. Moments later, Quashia is banging hard at the door. I plod out to open it.

'We've got an olive tree down on the lower-right grove. Its net surround and the tree itself have been trampled over. It was a good one too, doing well. There's no saving it.'

'Olive tree, tree of eternity, it regrows,' I argue.

'Carol, we can't begin another year like the last. Buy me a gun. Even if I have to stay up all night, every night, I won't sleep until I drive them off this property. One way or another, they have to learn that they are not welcome here!'

I respect Quashia's passion and I hear his vehement plea but I cannot buy him a rifle and I explain this to him yet again.

'If Michel were here, he'd have them shot.'

'I'm not sure that he would,' I counter.

'Well, there's little more I can do here, Carol. You gave me your word.' He wanders away and I feel as though I have let him down, which I have.

Back in my den, reluctantly, I pick up the phone.

'I'll be there before dusk. Tie up the dogs,' Alexandre warns.

The rest of my day is about waiting.

Alexandre arrives as promised, before the fade of day, in the company of a middle-aged hunter. I watch them from the window as they unload their carbines from their van. I signal that I am on my way down. A quick greeting, an introduction to his colleague, and Alexandre lays down the instructions. 'Keep away, even when you hear gunshots. Keep the dogs inside with you. You are not to venture beyond the house until I return and tell you that it is safe to come out.'

I nod obediently. Two hunters in the slackening light, on guard by the long wooden dining table on our summer terrace, off they stride into the woods, their gun butts resting on their shoulders. My stomach feels tight at the prospect of bloodshed on our land. I potter about doing nothing. It grows dark. Looking out of the window I see blackness. The world is silent. Until I hear a shot ring out, and then dead quiet. Eventually, after what seems like an age, the men return. Jacques is with them. I hadn't been aware of his arrival. I expect to see a corpse slung over someone's shoulder. Blood, at least. But there is nothing. They are despondent; the beasts have stayed away.

'But I heard a shot . . . ?'

'No, that was the spit of a damned exhaust down on the road. It could have alerted the *bêtes*, of course, warned them of our presence. Like you, they may have mistaken it for gunfire.'

We are in the hallway, huddled by the front door. I invite the three men in by the fire, offering them warm drinks No, they are hungry. It's late. They have families to get home to. We'll be back tomorrow, they promise.

I nod and wish them all a pleasant evening, thinking of them returning to their families.

Days pass. The men come and go with their guns but they bag nothing. Yet, the boars are still trespassing. Quashia and I find olive branches lying everywhere on the ground, ripped from the trees by the gang of beasts. Earth is upturned and roots upended.

Tracks everywhere. It looks like someone has been in with a tractor. I fear for the bees. Each day there is freshly turned earth down around the hives. I pray our beemasters won't propose an unscheduled visit.

Eventually, before the weekend, Alexandre decides to put his trap into action. He arrives with maize, stale bread and pellets of dried dog food.

'Come with me,' he orders. 'Look, I am encircling the meal with large, heavy stones and covering it on top with one substantial block. This will keep birds away, should the food still be here at daybreak. The boars have the strength to remove this weight with their muzzles. Most other scavengers do not. If the goodies are taken, set it up again tomorrow night. If it works on the third night, I will come with my rifle. Stay with this spot. Don't change it, whatever you do. It's high up on the land and a safe distance from the house. When the bait is taken, make absolutely sure that you replenish it again the following evening, are you clear?'

I nod. The boars come. They eat the food. I refill the stone circle. They come again. The following week the men return. Each evening after work they drop by, guns at the ready, in the dark, the cold and sometimes in drizzle, but whenever they are present, the boars don't show up. Eventually, the men give up. They cannot devote their lives to this. 'But we will install a cage. That will catch the brutes.'

The cage, an oblong container about the size of a child's playpen, hand-made by Alexandre out of sturdy metal sheets and wire-mesh netting, is installed. Basic provisions are arranged within it and I am called up to inspect the scene. Alexandre explains to me: 'Once one of them sets a hoof on that metal plate, there – wham! – the tripwire is triggered and this door here will slam shut.'

It is indeed a veritable prison.

'The animals have ten acres to feed off, why would they allow themselves to be caught by this snare for the sake of a bit of stale bread and maize?' is my question.

'They are pigs. Omnivores. They devour everything. They'll go in after the food, Carol, don't you worry. Just make sure you keep the tray well stocked and chain up your dogs because we don't want them sniffing about and getting themselves trapped.'

I follow the instructions to the letter, but the wild pigs do not touch the fodder. Day after day, morning after morning, Quashia and I unleash our howling, restless curs, who are crazed by incomprehension as to why they are no longer free to roam the hill at night, and climb the path intersecting the terraces to the ruin to see what the night's fortunes have brought. Nothing but an empty pen and stale, damp rations. These beasts are proving themselves to be smarter than the trappers and I cannot deny that I feel a mounting respect for the thieving creatures who are causing us so much aggravation.

'I think it's time to admit defeat, Monsieur Quashia. The trap is not working and I don't want the dogs to be tied up any more.'

'Carol!'

'Sorry, but it's not fair on them. We have reared them to live outside, to be at liberty, sleeping on their blankets and mattresses in the stables if they prefer on cold nights, or stalking the land. Their freedom is what they know. If the boars are smart enough to avoid the pound then I am perfectly certain neither Bassett nor Lucky will be fooled by it. Ella is no problem because she can't climb up here.'

Quashia protests, but I won't hear another word on the subject. The dogs remain unchained at night, and they stay clear of the pen. Until one evening later in the week, after Quashia has finished work and gone off to shop and I am still at my desk. I toss my biro on to my table and rub my eyes. Beyond the windows the sun has set. I glance at my watch. It is after six, later than I'd realised. I go downstairs to the stables to feed the dogs. Ella, as is her habit, is drooling by the food trolley – she may be rickety, arthritic and recovering from shock but her greed never abates. Lucky appears as soon as she hears the tin dishes clang against one another. Bassett, not unusually, is elsewhere and I am obliged to shout for him.

'Bassie!' I yell into the night as I fill up their bowls with their evening portions of meat and biscuits. The other two are slobbering and whining at my heels. I place their meals down before them. 'Bassett!' My voice reverberates around the hill and into the valley but still the little black and white hound does not appear. I take his dish back into the stables, cover it over and store it well out of reach of his thieving companions. I am not unduly concerned. It is his nature to disappear from time to time on one of his exploratory escapades, his forays into the world beyond our farmland, but he generally doubles back to spend the night with his playmates.

The following morning Quashia calls up to my den, where I am already at work. I lean out of the window. '*Bonjour*, Monsieur Q. *Le café est prêt*. Would you like a cup now?'

'No coffee for me, thanks. Have you seen Bassie? His dish has disappeared.'

I shake my head. 'It's on top of the black cupboard in the corner. He wasn't here for dinner last night.'

'No worries, I'll feed him when he returns. He's probably had a night on the tiles,' winks Quashia mischievously.

'I don't think the little fellow knows what it's all about,' I smile. 'Call me when he checks in.' I latch the window and return to the farm accounts.

No time later Quashia comes banging at the door, shouting. 'Come and look!' I follow him up the hill to the wild-boar snare where I sight our piebald Bass curled up like a puppy, staring balefully out at us. Between his front paws are the sucked remains of a large chunk of stale bread. He is perfectly quiescent, not the slightest bit traumatised and, when Quashia lifts the iron trap door, almost too lazy or reluctant to move.

'Come on, boy,' I pat my hands against my knees in encouragement. His tail begins to wag, he yawns and then deigns to join us at large. 'That's where stealing gets you, mate. A night in the clink,' I josh, bending to cuddle and reassure him. He rises on to his hind legs, yodelling with happiness, licks my face and bounds off down the garden in search of his chums. 'He thinks it's his private chambers, with room service thrown in.'

The boars begin to enter the cage. They successfully access the bait but somehow manage to sidestep the metal trap. I report the situation to Alexandre. He and his compatriots are baffled and I am losing patience. The beasts are laying waste to the grounds. The land looks as if meteorites have cratered it; walls are being dislodged on a nightly basis. There are not enough hours in the day to repair the disorder let alone keep abreast of the regular chores. I am worried for the bees but, above all, I hate having the pen on the land. I am about ready to insist that it is removed when, one evening, alone in the house, I go through to the kitchen to prepare supper and almost suffer a heart attack. There, beyond the window, is a massive peat-brown mammal, a sow, surely, weighing probably 90 kilos. I run to the phone, and reach Alexandre, who is fluey and cannot come out. 'I'll be there tomorrow,' he promises.

Tomorrow!

The following evening he and a colleague arrive before dusk, rifles at the ready. We discover how the hogs are managing to raid the larder without triggering the tripwire. A large chunk of bread has rolled under the metal plate and jammed it so that, no matter how forcefully an animal treads on it, it will not release the contraption that slams shut the cage door. Are these swine so intelligent, so savvy about deathtraps that they have disabled the mechanism on purpose, or is it a fortuitous accident? The hunters lie in ambush until eight in the evening, by which time they are cold and hungry. Still not a sniff of game.

The next night the dogs are in the yard, woofing and barking and yawping like a pack of chained dingos. I dutifully go out to check the premises and catch the desiccated whisper of turning leaves not fifty yards from the villa. I creep towards the distant plot of land and hear snufflings and hissings and the rustle of winter underfoot. I clap my hands, imitating gunshots, but no beast budges. They are not fooled. I return inside, worn down by the battle.

In the morning, the latest bulletin is that an Arab companion of Quashia's, dining with him in the cottage, spotted eight boars walking in file at the extreme reach of our fenced enclosure. I report this back to hunting base. The men promise to return, which they do. By this time, I am growing used to white vans pulling up in our *parking*, discharging male strangers unloading firearms and boxes of cartridges. Always they are accompanied by Alexandre and occasionally by soft-hearted Jacques, who never fails to remind me that he doesn't hunt – '*Je chasse pas, moi*' – but shows up anyway to abet his friends. This evening they are two, and without Jacques. Again they bury themselves in foliage up by the vine-keeper's *cabano* until long after dusk has fallen and, yet again, Alexandre comes knocking at the door to say they are going home. 'They were here. We saw them over by the fence beyond your disused vineyard but at the very last minute the wind turned and they caught our scent and fled the scene. Vamoosed.'

I nod wearily. These beasts are outsmarting everyone.

'I'll be back next week,' he assures me. 'Have a good weekend.'

Again I nod, offer my cheek for the customary *bisous* and lock the door. I just want this to be finished with. If the only solution to driving the swine off our property is to shoot one of these animals, I want the bloody deed done. I want the cage gone and the caravan of armed men away from here.

I work late and fall into bed exhausted, reading for a short while before turning out the light. At a quarter to eleven, the dogs take up their chorus. I throw my book aside. The cloven-hoofed enemy has returned. I switch off the bedside lamp, burying my head beneath the duvet, hoping for sleep, but the barking goes on, intermittently, until dawn, by which time I am dead to the world.

A thumping at the front door drags me from my troubled slumber and I crawl from bed, bleary-eyed and disgruntled, ill-prepared for the morning that lies ahead. Quashia is shouting excitedly.

'What?' I yell, throwing open the door to reveal myself wrapped in a creased towelling robe, my hair bird's-nest fashion, teeth uncleaned; ideally cast as either of Cinderella's Ugly Sisters.

'Look up at the enclosure!'

'What?' I repeat, squinting uphill, unsure of what I am looking for.

'Two,' explains Quashia.

I step towards the rear of the house. 'Don't go up there – the sow'll charge you.'

Yes, two. I make out a large brown silhouette ensnared within the pound and outside, crouched alongside it, much more visible, the captive's loved one. It senses or smells our presence and rises cautiously, paces, moving a few metres towards its escape route – its *draille* – and turns back, fixing a woeful gaze on the pound. It is unable to quit the scene, to leave its distressed mate.

It is this, this alliance, this beast's act of love, of sacrifice in the face of danger; its vigil by the cage throughout the dark hours of night, its pacing in anguish and confusion over the misfortune of its mate, mother or offspring, that sears my heart. I instantly burst into tears. 'Set the imprisoned one free, Monsieur Quashia, please.'

He roars with laughter – 'Don't be ridiculous!' – and then sees my tears, hears my shocked sobs.

'I want them to go free; I want them to be together. I can't separate them. I hadn't counted on this.'

'That's not possible, Carol. First, if I go up there, the liberated *bête* will charge me, so I am not going anywhere near that pen. Secondly, how many months have we been waiting for this? Call Alexandre, Carol, we are not setting it free.'

Alexandre is at work; he cannot get away. He sends his *beau-père*, his wife's father, who is with us within the half-hour. With his rifle on his shoulder, his close-set blue eyes fixed straight ahead, in brown calf-length boots he marches directly to the spot; he has been here on several occasions before and knows the lie of the land. Quashia and I wait two terraces below. The *sanglier* at large has spotted the human with his gun and bolted into the dastardly neighbour's jungle. The huntsman raises his gun directly at the cage – he is no more than a few feet from it – and pulls the trigger. I hear a thud; the fall of the beast.

'It's over,' I whisper. But, no. He raises his rifle and fires again. 'He can't have missed, not at that range!'

The hunter turns from the scene of bloodshed and begins to descend. But I stop him in his tracks, calling out to him, 'Is it over? Can I come up?' I have a need to confirm. He waves and beckons me excitedly. Quashia and I take the well-trodden path to the cage and there, to my horror, we find two animals in the pen, both lying on their sides. They are junior chaps, swimming in a ruby carpet of blood.

'A couple of brothers, I'd say,' remarks the huntsman.

'And the one who waited, was she their mother?' I ask, staring down at brown hairy lifelessness. But then I look closer, puzzled. Alarmed.

He shakes his head. 'A brother or sister, from the same litter. They're all about eighteen months old.'

'This one's not dead,' I state coolly.

'Yes, he's a goner. Death throes, that's all. The nerves. Don't you worry, he's dead. I got him right in the jugular.'

It is true that I have just observed its jittering body, thrusting in spasms like Michel on the hospital trolley, but I am not convinced.

'He's not,' I insist. I look from one victim to the next. The first beast to have been shot, the one deepest into the cell, is nothing more than a carpeted hillock of flesh while the other, whose snout is pressed up against the closed iron door, is inhaling through its mouth, lifting its upper lip as though snarling. Perhaps it is snarling. I hear the draw of its breath, like an old man whose lungs are packed with tobacco.

Quashia and the marksman are in jubilant spirits.

'It'll be very tender meat,' says the hunter. 'Have you got a wheelbarrow? Shall I strip them and carve up the meat here, in your garage, or shall I take them to my place and Alexandre can deliver some of the cuts back to you?'

'I'll get the wheelbarrow,' says Quashia. 'Yes, very tender meat.'

'Shut up, Monsieur Quashia – you don't even eat pork!' I am leaning in close, peering through the wire-latticed roof of the death coop, studying, hawk-like, the expiring pig. Blood is gurgling, popping bubbles out of its neck. Its tiny tail is wagging like that of a contented dog. The one slate-grey eye I can see – the other is out of vision – seems to be trained on me. I glance at my watch. It is almost fifteen minutes since the second bullet was fired. 'Wait! Please shoot this fellow again.'

The huntsman turns back and stares into the cage. It is blatantly clear that beneath us lies the last whispers of a life, but still it is life and it is suffering. 'I have no more bullets. I only brought two cartridges.'

I stare at him appalled. 'Well, we are not leaving him like this.'

Quashia and Alexandre's father-in-law struggle to lift up the pen door but the other animal has died on the spring plate and is holding it locked. Eventually they release it a few inches and the man begins to kick the beast's skull with his boot.

'Stop it!' I cry. 'Please, find a swift and dignified way

of killing this animal now. Don't you have a knife?' The man shakes his head. I don't bother to enquire how he had been intending to skin his prey here without one.

Quashia suggests his mallet and that is what is decided upon. The two men hurry away to fetch wheelbarrow and mallet. I remain at the side of the pigling whose death I have condoned. It makes a feeble attempt to lift its head. 'Please die,' I say almost inaudibly. 'Forgive me for this.' I am aware that anyone witnessing this would judge me ridiculous, even Quashia, who loves all creatures great and small, but I feel an obligation to stay with this adolescent boar until it departs this world.

The men return. The door is hauled open and the surviving animal extracted and given one solid crack to the centre of its cranium by Quashia. Not instantly, but seconds later, its eyelids close and its life finally drifts away, its soul set free.

I feel the charge of my own breath.

The men confirm that it was a young male and weighs nearly 40 kilos. While they drag the second, a female, from the pound, I continue to keep guard over the first, needing to be a thousand per cent certain that there is not a spark remaining. I have an overwhelming desire to faint or throw up, and I am forcing myself not to weep again. I must maintain emotional steadfastness, masculine sensibilities, in the present company. Both beasts are lugged by their haunches and slung into the wheelbarrow. Legs flopping in all directions, bare stomachs exposed, they look like a pair of cuddly toys dumped in a stock room. Quashia carts them away down the track to Monsieur's car.

The hunter lingers, waiting for me. 'You'll have peace and quiet for a good fifteen days,' he assures me.

'Sorry?'

'The rest of the pack won't come near your territory until the scent of blood has dispersed. They can't stand it.'

'And then?'

'Back to the business of keeping them at bay. The cage can stay here if you like. The Arab can wash off all the blood and then restock it in a couple of weeks.'

I am speechless. I had genuinely understood that one death here meant our grounds would be for ever off limits as far as these scavengers are concerned. For what have I admitted such bloodshed on our hill? For what has such a brutal death been perpetrated here? Two weeks' respite?

We are walking towards the villa and the pool. The view to the sea is unobstructed. The sun is shining.

'You have a lovely spot, very well maintained but, by George, they've done some damage.'

I nod, numbed. 'The biggest problem is the walls,' I murmur.

'Yes, they break into the walls searching for snails. That's their favourite dish.'

'Well, I suppose it will mean fewer snails all over the plants and vegetables.' I am determined to maintain a normal conversation though I am trembling with shock.

'That's nature. That's the cycle of life. Dog eats dog,' he replies.

We have reached his car. He shakes my hand heartily and thanks me profoundly. After the hunter, whose name I did not learn, has driven away with the two dripping, hirsute carcasses wrapped in plastic sheeting in the boot of his car, and Quashia has climbed the hill, quietly delighted to have a tranquil working life for the foreseeable future, to continue weeding around the feet of the olive trees, I go inside, shut the door, draw closed several of the shutters to create a crepuscular light and run a bath. Outside the day is bright and clear. I lie in the bath looking out at the morning. There is an eastern philosophy, Chinese Buddhism, I think, that speculates upon the engagement of responsibility. When a butterfly flutters its wing in China, they say, the impact resounds around the universe.

I have always been very taken by such a possibility and have most easily been able to comprehend it, relate to it, through the complexity of music. Of course, I have never seen it precisely as an isolated act, not as in one card that sends a pack of cards tumbling or one independent note or chord. No, rather more as woven or accumulated consequence. A wing lifts or a note is emitted, then comes a run of sounds, of movements, of notes; others are brought into play, from a variety of agents or instruments. Many resonate at once and, before we know it, we are listening to a symphony. One single wing flutters and its consequences release symphonies or, equally, a cacophony of cachinnating, barbaric sounds. The music of the universe: mellifluous, elegant, lyrical, or grating, off-key and discordant.

If the Chinese have hit the nail pretty much on the head then, surely, we are also engaged in that act of composition?

I lie in the bath, soaking, cleansing, immersed beneath gallons of grief – the departure of my husband, the slaughter of that young beast – until the water grows too cold to remain and I begin to shiver.

A Cocktail of Toxins

These early New Year days are bathed in sunshine. In another, more northerly climate, one might dare to call such mild weather spring. Here, it is a special season: a bright velvet warmth spliced in to cheer us after the holidays before the customary rains of February. Already the almond trees are in bud and the very earliest of the migrant birds are winging in. Our self-seeded almond up by Quashia's construction is growing out of control. Its branches spread forth, monster tendrils overshadowing the more reticent fruit trees, intent upon the shed's semi-tiled roof. I tease Quashia that the tree is in revolt against all the masonry detritus he has bestowed upon this once fecund corner. We must prune it, before it flowers. Together we go at it, cutting timber in the fresh sharp air. Setting the chainsaw zizzing; splitting, cracking, thudding and rolling its limbs into the birdsong of morning. We argue about this branch or that, whether we should keep it or hack it, like an old married couple, and while we are puffing and sweating he requests a leave of absence for two weeks to visit his family in Algeria. He's long overdue a break. One of his granddaughters is screaming to get engaged, he moans. Sixteen, she is. He has given strict instructions to his wife that no decisions are to be made until he gives the suitor the once-over. Our dear Quashia remains head of his family and any nuptial bondings involving the grandchildren must be blessed, not by his son, the girl's father, but by him, the paterfamilias. The lad is a stranger; he hails from a village one hundred and more kilometres away from their village.

'Does it matter that he wasn't born in the same region?'

'We have no idea how he earns his income and there is no one nearby to fill us in on the matter. Don't you worry, as soon as I clap eyes on him, I'll get the picture and make my decision.'

Poor young girl, that her romantic future should rest in the hands of her grandfather who hasn't lived in her natal land let alone her Arab community for more than fifty years. We settle on a date in early February when, due to the rains, little exterior work can be achieved. Satisfied by our efforts, once the tree looks as though it has been at the barber's, he hurries down the hill to phone his wife while I lop off some extreme twigs from the severed branches and carry them into the house as a bouquet. They might still flower.

The almond sprigs retrieved from our bout of pruning, splendid in a vase from the Nice market in the dining room, have burst into delicate bud. Elsewhere, the hills are egg-yolk yellow with a perfume from heaven. The mimosa season has sprung early. It is late January. I return from Tanneron, village of the mimosa, where the entire hilly hamlet was swathed in the ferny branches and fluffy, chick-like flowers and where I have invested in armfuls of the tightly balled blossoms. Driving up our lane, I spy Quashia in his black hat and black leather jacket, hands clasped tightly, waiting by the locked garage doors. He must have forgotten his keys. I wave, proffering the sweet-smelling branches, yelling. 'The pool house looks great, Monsieur Q.' He has just completed its repairs. 'Would you like some flowers for the cottage?' Then I realise he is crying.

'I must leave for Africa immediately. I'll be back as soon as I can,' he stammers, as I run to him. His second son has been killed by a lorry in a road accident on the borders of Algeria and Tunisia, leaving a wife and six small children. It is heartbreaking to behold him sobbing like a boy. I drive him to a local travel agent, purchase a plane ticket and deliver him to Nice airport. He is travelling with nothing but his identity papers.

'Are you going to be all right on your own?' he asks, when we arrive at the terminal.

'Perfectly,' I lie.

'I'll be back as soon as I can.'

'Stay as long as you need to. Look after yourself. Best regards to your family.' We hug forcefully and I wait, watching him, head bent, disappear.

When I return to the empty house, I box up long stems of the mimosa, carefully sealed in cellophane, and post them to Michel. 'Enclosed, a golden perfume from Provence. I visited Tanneron today,' I write. 'Gazing from the sill of the clifftop out towards the distant sea, the hills in every direction beneath me were a curtain of yellow. I could have believed I was sitting on the sun. *Je t'aime.*'

I refrain from mentioning Quashia's tragedy or his departure.

I am alone with the farm's responsibilities.

A day or so later I receive a call from Alexandre. His tone is mysterious. 'Are you home?'

'Of course, you rang the house.'

'I mean, are you staying in? I'd like to drop by.'

'I'm here,' I confirm.

Within the hour he pulls up in his van. He is carrying a large fortified paper sack. It reminds me of the ones they used years ago on my grandparents' farm in Ireland to transport the potatoes. He carries it over his shoulder, swag-style. 'Here,' he says, swinging it to rest on his feet. 'This is for you.'

'What is it?'

'Your share of the spoils. Two *très bons gigots*.' He is offering me the two hindquarters of one of the young boars. 'These are from the girl because hers will be the most tender meat. The carcass has been hanging since the beasts were shot and skinned and now these legs need to be refrigerated for a minimum of fifteen days before you eat them. Roasting is the best method and simplest. Make sure the oven is exceptionally hot—'

'Please, Alexandre I cannot take these. I didn't hunt them and—'

'Carol, we have divided up the meat as is our custom, and this is your share. Now let's get them to a fridge.'

I unlock the summer kitchen and our hunter begins to rearrange the few morsels already stored in the deep-freeze. He lifts the two haunches out of the sack causing blood to fall in droplets to the floor. He doesn't notice the stain and I don't say anything. The cuts are so considerable he is having difficulty packing them into the compartment drawer. The cloven hooves and ankle hide are still attached to both lower legs. I close my eyes. He catches me.

'Of course, you must saw off the hooves before you cook the meat. I left them to assure you I was delivering you your own beast.'

'I trust you,' I manage.

Eventually the butchered produce is stowed away and the freezer closed. Alexandre requests a sponge and kneels to clean the floor.

'Please, don't bother, I can . . .'

'You're not going to cry again, are you?'

'Cry?'

'As you did the other day, when the beasts were shot.' He rises from the floor grinning and walks over to the sink to rinse the sponge.

'When we went hunting I was fine. What upset me the other morning was the mate waiting outside the cage.'

'You think it waited because it was grieving for its loved ones?'

I shrug. Well, yes.

'You know why it was there?'

I shake my head.

'The girl,' he points to the fridge, 'was on heat. One male went in after her and they got trapped. The other lad would have followed too if he could have. He hung around – animal instinct, Carol – hoping for a sniff. You know how it is when a man is attracted to a woman's scent.' We remain within the cool crepuscular half-light of the summer kitchen. The hunter is at the sink again, running the tap on the sponge. He lets it fall into the basin. He is smiling at me audaciously, amused.

'Where's your Arab?'

I wince; I hate it when anyone refers to Quashia as the Arab. 'Erm, he had something to deal with. He'll be back shortly. Let me get you a towel to dry your hands.' I make for the door.

'It's fine. I've got to get to work. Instruct the Arab to reset the trap and call me when anything happens, OK?'

I nod.

'No more tears. They are beasts with beasts' impulses. They know nothing of love or feelings.' He leans in, kisses my cheek lingeringly and swaggers off with a wave. I decide against preparing the trap. In any case, alone, I cannot hitch it up. Its iron door is too heavy for me.

Later, to cheer myself, I take a stroll to the hives in the afternoon sunlight to find the bees out and about, in swarms. I stand up close behind the boxes, not in front where I may alarm them and they, in defence, might sting me. What I notice is a great deal of activity around some of the flight paths and none at all in others. I walk the two rows and hear loud buzzing within the boxes. Twenty thousand bees in each hive in communication. I run to fetch my mobile to ring Michel. His answer machine kicks in. Still, I hold the handset over the hives, transmitting a message, a bees' song from the south of France.

The following Friday when Jacques comes to work I pop down to say hello. The air is tangy with wood-smoke from a bonfire in a neighbour's garden. 'Would you like a coffee? It's ready.'

He shakes his head while unreeling metres of swimming-pool hose.

'Got yourself a boar, then.'

'You heard? There were two, well, three with the fellow outside.'

'Yes,' he smiles. 'Alexandre regaled us with the account. How I laughed!'

'What at?'

'You.' The memory of his amusement tickles him again and he begins to chortle.

'Me?'

'We nearly bust our guts. Alexandre, me and his father-in-law. Every time we thought of it or mentioned it.' He is laughing again now and shaking his head in disbelief.

'Blubbering about a beast that *didn't* get trapped.'

'Well, no, it wasn't exact—'

'I haven't been that cracked up in a long time. Oh, Carol.' He is crying with mirth, hand pressed against his stomach.

He wipes his eyes while I lower mine, hurt. This is the man who doesn't hunt. How often has he reiterated that fact. Somehow, inaccurately, I had judged him to be the finer, the more tender-hearted and sensitive of the group.

'Well, that's me, I suppose,' I whisper. 'I had better get on.' And I return inside, to the security of my library, where seated amongst my books, I bury my head in my hands, feeling defenceless.

★

The almond twigs I brought into the house, now on my work table, are sprouting scrumptious delicate leaflets and I discover that deep in the water, peeping out from the severed end of one cut limb, is a tiny pinkish stub: the eye of a root, with the appearance of a shy earthworm. I decide that I will keep the twig in water and when the shoot is ready to pot, it will be for Michel, for his studio in Paris.

When evening falls, I call him. I chatter on for a while, a little nervously, till, delighted, he tells me he has news to relay. He has an idea for a film and a director to work with, very early days but . . . The mimosa arrived safely. It brightened his day. His little studio is redolent with the scent from the south.

I recount the hunting episodes. 'You are worse than I am,' he teases. There was a mouse in his Paris kitchenette. 'I spent two weeks shopping for a trap that wouldn't kill it.' When eventually he found what he was looking for and caught his prey he carried it in a jar to the cemetery at Montparnasse where he set the little rodent free. I smile at his tender heart, wishing that we were together, wishing that all was well. I want to tell him that I love him, I am waiting for him, that all will turn round again; I believe he'll win through, we'll win through, but I refrain from mentioning us at all. Instead, I ask after the girls, his twin daughters. Vanessa has just learned that she is pregnant. It will be an autumn baby. Clarisse already has a child, a little girl. She and Serge married two years back and have a small house in the countryside east of

Paris. Vanessa is married too, and lives in Manhattan, where she travelled to finish her degree.

'Send them both my love.'

And then he rings off. No further mention of divorce has been made.

The following morning I am out sweeping the terraces when the postman buzzes up the drive on his scooter, which is most unusual. While he is rummaging in his satchel for our letters, I hasten to restrain Lucky. 'The beige one went to the refuge and the others are fine,' I assure him, noticing that he has lost weight, shaved off his beard and looks ten years younger. Of course, it would be impudent to remark upon it.

'You've got bees,' he says, as he hands me the envelopes.

'Yes, but they're harmless, I swear. Hardly ever sting. Not at all, in fact. Please, don't concern yourself.'

'I love bees,' he states blandly. 'Could I have a look at the hives?'

I am completely bowled over. 'Well, I can't open them up, I'm afraid, but you are welcome to . . . are you sure you want to? I mean, they *might* sting.'

He nods intently and, bemused, I lead the way to the makeshift apiary. He watches with a child's glee as the bees enter and exit by their flight holes and circle in the sparkling morning air. Disarming himself of bike and leather satchels in the drive, ignoring the two mutts, who have joined us and are yapping manically at him, he shuffles to the silvery grove, a man entranced.

'I wouldn't go too close if I were you, best to stay behind the hives!' I am picturing the full force of La Poste at our door when this man returns to the sorting office, swollen-faced, cursing us and our livestock, but he removes his postman's cap and stands in the morning sun, head tilted heavenwards, glorying in the circular poetry of the bees. I move in to join him, more taken by him than by our furry arthropods.

'I always said that when I retired, I'd keep bees. It's been my life's dream.'

'Well, the owners of this lot have done exactly that,' I smile encouragingly, puzzled by the extraordinary transformation in this man. 'Happiest couple I know. Follow your dreams, I say.'

He turns his head, looks gravely at me and gives a half-hearted nod. 'Yes, well, I best get on. Letters to deliver. See you tomorrow.' And with that he retrieves his yellow scooter and putts off on his way, leaving me utterly astounded.

Alone, I struggle on with the tasks demanded by the farm, determined to manage, to find a way through, convinced that if I can hang on in, life will turn around. It begins to rain. At first it is a soft mizzling fall, invisible to the eye. I watch it pocket in translucent drops on the trees' limbs made shiny by it, but little by little the heavier winter downpours set in: overnight soakers; eddying and swirling in the pool and the gutters; thunderclaps splitting the distant pewter horizon, while inside the house flames roar in the fireplace. The hunting season draws to a close, save for foxes and migrating birds. I leave a message for Alexandre: please remove the cage from the land. Without Quashia, I am obliged to chop and lug wood from the shed alongside his hangar to bank the blazing fires. I keep candles burning so that when the storms cut off the electricity, which they do regularly, I am not staggering around in the dark, in the garage, grappling for the trip switch. And then, late one afternoon, the electricity shuts down and no amount of flicking or smacking at the mains makes the difference. There is a fault. Four calls to our electrician remain unanswered. My work is at a standstill; no computers. And no music to accompany my solitary evenings. Candles illumine the house; I bath in cold water – fortunately, my daily swims have prepared me for such a situation – and, even more fortunately, our stove has three gas rings so I can still heat food. Into this rainy state of affairs, I hear the chugging of Jacques' truck. I hurry down to explain that though the pool is turning green it cannot be cleaned because I have no electricity.

He eyes me with incredulity. 'Where's Monsieur Quashia?'

I hesitate. 'Had to go off, a family crisis. Obviously, I'll pay you for the visit. Please don't worry.'

'How long since you had power? The last storm was three days ago.' He strides to the garage and begins to ferret about, unplugging oblong thises and thats, testing wires, opening boxes until he discovers whatever it is that he has been searching for. Then he nods. 'Where are the toolboxes?' Whatever he requires I manage to furnish and I am secretly chuffed at how well equipped we are here. The problem is solved in a jiffy. A question of blown fuses. Jacques turns to me. 'If ever you are in trouble like this again, I want you to telephone immediately. Promise me.'

'How much do I owe you?'

He walks away in disgust, play-acting insulted. 'Hey, I know what!' he cries. 'If you have the latest 'arry Potterr in English you can lend it to me. I am brushing up on my rusty vocabulary.' I do; I run upstairs to fetch it and he sets about cleaning the pool in the light rainfall while I make us both steaming mugs of coffee, grateful for the presence of this gentle Provençal man whose philosophies I have not quite got to grips with.

No matter what the weather, I must check the water level in our basin. So, after the weekend, I make a visit to the hill's summit, head covered by my flapping raincoat, where I find the sad remains of a trapped bird floating, bloated and decomposing, on the water's skimmy surface. How to extract it? I could telephone Jacques but I decide I will save his kind offer for emergencies and deal with this myself. I hurry down to the pool house, slipping and sliding in the mud, feet swashing in puddles of gunge, Lucky and Bassett keeping me company, and pull out the net used for extracting fallen leaves and flies from the pool. This I secure to a long metal pole that normally holds the pool brush, cart it back up the incline and set about fishing out the carcass. But I am not tall enough, and no amount of arm-stretching delivers the net to the basin's centre. I trudge back down for a garden chair and hike the hill with that. Eventually, the bird is salvaged. It stinks to high heaven so I decide not to throw it in the dustbin. Instead, I dash with it in the escalating rain to ditch it into the hunter's grounds. I bid the dogs stay at my side which, for once, they do. I hurl the dead bird. It flies high through the wet air. I await the soft thud of its landing in the brush but instead I hear a rifle shot, muted by the noise of the rain. It shocks me. I hadn't expected anyone to be there. The season is over. What's he up to? Of course, rabbits and small birds are not protected. Warned of the trapper's presence I retreat at a lick down the hill but I am halted by his cry. He is calling my Christian name, which confounds me. I turn. Covered from head to wellington tops in a soaking black oilskin, and resembling a gigantic seal, he strides my way, gun swinging loosely at his side. He is on our land and I am on the point of rebuking him when he shouts, 'Heard you've taken up hunting!' The rain is falling fast over my face, running in driblets from my hairline, making me squint. I am panicked, threatened.

'How's your dog?' He continues, unshaven, smirking, moving closer. He has thick-fingered hands.

I glance quickly to confirm that my two faithfuls are safe, have not been shot. They are. Why aren't they barking at him? 'What do you want?' I snap.

'Your redhead got back all right?'

I frown.

'She was caught in one of my traps. I delivered her to your gate. Next time I won't be so generous. I'll send your beast to Jacky, shall I?' And with that he is gone. An armed, black-cloaked figure disappearing into his sodden kingdom.

I stagger back to the house, freezing, soaked. That cut on Ella's foot was caused by one of his traps. She would have died if he hadn't released her. I should have thanked him. 'New cover for basin', I scribble furiously, gibbering from cold and confusion. Next time, I must.

Quashia closed over our basin with iron sheets a while back. Unfortunately, a storm-damaged pine blew down and split the corrugated roof asunder and we have never got round to replacing it. I promise myself that when Monsieur Q. returns . . . when he returns . . .

The following evening he calls me from Constantine from the local café, hollering into the handset as though the force of his voice alone will transmit his message to France.

'How are you, Monsieur Q.? Oh, I am so pleased to hear from you.'

'I have to delay my return.'

My heart sinks like a stone.

'It's La Fête du Mouton. I can't leave my son's youngsters with no one to buy their sheep. I must stay on, play father to them.' La Fête du Mouton, the sheep festival, is the Arab equivalent of Christmas. It is celebrated by the roasting of a whole sheep. Each family prepares and cooks one.

'Yes, of course.' I force myself not to refer to his return. Selfish to put pressure on him and his bereaved family.

M. and Mme Huilier drop in. They need to open up the hives, check on how the colonies have fared through the winter and, if any of the hives have grown short of honey, feed in reserves of liquid glucose. They arrive bearing gifts, golden sprays of mimosa and a book. 'This'll give you all the information you need concerning Karl von Frisch, who won the Nobel Prize in 1973 for his research on the interpretation of the Dance of the Bees,' smiles Madame, handing me my presents. 'I know that you are interested.'

I confirm my pleasure.

'Of course, not everything that prize-winning Monsieur has deduced is accurate,' remarks Monsieur Huilier over coffee and cake. 'Scientists don't know everything, but it's worth reading nonetheless.'

I thank them again. 'I will enjoy studying it and I am looking forward to playing beekeeper's apprentice,' I remind them.

'We'll arrange an outing for the summer because soon it will be time to take the little 'uns away.'

'Yes, I understand. It is as we agreed.'

After our snack we set off for the lower terraces. They have brought an extra protection suit and face mask for me. Each of us dons our costume. Madame lights the *enfumoir* and I am charged with the responsibility of maintaining calm amongst the furry newcomers. Monsieur heaves off the lid of the first box and I stare for the first time in my life at a living hive. Bees are crawling everywhere but I cannot see the queen; she is hidden away in a lower compartment. While Monsieur explains this to me and lifts out the honey sheets to confirm that this brood remains well fed and in good shape, Madame records the information with box number into a dictaphone. After the lid has been replaced, the hive is weighed. This one tips the scales at 20 kilos and our apiarists seem content. We move on to the next. I puff the fumes everywhere around the flight hole but there seems little activity here. The lid is removed to reveal a very different scenario. Within is an ominous stillness. The hive is dead, declares Madame. I am utterly shocked. 'Occasionally, over the winter period we lose one or two. We calculate for it, particularly when the queen is older.' She reports the data into her machine. However, in this instance, the queen was a one-year-old, and it was a robust colony when it arrived here. I say nothing, fighting to contain my questions. We continue on down the line and discover that out of the fourteen, five swarms have expired. The cause is not starvation. Monsieur returns to each to confirm that their reserves were sufficient to maintain well-fed colonies. The couple cannot hide their dismay. I fear that our site has let them down. Monsieur shakes his head. 'All over France apiarists are losing vast quantities of stock. There is an insecticide produced in Germany for use on maize and sunflower farms; it has proved lethal for bees. I fear we have fallen foul of that.' The couple, so enchanted when they arrived by life in their newly constructed chalet in the mountains, depart taking two empty hives with them. The others will be removed later, along with the living colonies. They did not come with their trailer. I wish them *bonne route* and return slowly up to the house.

Soon it will be March. The pale almond blossoms have fallen; the branches are shooting lime-green leaves.

Rooks caw loudly above the hillside, wagtails hop to and fro across the driveway, the cedars are heavy with a rusty pollen, which, when the winds come, spreads a canopy of yellow dust everywhere. Borage is a carpet of blue in the grass, the sun shines silver on the sea and I can work with all the doors open. Myriad songbirds are settling in, intent on nest-building after their long flights. New research suggests that as well as being guided by solar and star navigation and visual clues or landmarks such as we humans use, migratory birds also possess an ability to use the earth's magnetic field as a compass for their arduous journeys. Now safely landed, they greet the mornings with their crystalline tunes, their bell notes. The temperature is 24 degrees. Spring is truly on its way and I cannot say how glad I am that this winter with its hauntings, its death and decomposition and loss is at an end.

Michel and I remain in regular contact. Our relationship is amicable and I am determined to rebuild from there. From this southland I send him samples of all that flowers or grows. These are my couriers, my love letters, my optimism.

The young olive trees are shooting up at an astonishing rate; tender new foliage is in evidence all over the estate. As I turn their newly thrust sprigs in my fingers and marvel at their life-force, I fancy they are displaying such tenacity to encourage me, to spur me on to dizzy heights of faith.

Their eminent stature, though, on such slender trunks, makes them vulnerable to the harsh winds that surely lie ahead at the tail end of February and beyond the ides of March. I must protect them. I motor to the *co-opérative*, choosing a Monday, knowing that it's Alexandre's day off, and buy 200 2-metre wooden pickets. Days it takes me to carry them up the hill on my shoulder, or drag them like a carcass when they grow too cumbersome. If I am to remain here alone, I tell myself, I will invest in a donkey. I am a woodpecker at work – tock, tock, tock, tock – driving the thick sticks into the stony hillside with Quashia's mallet or, when I cannot negotiate it, with a rock that fits into the palm of my hand. Once they are secured, I fetter them with a cushioned thread that cannot cut into the trees. And when the work is done and the day is at an end, I fall like a log into bed.

With such growth comes the need for pruning; indeed, the season for olive-pruning is drawing to a close – soon their lacy forked flowers will begin to bud again. But alone I cannot lop the trees. I cannot even shift my splendid wooden ladder from its resting place by the stables. Our apple orchard badly needs attention as well, and then there are the mixed fruit trees I planted up by Quashia's neglected shed.

I telephone René but he has had an accident: he fell out of an *olivier* and sprained his wrist when his mobile phone rang and frightened the life out of him. He and Claude have only recently completed their harvest. The olives never really ripened. 'In the end we pressed them all green. I've never known it in all my years,' he groans. 'Just goes to show, there's always something you don't expect.'

Laurent from the co-operative is still convalescing after his own arboreal mishap and Jacques does not prune trees, he informs me.

'But I thought you were a gardener?'

'My specialities are grass and swimming pools. Why not call in Alexandre?'

And that is what I am obliged to do. Together, in the young year's sun, we trim the small fruit trees and then the apples. 'I'll take you fishing, if you like. In the mountains, close to where we shot the chamois. It's beautiful up there in the spring. I spend days camping at the lakes, watching the fauna and fishing.'

'Doesn't it frustrate you not being able to shoot them?'

He shakes his head. 'I'm just as passionate about studying animals as I am about shooting them.'

I shake my head. I don't get it.

'Where's your husband? He hasn't been here for a while.'

'He's working.'

'I'll stay around and help you prune your olives.'

Although I believe his offer is well-intended, I thank him but refuse.

'As you like, but you had better get the dead wood out soon or it'll hinder the growth of the new crop.'

I urgently need his assistance, so my refusal is born of what? Caution, hurt. I haven't recovered from his derision over the wild boar. If the worst comes to the worst, the farm will suffer a second consecutive harvestless year. There has been nothing but silence from the AOC bodies so our rating appears to have gone nowhere. I am almost past caring. In any case, how can I hope to manage the upcoming olive seasons single-handed? Nothing of these concerns, nor my swing to despair, do I disclose to Michel.

And then, when I least expect it, Quashia returns. Strolling up the driveway in his old black lambswool hat, swinging one solitary carrier bag crammed to bursting with freshly picked Algerian palm dates: his annual gift for us. I have never confided to him that I don't like them too much. Michel, on the other hand, loves them, so I post them all to him. Quashia cuts a less ebullient figure than the smiling Monsieur Q. I have worked alongside for so many years but he is glad to be back, he owns, and I am desperately grateful to have him here.

'Work,' he says, 'is what heals. Let's get to it.'

After everything, even though he has returned, I make the decision to forgo drastic pruning of the groves this year. 'We'll clean out the trees, fillet them and see what happens. It might, just might, produce a bumper crop.' So we snip away the rogue suckers from the base of each trunk – these will sap the growth force – and set about cleaning out the dead twigs within the trees' silvery crowns, letting in the light, making a passage for the swallows to fly through, while the outer branches we leave alone.

The farm chores are endless. We work as a team. I lack the strength and skills of a man but I participate with commitment and reasonable good humour. I decide to modernise our ancient kitchen and, in preparation, I strip and paint and clean. Then I attack the bathroom, choosing an ice blue for its walls, cracking the sink while climbing a ladder. Late into the evenings, when the sun has set and outdoor chores are impossible, Monsieur Q. and I replace the tiled skirting board throughout the entire house. In daylight hours we restore the corrugated cover to the water basin and till the land. I am his assistant, running errands to the builders' merchants, shunting, carrying, ordering materials. I call in the plumber, the fellow who shouts and takes five sugars in his coffee, to repair leaks we have lived with since time immemorial. I book the electrician to lay cables for garden lighting. I plant bulbs, I sow veggie seeds. I scour bric-a-brac markets for old chairs, metal tables, stone water basins, broken amphorae, anything I can cheaply lay my hands on to put to inventive use on the land. We toil in rain, in driving winds, in spring sunshine, into the night. I develop a rash from weeding the flowerbeds. On free evenings I burn the midnight oil, studying the local language and lores and writing. The plant I am allergic to, I discover, the one that creates the rash on my arms, is bizarrely named pellitory-of-the-wall. It is part of the sandalwood family and grows out of the stone walls.

Exactly like my Arab companion, I work to assuage my sadness. He reports that he refused the suitor his granddaughter's hand and took the girl out of school, believing that she would be better off segregated from boys, learning cooking at her mother's side. I beg him to reconsider this decision. 'Every young woman is entitled to education,' I plead, but he shakes his balding head adamantly.

He never makes reference to his deceased son though from time to time he talks of the orphaned grandchildren and how he worries about them. And I, in turn, speak of Michel only when Quashia asks after him. But I never let go of my love for him. All that I am doing is for his return; holding faith with our dream, our olive farm. Whatever our land produces, no matter how modest, I box up a share and send it to him. Herbs, bay leaves, pressed flowers, oranges. I take snapshots, fairly amateurish ones, of sunsets over water, of changing colours and seasons on the land. Even after all these years, I regularly find shards of old earthenware pots or hand-painted tiles buried in the rocks and when I do, if they please me and I think they will inspire him, I parcel them up and send those to Paris too. I hold fast to the picture of his crazily painted studio. The colours he chose were our colours, and so I offer him whatever the land throws up. Lest he forget.

The bees must leave. Off to work, says Monsieur Le Beekeeper, to mountain escarpments in the Var, the pollen-rich rosemary fields. The spring *transhumance* is underway and the little girls are being packed up like so many boxes in a shoe shop. Each hive is weighed again before they depart to establish the kilos it has gained, how honey-rich it has become. And the joy and relief of opening up *les ruches* to find bees buzzing noisily and a healthy queen laying nigh on a thousand eggs a day. Perhaps the most memorable moment is the sighting of one bee, returning home in the nick of time before the circus hits the road. Somewhere she must have found a late-flowering mimosa. She lands with a cache of mimosa pollen, like two miniature gold bullion bars, strapped to her hind legs. Miraculous.

Their departure saddens me. I lend a hand, as Mr

and Mrs stack the hives into the trailer behind their four-wheel-drive. 'I look forward to seeing them back next year.'

'Next year it will be so much better for them if they could be housed higher up. You must create a realistic approach to your hill's extremity. You'll need one yourselves when all those olive trees start bearing fruit. Those splendid future harvests will require transportation.'

I reconsider the idea of a donkey. If that is how these terraces were farmed in earlier days then why not now? But who keeps mules these days? I could visit Thierry, the shepherd in Castellane, seek his advice. Who knows, perhaps Zamzong has produced a youngster? But Quashia shakes his head. 'A donkey?' He roars with laughter. 'I had two in Algeria but when we moved closer to the city I sold them. No point bringing them here, of course, they only spoke Arabic. No, we don't want donkeys. They will bring other burdens upon us. Buy me a tractor. One with caterpillar feet that is designed to scale these rocky surfaces.'

'But we have no tractor access and you don't drive.'

As spring advances, and to our delight the olive trees are showing every sign of a decent fruiting season ahead, a letter arrives from the olive institute in Nice. I have heard nothing since the Marsellaise letter I ignored. I open it, steeling myself for further difficulties, but this is a very different missive. After everything Michel and I have struggled through, after the countless inspectors who have visited us, the forms we have filled out, the expense and work we have let ourselves in for – can it be true that the paper I am holding is informing me: 'Your farm has been given its ticket, its identification by the Institut National des Appellations d'Origine'? I read it and reread it, telling myself it's my French. I've misunderstood. I've got it wrong. I sit down and read it again, but there is no mistake. *Your farm has been given its ticket, its identification by the Institut National des Appellations d'Origine.* The identification number is right there on the page in front of me: 0604000001. I read on. 'Please contact us with your pressed oil in order that we can make an analysis of its chemical content. No AOC will be authorised without confirmation of the analysis.' We are asked to deliver to the institute three examples of this winter's newly pressed oil. But we have none! Does this mean we are back to square one, must begin again from zero? I telephone Michel, wishing that he were here to share this long overdue moment with me. 'I'll write to them,' he promises me flatly. 'All farms have poor years. I am sure they will agree to hold our status until the next season's fruit is delivered.'

He does not tarry on the phone to discuss his own affairs and I do not press him. He sounds tired, strained. Whenever we speak these days I find myself examining his words, listening for nuances, clues, sounding out the depths of his warmth, his distance or proximity and his state of mind. I replace the receiver promising myself abundance for us. The very next morning, our first newsletter arrives from the AOC bureau in Nice. It is addressed to all colleague farmers. *Chers confrères*. I relish every word, hellishly proud that Appassionata is now amongst their esteemed *oliveraies*. I learn that it has been a bumper year for local producers. Three hundred and fifty farms have requested AOC recognition for the season's olive confections. Alas, not us, but so long as we can keep the trees healthy, free of insects and disease and we can invent an efficient method of servicing the upper hillside, we will reap ourselves scads of olives next autumn. I scout the hills to reaffirm my faith. The dogs accompany me as warm sunlight breaks through the groves where I gaze upon silvery bearers in doughty health. With hard work and good fortune, my hopes for our autumn harvest will be realised.

Spring delivers nothing but good news. My spirits are lifting. Blossoms abound. Quashia finally completes his shed, though without Michel to oversee its structural fine-tuning I have to admit that, in places, it looks decidedly tipsy. Monsieur Q. argues hotly against this conclusion. He takes up his spirit level and presses it against walls and pillars, crying, 'There, you see, dead straight.' So we let the matter rest. In any case, I quite like its helter-skelter appearance. The wild boars have not returned. It would seem that two deaths here were ample sacrifice and I am deeply grateful for that. Alexandre, aided by his father-in-law, removes his cage. I harvest the oranges – their yield is pretty spectacular – and store them to give to René to metamorphose into delicious marmalades and orange wine.

I walk the land with the dogs in the golden spring

evenings, alone but optimistic, always on the look-out for gifts for Michel. The finely forked flowers on the olive trees are plentiful. Fruit nodes are peeping out from beneath perishing petals everywhere. Only the orange trees seem in decline. Their leaves are losing their verdancy and on their undersides I discover encrustations of what resembles white shingle. When René comes by, arm strapped up, to collect the oranges I show him the foliage. He shakes his head. 'Well, you didn't treat the olives last year, and this is the result.'

I feel frustrated with him. 'What has this got to do with the olive trees?'

'You'll see, but my advice to you is budget for three, even four, treatments this year or you'll have infestations of trouble.'

I don't believe him.

'Gauging it by the flowers, you're going to have a spectacular crop, but you must safeguard it,' he reiterates, before tottering off with our crates, promising to return soon with wine and jams. 'If you want me to come and spray, let me know.'

I nod, waving him off without the slightest intention of calling upon his offer.

Summer arrives and the *oliviers* are straining beneath the weight of their early fruit. As long as no natural disaster intervenes to destroy them, we are set for a whopping harvest. The zenith of the year, and this one promises to be as sweltering as the last. So far, no major fires. And no promise of a visit from Michel for the holidays, but he has begun to send gifts too. Jazz

CDs he has copied, articles from newspapers. I treasure them as missives of love in response to mine.

While I am lingering over breakfast and a book on the upper terrace, my attention is drawn to a squad of purple-grey insects on the bougainvillaea blossoms. I rise to investigate and recognise them as those I spotted late last year on some of the upper-grove striplings. I leave my coffee and set off on a quick recce. My search reveals the young olive trees to be covered in these small helmet-shaped flies. They have a metallic, space-age appearance and some have a few darker markings. Might they be a variety of moth with opaque wings? When I raise my hand they flit from the trees and settle on me, stinging my legs and arms. They are nesting in the crooks and angles of the young branches. I press my fingertips against the clustered larvae; they are white and powdery and sticky. And they are everywhere. On the roses, vines, tomatoes, but most worrying of all, on the olive trees, young and old. How have we not noticed them? I spend the stiflingly hot midday hours in the house, leafing through my various reference books in futile, drowsy attempts to pinpoint the precise identity of these bugs. I narrow the possibilities down to five insect families but cannot be more specific. I read that 'insects are the most successful animals on earth. They account for more species than any other class: over a million have so far been identified, but it is thought that the true number may be between 5 and 10 million.'

I close the book in despair. I need unbiased advice, and fast. If I could catch a few of these silver-grey, gossamer-winged beauties and bottle them, I could drive over to the co-operative with them and ask Alexandre or Jacques, but the critters are elusive. Finally, after patient hours, I manage to trap three in a washed yoghurt jar set aside by Quashia for such emergencies.

Laurent has returned to the gardening co-operative but he does not have the expertise to identify them. Alexandre would know, but he is away until the end of the week. Jacques is with his family in the mountains and won't be returning for another fortnight. I am frantic. The examples I have trapped in the jar expire and on Friday I set about capturing new ones. Eventually, after much frustration, I bag a pair and return to the farmers' co-operative in search of Alexandre, who recognises them instantly. *Cicadelles blanches*. 'Don't worry about them,' he says. 'When you treat the olive trees, they'll be taken care of.'

I refrain from mentioning that I have not been intending to treat the trees and that my resistance to insecticides is all the greater since I stared down upon dead beehives.

'There are two kinds of insects,' he explains to me, 'those that sting the vegetation and those that suck. These are suckers. If you climb the old trees you will see that they are everywhere on the young shoots, new growth. They are always there, but you haven't seen them. When René treated your old trees against the *mouche de l'olive*, the olive fly, that same product shielded the plants against these white invaders. They have bred like this because the vegetation lacked protection last year. Heat incubates the larvae of various insects, including these chaps. If you are registered with us as fully fledged olive farmers I can sell you a liquid, but we cannot supply insecticides to you otherwise.'

I confess that I haven't listed us because I have never intended to purchase sprays.

'Well, try this. It's pretty benign and though not specifically for olive trees, it should see them off. Next time you come by bring your ticket of affirmation as *oléiculteurs* and I'll add your name to our files.'

When I return home Quashia and I set to with the bottled pesticide, diluted with water in two shoulder pumps, and cover the entire estate. It takes us the rest of the day and the following morning. And then we wait. Forty-eight hours, the instructions claim it takes for the flies to begin to drop away. Two days pass, then three, then four. The bugs go nowhere. They appear to be immune to the blue insecticide and remain on the stalks and branches and, in the case of the young olive trees, they are also setting up home on the trunks, sucking the sap. I look them up and find *Cicadellidae*, leaf-hoppers, but they seem nothing like the moths we have. I am desperate. Not knowing who else to turn to, I put in a call to the Chambre d'Agriculture. It is August – almost impossible to find assistance anywhere – but finally I manage to contact a young man who can advise me.

'Sounds as though they are of the *Aleyrodidae* family, whiteflies. Serious pests.' He recommends another product. However, we need a licence to purchase it. Might there be an organic alternative? He has absolutely no idea. But how can I be sure his verdict is accurate? I cannot afford to invest in costly insecticides and I have no desire to bombard the hill with a cock-tail of toxins out of ignorance and alarm. I decide to hold off in the hope that the gentle chemical we have used will start to kick in.

Hosing down the garden furniture, I discover the pale lavender bugs at work in lines of sixes and sevens on the pear-tree boughs. I approach and they take off; a gauze scarf fluttering in the breeze. If they were not leaching the vegetation I would find their colours and form rather lovely.

We are now into the heavy watering season; an hour at dawn, two hours at sunset. I collapse into bed but cannot even close my eyes. In the moonlit dark-ness, I count six of the winged insects on the ceiling. Are they intending to take up residence inside the premises as well?

Quashia suggests we call René and he insists on Michel's advice. I haven't shared the problem with Michel who, in any case, is in China, where he is on the judging panel at a documentary film festival. I telephone René and then stroll down to collect our mail – I haven't seen our postman for a while – and find a letter from the Chambre d'Agriculture. It re-quests completion of an enclosed form – something about products in use on the land. They are offering to collect free of charge all empty or semi-used defunct containers. I set it aside, my mind occupied with our current bug battle and because I am not quite sure what precisely it is requesting.

René arrives, sporting dark glasses, which is a sight I have never seen before. He has a mild eye irritation, he explains. Nothing serious. He was working one of his farms when his mask was caught in a low-hanging branch and pulled off, exposing his face. A pesticide shower caught his eyes. He dismisses it, concentrating on our problem, 'They are of the *Coccoidea* family. Scale insects. The females are wingless, legless, spend their lives attached to plants, sucking them. The males have the wings. They are steadfastly extracting the juices from the trees and are particularly dangerous for the saplings, which haven't developed the where-withal to withstand a plague such as you are ex-periencing. If they've found a good grazing ground, which they have *chez vous*, you'll have a dickens of a job ridding yourselves of them. You should have listened to me and prevented this. Not a single one of my farms is blighted. Not surprising, by the look of it – the bugs are all here! The shingle you showed me on the orange leaves was their larvae. They have hatched and are spreading rapidly in the heat. Treat the olive trees, Carol, or lose your crop.'

'We have sprayed them,' I confess. I display the product we have used. He shakes his head. 'I'll provide you with a much more efficient juice – it's in the boot of my car – and I'll hire the machine for you, but I can't lend you a hand because I am committed else-where for the next couple of weeks, and what with my eyes, I'm not feeling terrific at present . . .'

'Alexandre claims they are leaf-hoppers and the agricultural office diagnosed whitefly . . .'

'The product I use destroys those too. One proviso: don't harvest anything for twenty-one days after use.'

I drop my gaze. It looks as though I am beaten. My dreams of organic farming are gone. For our AOC ticket we are not expected to produce organically, only to deliver first-class oil. If I continue to strive for a chemical-free farm, I will probably lose this season's fruit and have no oil of any kind to offer for examination.

'I'll take it,' I concede.

He supplies me with the extremely expensive 'juice' and returns with the machine late in the afternoon. Quashia and I set to work treating every single tree, every flower, every plant, every vegetable against the *cicadelle* or the whitefly or scale insect, whichever it is. An hour or so later Jacques, fit and smiling, returned from his family holiday, arrives to clean the pool. Quashia has gone off to shower. We have douched over a hundred of the *oliviers* as well as all the small fruit trees. The rest, which involve hiking the hill, we'll attack bright and early in the morning. My muscles are trembling with fatigue.

I mention the letter from the Chambre d'Agriculture and Jacques asks to read it. 'Ah, it's reclaiming all banned pesticides. They're getting strict, and they're jittery.'

'Jittery, why?'

'Haven't you been following the Fiprinol saga in the newspapers?'

'The active substance judged lethal to bees? Yes, Michel has been sending me cuttings.'

'There is concern for human contamination from the same product. Cancer research centres are testing it now. There's another, also lethal to bees, a spray used on sunflowers.'

I am angry, recollecting the five hives lost here.

'Fortunately,' I assure him, 'we have no banned products here. I have the residue of a bottle purchased from Alexandre and an insecticide René sold me.'

'Let's check them. I'll fetch my Bible out of the truck and we'll take a look.'

'Your Bible?'

He nods and disappears.

I offer up the semi-empty container from Alexandre and Jacques confirms that it is of little use. 'Moderately harmless, except that it shouldn't be used on any plant visited by bees.' Which strikes me as a very real reason to avoid it. Then I fetch the liquid we are squirting everywhere now.

'Where the hell did you get this?'

He riffles furiously through the pages of a hefty paperback, runs his finger down a column of names and hands me the book, entitled *L'Index Phytosanitaire*.

'This,' he says, 'is the agriculturists' bible. It lists the pros and cons of every available and withdrawn pesticide, fungicide, organophosphate, you name it. The produce you've used on your trees is illegal and highly dangerous. Read the list of side-effects.'

Which I do. It includes several cancers.

'By law, you cannot even throw it in the dustbin. It has been banned for some time and even empty bottles must be delivered up to the Chamber of Agriculture's collection service for safe disposal.'

I gawp at him in horror. 'Will it harm Quashia, me, the fruits and olives?'

He stares at me gravely and chooses not to reply.

'Show me the trees.'

Jacques confirms Alexandre's diagnosis: '*Cicadelles*

blanches, also known as *Metcalfa pruinosa*. They arrived in France from the United States about fifteen years ago. Currently they are feeding off more than two hundred plants, including fruit trees and vines.' Then he explains that I have muddled two insect families. 'The bluish moths you have here are *cicadelles*, of the *Cicadellides* family. There are over four thousand species worldwide and their colour can vary, which is why it is sometimes tricky to recognise them, but there's no doubting they are what you have got. *Cicadellidae* are also leaf-hoppers. They are suckers too, and pests to crops. Interesting little critters, though: the males attract their mates by low calls transmitted through leaves and stems instead of carried on air.'

'So what should I have treated the *cicadelles* with?'

The solution Jacques would have suggested was a dash of washing-up liquid diluted with water hosed on the bugs with a high-powered jet spray. 'You could've waited till after summer. No real harm would have been done. But now it's too late.'

'And the insecticide we've drenched the olives in?'

'Poisonous. When did you spray?'

'We began a couple of hours ago.' I am considering the fact that I have deluged almost 50 per cent of our *oliviers* in a banned product, listed as a carcinogen. Any oil pressed would surely bear traces of its elements. The AOC chemical test is bound to register this.

'My advice to you is to get the trees washed down immediately.'

I run in search of Monsieur Q., who is preparing his supper. He looks shattered but he follows me up the hill where we find Jacques unreeling the hosepipes. 'I'll stay and help you. I've called Alexandre, too. He's on his way over.'

Fortunately the days are long. We each take a separate section of the land and work through until late, late in the evening. Quashia has already seen to it that our water basin is being replenished from our pump house on the other side of the lane. I am allotted the lower eastern flanks because these involve the shorter lengths of hosepipe and are the most accessible. Even so the work is crippling and my arm muscles are burning, screaming with pain. I am transporting weights my body has never been trained to bear, hoisting unwieldy pipes in the fading light. The trees are dripping, raining. I am soaked to the skin, and praying. It is an awesome baptism. Around ten-thirty, when we pack it in for the night, I open a bottle of wine and, together with the two men, relax on the upper terrace. We polish off that red and another. Quashia, of course, does not partake. He has returned to his cottage and a solitary dinner. It is agreed that we will all reconvene at dawn and go through the entire process all over again, just to make sure that the trees are thoroughly cleansed. The cost in water alone does not bear thinking about.

Before crashing out for the night, I play my messages. There is one from Michel, who has returned earlier in the day from China. It says, 'Back safely. Falling into bed now, jet-lagged. I've been thinking. We have to do this differently. I love you.'

When I wake the next morning, my right arm is frozen. I have torn both upper and lower tendons. I can barely lift a pen or cup and certainly not agricultural equipment. I am obliged to cease work. There is little I can do to assist the men. My arm is trussed up. I call Michel: 'Come home, we need you.'

He drops everything and flies south.

I pick him up from a plane that is delayed by hours. He is shattered after so much travelling, but perhaps not as shattered as I am. What has happened to my arm? He takes the wheel, talking nineteen to the dozen, describing developments in China since his previous visits, the films he saw, those that won, those he fought for. I turn my head and study the man at my side. My silent husband grown confident again, loquacious even. He wants to hear all my news. 'We have much to discuss,' I murmur.

But I am content just to have him home.

A Harvest, at Last

Today is 25 November, the feast of Sainte-Catherine. Traditionally, it is the first day of olive-gathering but earlier rains have brought large quantities of the drupes to the nets already. They are plump and fleshy and delicious-looking but still too green for an oil-lucrative pressing. Still they must be gathered, on hands and knees, picked from the sodden earth. Rummaging about amongst the first of the fallen leaves, slicks of light minky oak mulch and the first of the earth-bound fig leaves, yellow and curled, working with my left hand only, I inhale the scent of bonfires on the surrounding hills. A popular Provençal dictum is that on Sainte-Catherine's day *'tout bois prend racine'*, all wood takes root. It is the perfect season for planting, particularly fruit trees. A warm, humid earth is the gardener's dream and *arrière-automne*, or *vers la fin d'automne*, the late autumn season, promises exactly those conditions. Michel and Quashia take advantage. I see them through the kitchen window planting up the surround to Monsieur Q.'s completed shed extension. Alongside it, we are planning a splendid custom-built greenhouse for tropical fruits. Mr Pear, the blacksmith colleague of Guillaume Laplaige, has been by to measure for the frame.

The outskirts of Marseille are under 2 metres of water.

Landslides are being spoken of everywhere in the hinterland hills, the *arrière-pays*. Roads are closed off. Red triangular signs warn of floods. Bad weather, moving east, is forecast. A scirocco wind blows our way, carrying with it red sand from the Algerian desert. Accompanied by heavy rains it settles like roseate mud at our doorstep. The base of the swimming pool is carpeted in it and the water turns deep rust, the colour of freshly dug carrots. Still, I swim, or paddle one-armed. But the force of the relentless wet sandstorms begins to break the olive boughs laden with piebald fruit. They are falling fast and the magpies are having a field day, tearing the nets as they feast. Michel and Quashia are working in the gales to beat the birds to it. My support is given in cooking and brewing pots of steaming tea for although my arm is no longer trussed up the doctor has advised no heavy lifting for six months.

Out shopping in the village, I bump into Alexandre.

'How's your arm?' he asks.

'Better.'

'Look at me.' His right hand, his trigger finger, is bandaged and besmirched with bloodstains. The hunting season is in full flight and he cannot participate.

'What happened?' I cry. 'Did you shoot yourself?'

He tells me solemnly that it was an unfortunate accident. The previous Sunday, he was out hunting in the mountains and having a terrible time of it with the weather. It bucketed down all day. He and a couple of his hunting colleagues, along with his two retriever dogs, attempted the ascent of a sheer rock face directly behind his mother and stepfather's chalet. They were tracking wild boar. The ground was slippery. He lost his footing and his gun went off.

'Lord, you did shoot yourself!'

He shakes his head. The gunshot spooked the dogs. He immediately grabbed one of them in an attempt to restrain her but the creature panicked, turned on him and sunk her teeth through his tendon. 'My own dog!' he wails. 'When I let out a cry of pain, she and the other hound bolted and neither of them returned home until Monday evening. It was a catastrophic weekend.'

Could it have been the irresistible Beethoven? I wonder.

Alexandre shakes his head, staring at his disabled hand.

'Do you ever take him hunting? He is a retriever mix, after all.'

'We took him once, a long while back. Jacky and I thought that he would make an excellent hunter but as soon as the guns went off he fled home like a scared rabbit.'

I smile silently. My instincts about that shiny-headed black brute were sound.

As we part, I thank Alexandre once again for the enormous support he has given me this year. He beams like a schoolboy and begs a kiss. I acquiesce, grinning, and peck him on the cheek.

The rain that Alexandre talked off in the mountains is settling along the *pays côtiers*, the coastal regions. Everywhere is sodden. Fortunately, the scirocco has abated. We pick and gather the drupes in between downpours or even, when needs must, in the rain. It is

Ramadan and Quashia is fasting. He finishes in the early afternoon so that he can rest and prepare his post-sundown meal. Michel works on alone. I participate a little. Standing at his side, holding steady my prized fruit-tree ladder, I watch him and wonder. Hair plastered flat by the recent rain, I follow the shadow of a raptor gliding across the cypress trees and listen to the distant hum of traffic. Our fruits are being drummed into the earth by the force of these incessant torrents.

'We must deliver what we have collected to the mill or the wet drupes will turn *moisi*' – mildewy – 'and the pressed oil will be acrid and barely useable. They smell like mushrooms already,' I mumble.

The following morning Michel and Quashia press on with the *cueillette*, the gathering, while I take charge of the first of this year's pressings – the windfalls only, but they tip the mill scales at 123 kilos.

All around me, men arrive from out of the inclement morning with sackloads of fruit; hessian sacks with 'La Poste' stamped across them or bread and flour bags. I thought sacks were forbidden now. Are these people moonlighting postmen and bakers, pressing their olives in their spare time? I am reminded that I haven't seen our postman in a while. Perhaps he has thrown it all in and taken up beekeeping?

A handsome, grey-haired man and his very tall son tell me that they have eighty 400-year-old trees and compliment me on the superiority, the plumminess of our drupes. They ask me what I feed or treat them with. 'Nothing, if we can avoid it.' I refrain from relating the saga of René's poison. It is too troubling to reflect upon. 'I'd rather have a small white worm or two than the cocktail of toxins those wretched sprays give off,' the father claims. I am amazed to hear this. He is the first olive-producer I have encountered down here who is pursuing an organic philosophy. 'Not that we sell our oil,' he adds. 'A few litres here and there, yes, to cover costs, but we store the bulk of it for family consumption. We do this for the pleasure and the sense of achievement that accompanies the work. It's back-breaking and it's demanding, but when I see my trees pruned like poetry . . .'

I smile at the image. His oil is spilling through. He bows and hurries away.

I turn my head in response to a nudge to my sore arm. A man alongside me bellows in my ear: 'Alain's wearing a corset. Have you noticed?'

I couldn't say that I had, not until this farmer seated alongside me, holding fast to a Doberman, pointed it out. Alain is the chappie who carts the olives from yard to machine. He always has a fag in his mouth, rarely speaks and strikes me as a bit of a miserable so-and-so. In spite of the number of years we have been frequenting this establishment he never acknowledges my presence.

My neighbour reins in his fearsome dog's chain and gives the animal a swift kick in the ribs. 'Sit!' The poor mutt dithers, looking terrified. The level of noise down here is threatening and unfamiliar to him.

'Where are you from?' the farmer quizzes. It is almost always the first question any of them ask me. I am an oddity to them, a puzzle they can't quite figure out.

'Ireland!' I yell.

'Oh, Holland.'

'No, Ire . . .' Faced with the effort of hollering above the machines, I drop the subject. It is far too arduous to bother. So what if he thinks I am Dutch? But in spite of the racket he seems intent on conversation.

'You look like you enjoy your food,' he shouts. I smile politely and he embarks on an account of a most marvellous dinner he ate a month or so back.

'Simple people. But would give you everything they have in the house. True Provençals, and there are not many of them left. A dying breed. Yes, indeed. They live near Valberg, do you know it?'

I shake my head.

'It's a ski station in les Alpes de Haute-Provence. Their village is Touët. An entire pig they served on the table for dinner. Cut it up right there. Cochon de Lys, stuffed with mushrooms I gathered myself that very afternoon from the mountainside. I drove the length of the gorge, found their village, parked my car and scouted about from there. Delicious. Litres of local wine. They are the kind of people you should be mixing with.'

I smile again and look about me to see who else is here. My attention returns to an old codger who has been amusing me with his incessant attempts to pick a piece of fluff off the cuff of his sweater. He has been fiddling with it since I arrived. Finally, after one last go, when it still refuses to lift off, he lights a match and sets fire to his sleeve. No one pays him any attention, except me. Alone in a slippery corner of this thundersomely noisy mill, he is now slapping and flapping at himself in a desperate bid to extinguish the fire raging the length of his arm.

Why on earth, I am asking myself, would he think that a lighted match would remove the fluff from his cuff? Later, he disappears, looking very sorry for himself, with his demi-johns swimming with freshly pressed oil and his one charred sleeve and burned wrist.

It's curious how I never seem to encounter the same faces twice. Gérard, the miller's son, calls to me, beckoning with his hand in a backward wave, the way Italians do. He wants to introduce me to a man wearing a flat cap as green as fresh nettles. 'This here is the village chief. He wants to make your acquaintance!' teases Gérard, pulling his companion's hat askew.

'Don't you listen.' A man with one badly bloodshot eye grins at me lasciviously.

Close by us, a little grey-haired man in army boots has just arrived. He is squawking to himself and marching through the mill as though square-bashing. Alain drags in the fellow's crates of olives and grunts at me to move my handbag out of his way, which I do. The gathered drupes look disgustingly mouldy and Gérard is loath to accept them, but the man grows so irate that our young miller shrugs, gives Alain the go ahead to put them on the scales and the process begins. Gérard's father, Christophe, the owner, comes toddling through. He glances at the recently arrived load and shakes his head disapprovingly. He looks deeply troubled, but then I have rarely seen him with any other countenance. Hands in pockets, he stares at his noisy steel machines as though they have just broken his heart. Today he is wearing holly-green and mauve. His face is as red and shiny as a berry. He imparts some news to his *fils*, shakes his head tragically and totters off again.

I wander over to the giant vat which is churning our chocolate-brown paste. These will be our first pressed fruits in two years. From this paste will be extracted our oil and from those golden bottles will be chosen our first specimen to be offered to the inspectors to confirm our Appassionata AOC, and I am praying that it will be fine, that René's insecticide never penetrated the fruit. Gérard joins me. 'Smell it,' he breathes. 'Its perfume. Mmm, truly excellent.'

And it is. Today our newly pressed oil tastes creamy and very peppery. He and I shake hands.

'Looks like you are set for an excellent season, Carol, if the rest is of an equal standard.'

'Let's hope so. See you next week.' I smile. But until the oil has been tested and passed by the experts at Nice we cannot be certain and I won't rest easy.

Upstairs in the shop above the *moulin*, Gérard's wife, who runs the accounts and the till, gives me the news.

'Have you heard about René?' she asks in a tone that troubles me.

We haven't heard a word from him in weeks and weeks, but this is not unusual, particularly during the olive season. I haven't bothered to phone to find out why he hasn't collected the 150 steres of wood piled in our drive that he promised to take away and sell for us and why he palmed me off with that illegal poison, because it is hopeless trying to reach him during the harvest anyway and because I cannot bear to rupture a longstanding friendship. After all these years, could he really have intended to cheat me or could there be another explanation?

'He's in the Hôpital Pasteur. Four bypasses, he has had. All the arteries are blocked.'

I picture René in my mind's eye. I cannot imagine what it must be like for one as active as him to be in hospital. Recently turned eighty and still climbing in and out of trees every day. Pruning, gathering olives, making money.

'I'll call his wife tonight and see if there's anything I can do for her,' I say, as I pay the requested 700 francs for our pressing.

Outside, loading up my *bidons* of oil, I come across a poor bugger shouting and swearing in the *parking*.

'Jesus! I'll be in the doghouse when my wife sees this!' The man, in a tracksuit and worn plimsolls, has unloaded what must be close to 1,000 kilos of olives. One of his plastic crates – *la cageotte* – has split and his drupes, so laboriously gathered by hand over many wet days, have spilled all over the crowded car park. Now they are rolling away faster than he can retrieve them; streams of purply-black fruits disappearing down the steeply inclined lane.

'Can I help?' I call, hurrying to his assistance.

'What? No, go away, leave me in peace. I'll manage. My wife is going to wring my neck for this. Well, I won't tell her. I'll say it was a miserable pressing.' He gives up on his crop. He has spotted a parking place – others are leaving with their oil, smiles all around, save for him – he leaps into his four-by-four, releases the handbrake, lurches the car into gear, accelerates hard and smashes directly into the rear of a stationary van owned by another *oléiculteur* waiting below in the mill. 'Shit!' he screams in fury. 'Shit!'

I smile and turn my head, eyes squinting in the sunshine, to listen to the birds. Today, the sun is shining. It is the end of the first week of December. Brightly coloured birds caged in an aviary higher up the hillside are singing their hearts out.

Another year, another day at the mill.

It is the end of the Christmas holidays. I hear the familiar sound of the yellow post-office bike struggling up the drive. I didn't see our postman before Christmas to give him his tip in return for the annual calendar he presents to us, so I hurry downstairs now to meet him and wish him the best of the season. I am greeted by a young blond woman who introduces herself as Marie and hands me the usual picture calendar.

'Where's our regular fellow?' I ask, handing her a banknote, realising that we have never known his name. Her face falls. 'Unfortunately, Philippe passed away a couple of months ago.'

I am speechless. 'What happened?'

'He'd been fighting cancer for a while and . . .' she shrugs. 'I'll be doing this route now. Happy New Year.' And off she goes, leaving me staring after her, remembering our postman engrossed by the bees.

January, a new year, is upon us and Michel and I are home together. René remains in hospital. Quashia has taken the boat for Africa for a hard-earned two-week break with his family.

Our harvest has been completed. Our fruits have been processed and Michel has delivered a sample bottle from each of this year's pressings to the olive authorities in Nice, who will send them away for testing and quality control. We await the results. Is the oil from this season worthy of the AOC stamp to which our farm is now entitled? I still harbour a niggling doubt.

Blessed June

This weekend has been designated Party Time. What are we celebrating? Our golden olive oil, of course, or *oli d'oulivo* in Provençal. Six separate lots from our winter pressings were delivered to the Olives of Nice organisation down at their seaside offices and each has received the official stamp of approval. It has taken us over seven years of inspections, visits and agricultural challenges to achieve this badge of merit. Michel describes it as 'our tribal initiation'. Now we are members of the brotherhood. Yes, we are bona fide producers of top quality *oli d'oulivo*. A cause for celebration? Oh yes, indeedy.

As the sun comes up and circles round to the front of the house, most of the guests who descended upon us last night are still sound asleep in tents dotted around our grounds. Michel appears and then disappears from view, carrying a small wooden ladder. 'The ladder of adventure,' he winks as he passes. 'To keep the children happy.' Off he goes, climbing up behind the house, to place it outside Monsieur Q.'s splendid hangar. There he stacks ancient, broken roof tiles gathered from our still-neglected vine-keeper's ruin to support it. Within the hangar our tools are neatly laid out. Creeping up its exterior, jasmine and bougainvillaea are flowering. Flanking it are my fruiting trees. It is a heart-warming sight.

'What are you doing?' I call.

'Creating a dungeon. It will keep the little ones occupied for a few hours,' giggles my husband. His long curly hair reminds me of Frédéric Mistral's. I wave, marvelling at his ability to invent non-stop games for the kids. He understands the need for the marvellous, for children to give rein to their imaginations. He is a bizarrely inventive grandfather, if a rather young one. More importantly, I am thrilled to observe this mirth and fun in him again, his renewed health and rediscovered carefree spirit. After he and Monsieur Q. have completed preparations for the 'dungeon', he heads off to the town hall of an inland village to borrow tables and chairs for the sun-drenched meals that await us this evening and tomorrow. A short while later, he returns with the mayor himself in tow, a gangling apricot farmer whose passion is go-kart racing. I have no idea where or how Michel met him. Together they set about unloading the furniture and carrying it to the designated dining site.

While the men are at this work, the butcher drives up with a suckling pig for spit-roasting. It will need to be stuffed with apples and herbs and then the stomach restitched, he informs me while I attempt to control the dogs, who are set on consuming the entire carcass right now. Much debate ensues about what thread to use. I haven't a clue. I don't like pork and it would not have been my choice of principal dish. The spit, *la broche*, is a hand-operated iron contraption discovered by Michel in a knick-knack yard, bought for a song and cleaned up by him a few days ago. Michel's brother-in-law, Ralf, has woken up for a swim. I observe much male discussion about whether the spit will be long enough and sufficiently sturdy to support the weight of the pig which, according to bald-headed, puffing Monsieur Le Boucher, is 30 kilos. Eighty or more guests are to be fed and, this being France, the worry that provisions will be insufficient or not handsomely prepared is cause for serious consternation. But Michel will have none of it. He reassures present company that his purchase will prove itself to be sturdier than any costly, modern electrical device.

How many hours will the beast take to roast? Five, the butcher has advised, as he takes his cash and waves *au revoir*. But at what height from the fire should the pig be hung? This is a question that no one has thought to pose and now it is too late, for the butcher has departed; gone fishing in the mountains for the rest of the weekend. While the men of the party assembly committee discuss the finer points of medi-aeval roasting, others are digging a bath-sized shallow trench and encircling it with large stones to stabilise the spit while Michel's sister, Angélique, and female friends from London and Paris are clustered about our wooden table grating finger-length sticks of *cannelle*, cinnamon bark, with cheese-graters.

Ralf and Quashia have gathered wheelbarrow-loads of substantial logs to fuel the fire. Ralf appears to be leading the spit-construction team while Michel has appointed his nephews, three enterprising lads, apple commanders, furnished them with woven baskets and charged them to go gathering early-fall fruits from the orchard I planted so many years ago in memory of my late father. If they don't suffice, I have a box or two stored away in Quashia's hangar, reeking richly of cider. The boys return with a few knobbly, insect-infested windfalls and the sloughed yellow and brown skin of a mountain snake they have found in the dried grass.

A moment of animated panic unsettles the preparations of the sweltering morning when my cousin Noel and I bring the stored apples out into the sun. Long-bodied wasps swarm every which way and an investigation reveals that they are nesting in the chimney. With so many guests expected and children about, I run to call in my heroes, the fire brigade, to clear them away.

Michel christens one very persistent wasp Christopher. This causes the children to hoot with laughter until Noel is stung by the very same fellow. Pandemonium ensues. 'Anti-histamine!' cries his wife. 'He has an allergy!' There is talk of hospitalising my beloved cousin. A group gathers around him, looking on while his finger swells up. I beckon to Jacques, who has just driven up with his wife and daughter and is about to clean the pool in readiness for later, to come and help. While I am hunting for our first-aid kit the red engine and its team of firemen hurtle up the drive, on the scene within fifteen minutes. Whence the panic subsides. The allergy is very minor and there is no real crisis.

'*Vespa crabro* is the Latin name for *les frelons*,' a handsome young fireman explains when the nest has been smoked out and he and his companions are enjoying a chilled glass of lemonade out of the sun. 'They are hornets, not wasps.'

Michel is gathering the children together and off they go, following my Pied Piper of a husband for the ceremony of 'burying Christopher, the long-bodied wasp'. As they lay the hornet to rest, my red-headed Irish nephew is heard to say, 'Rest in peace, Christopher. You'll never sting Daddy again.'

I thank the retiring firemen and invite them to return later when their duties are finished to join us for our Olive Oil Party.

Wine is delivered in a vat: a Côte de Blaye, great value at 18 francs a litre. Flowers arrive. And champagne. Followed by a van delivering cheeses. Four friends are in the vegetable gardens plucking lettuces and tomatoes. Oh, the preparations are exhausting. As the sun begins to slip behind the hills, endless processions of plates piled high with offerings of food are being laid out in the shade on the summer tables, including dishes of marinated olives from our own trees, which have proved a great success. Clarisse and friends are rigging up a disco and wooden dance-floor over by the disused vineyard. Cars are arriving at an astonishing rate. Children are shrieking, throwing themselves in and out of the pool, splashing water everywhere, arms outstretched, imitating hornets; dogs are jumping and leaping. The firemen return, now off duty. Corks are popping. And here comes Alexandre. And Gérard, our vet. The party is kicking off. Strike up the band. Let's boogie the night away beneath the warm starry sky.

Sunday morning. I open my eyes and inhale the aroma of brewing coffee drifting into the bedroom. I hear cups rattling as they are placed on to saucers. Breakfast, narrated in sound and smell, is in preparation. Time to get up.

Outside in the rising morning sunlight, our wooden table, the length of a railway sleeper, has been laid and several of our house guests are already attacking their breakfasts: toasted chunks of yesterday's baguettes, *tartines* runny with golden butter, topped with melting jams, Corsican clementine marmalade, chunky Appassionata orange marmalade or poached free-range eggs. The dogs are hunched beneath the peeling and faded garden chairs, hiding from the heat, scrambling from seat to seat in search of attention, affection and titbits. Animated chatter, sunburned faces, open smiles greet me. An extended family at feeding time. The children are heaving themselves noisily from lap to lap, giggling insanely, encouraging or goading one another while their young mothers' attentions are elsewhere. I descend the steps slowly, making for the pool; a gentle dip before joining the gang. A symphony of birdsong accompanies my laps. All around me the trees are sharp green with early summer growth. I inhale warm June scents and take in the satisfying sound of the whirr of hosepipe nozzles watering the already parched flowers. Spring's wild flowers have been felled. The earth is growing thirsty again, as is the vegetation. The cicadas are in full lusty throat. Black and white butterflies, their pulsing wings unfolding like parachutes, lift off the water and drift in the air. Midgy insects, no bigger than dust motes, speed through the morning light. I swim lazily through spangled sunshine beneath the fig tree.

After my swim and several gulps of coffee, I amble about the grounds for a while with Vanessa's eight-month-old son in my arms, to give her a break and to be alone with the baby. How he gurgles and dribbles. I look back across the land to the table where Michel is seated with the girls either side of him. These lovely daughters of his who were jealous and uncertain of me in the early days are young women and mothers now, handling the responsibilities in their different ways.

And I used to wonder how it would all turn out.

While I am on my lap of the garden, our wine-variety expert, M. Laplaige, zooms up in a pure white Citroën, another of his classic cars. Accompanying him is Pascal Poire, Mr Pear, the blacksmith, who I have warned Alexandre is also a *garde de chasse*, a hunting warden. Although it is only ten in the morning the men request glasses of port or, if we have none, tequila. Laplaige comes bearing many kilos of lusciously red strawberries from his greenhouse. Strawberries, what a treat, and we will have them too when our own greenhouse alongside Quashia's hangar has finally been constructed. The babe still in my arms, I thank him and run to the summer kitchen for dishes for the red fruits, which I place on the groaning breakfast table where our guests and families are feasting, conversing in three languages at once, smoking cigarettes, opening bottles of wine and discussing what will be served for lunch.

A country weekend in high summer in France.

A time to be idle, to linger in the company of friends and loved ones, to drink in the luxury of this hard-won moment, this precious day. I close my eyes in appreciation. A row of turtle doves on the electricity line coo in deep-throated resonance. They are becoming almost more common here than the myriad songbirds who chatter and flit from tree to tree, I remark to anyone who might be listening. Laplaige explains that there are so many areas in France where they are hunted now that they are emigrating ever southwards.

A debate has broken out. Voices are raised in amicable argument. I lean along the table to find out what the trigger for so much passion on a Sunday late morning, almost lunchtime, could be. Cheese, I am told. Three young friends of Michel and Clarisse from Paris are offering opinions about cheese. A most serious matter, until the exchange breaks down. Now there are peals of laughter and lolling of arms across the tables. Couples are kissing, more cigarettes are lit up, yet more bottles are uncorked. Who cares what time of day it is?

Clarisse regards her light-haired daughter, Celine, skipping with Titus, their dog, a mammoth beast but gentle and playful with the children. I watch the little girl too. Amber-skinned with hazel hair, dressed in a white T-shirt and black-striped shorts. She is attempting to throw the dog a ball but the huge black hound bounds towards her and seizes it from between her fingers. She shouts his name but he pays her no attention and then, when he is tired of his private game, he returns and lays it at her feet. Celine, who resembles both Michel and Serge, her father, shrieks with glee. Clarisse comments on the miracle of motherhood. I smile, saying nothing.

Sometimes, even now, after everything, I feel as though I am the outsider, as though I belong with and to no one, as though an act in the story was cut or pages were lost before I was given the opportunity to play them out. As though my role in all of this is to observe. But when I sink into such thoughts, there is Michel, who holds out a hand and smiles with eyes that beckon me close, 'Come, *chérie*, don't sit alone. Be with us.'

Michel with his smile that lights up the world, Michel who draws people from the four corners, who builds castles at dinner tables and dismantles them with equal facility. Michel who left but has returned.

I watch Clarisse calling dogs and children to order. How she resembles her father: introspective, sensitive, creative and, above all, charming. How unlike Vanessa she is, who is more Latin, open and maternal, always laughing, passionate and pragmatic. I love to see them together, these girls who link arms and chatter like monkeys; twins but so dissimilar. Twins with individual souls. I am reminded of their adolescence and our early days here. I remain their stepmother but we have grown to be friends. And I am a grandmother, I suppose, of sorts. *La belle-grandmère* to the children. Titus comes loping across the terrace, intent on theft, and grabs a badminton racquet lying forgotten in the grass. Off he goes with it in his mouth, leaping terraces triumphantly. He could be an incarnation of Henri, the very first dog we ever welcomed to this property but had to return to the refuge because he was such a hooligan. Alas, *cher Henri* must have perished long since, unless he has made it to seventeen. Our own two hounds give chase, yapping and dribbling contentedly. Ella stays in her stable or sits outside in the shade. She is far too old to participate in such antics.

Michel's sister, Angélique, with her three strapping boys and husband at her side, joins us at the table and pours coffee from a flask. She gives me a wink, a private moment shared between us. She has been dismantling tents and storing them in a corner of the summer kitchen until tonight when, after more festivities, she will re-erect them. From the house I hear music. Someone has decided to silence Kiri Te Kanawa at her *Songs of the Auvergne* and switch to one of the Buddha Bar compilations. Our dogs are sniffing about in the summer-dried grass in the hope of *les bonnes surprises*. The children are building universes of their own in various corners of the garden. The bees are hovering and circling about the innumerable blossoms, bent upon their tasks of gathering nectar, spreading pollen. Our beekeepers will call in later to join us for an early-evening *verre*.

I hear cries from across the grass, beyond the Florentine cypresses where we have sited our badminton court. I lean to look. Michel and the girls are at play in the hot afternoon sun, shaded by a line of wild oaks growing on the terrace below. He is in competition with the pair of them. I hear female cries: *'Bien joué, Papa!'* He is an excellent player. I am surprised. I hadn't known it. A documentary film-maker friend from Austria with his French wife, an underwater photographer, join the team and play resumes. I love that thwack of racquets. Out of nothing Michel creates play and adventure. He requires little money. His charm draws people to him.

Many coloured roses are blossoming again in this season of efflorescence. Valerians are shooting up out of the walls, red and pink flowers everywhere. Yellow and white marguerite daisies crowd the flowerbeds. Pots of lipstick-red amaryllis are in full bloom. Our grapes are ripening fast in this exceptional heat. The blacksmith, a cool glass of beer at his side, is measuring the stone staircase with a view to installing the sweeping pergola Laplaige suggested on his first visit here, two summers ago. Quashia is nattering to René, frailer than ever before but still at work. His eyesight is not what it was and that, he claims, was the cause of the near-disastrous spraying incident. They are in debate about methods of pruning and harvesting. The trees are bending beneath the weight of the drupes. They are looking forward to our next harvest, and a bumper season it promises to be again.

Olives again. Yes, here on this fabulous hillside, this sea-fronting escarpment, there will always be olives, always be harvests, whether the farm is paid for or not, whether families unite or lovers, partners drift apart.

Without this olive farm might Michel and I have drifted apart? Certainly, it has bonded our story.

Our love has changed: it has grown sturdier; there is a broader understanding of one another. The mosaics of Michel's mind are a little clearer to me now. Sometimes, when we are alone or lying close within the safety of our private universe, he touches upon the 'recent dark days', when he 'nearly let me go'. Days, he says, when he was in an extreme place, 'where no one was'. But those days have passed now and he has learned to live again, to allocate his career its rightful place and not make it the whole of his life, to wake each morning to *life*, to a world where colours reign and there are many reasons to be joyful. He remembers everything, he says, but he prefers not to talk about it. 'I, we, are fine again now. That's what counts.'

I close my eyes and wonder if he understands that it is the same for me. I also remember everything. How could I forget the abandonment, those lonely, lonely seasons? The world can be a brutal place, often extreme and random in its cruelty, but there is beauty too, generosity, romance, laughter and, at its core, there is boundless love and the ability to be reborn. Our ability to keep our hearts open to it is what counts, what keeps us liberated and alive.

Many years ago, long before I cared a sou for an olive tree, long before I was able to describe its form, I heard a tale. Why are olive trees made up of two forked trunks growing from one single base? The tale's answer, as far as I remember, is that two mythological lovers became separated, were driven apart, but no matter where their journeys tossed them, their souls returned to the olive tree in their search for one another's embrace, and so they were reunited, joined together for eternity by the solidity of one root, one love; they were two halves of the same soul. The olive tree, its silhouette, is the physical representation of their love.

While, all about me, friends and family enjoy this lusciously warm summer weekend along our cobalt-blue coastline, I turn my head and gaze up the hillside at our young saplings shooting skywards like silvery rockets. To the Provençal way of thinking a hundred-year-old olive tree is still a baby. It will give of its best harvests in the centuries to come. Of course, Michel and I won't be around to gather these mature gifts. We will have passed on to other incarnations of ourselves, but we will have left a part of ourselves on this hillside.

When we first discovered this Mediterranean paradise, sixty-four abandoned, 400-year-old olive trees stood here. Over time we have extended the groves, planting many juniors. In three centuries from now, when our young fellows are grown up and bountiful and we are long dead and forgotten, what will remain?

I like to fancy that the part of Michel and I which is our joint soul will continue to inhabit this farm. I also like to fancy that one of the gnarled old trees, its branches fecund with fruit, its twin trunks forked and twisted, long since transformed from the silvery-green sapling growing promisingly on our property now, will be our harbour. Within that twin-trunked *olivier*, two limbs growing jointly from the one root base, will reside the *âme sœurs*, the twin souls, for ever locked in embrace, of Carol and Michel. And who knows whether, in one of those centuries to come, another thirty-something couple might chance upon this hill-side, left to its own devices once more, and decide to sing it back into existence. Might they, on a hot summer's afternoon like this one, gaze upon the gnarled and twisted branches of the two-forked tree and speculate upon what stories that ancient could tell them?

And when the breeze stirs our olive's boughs and its pearly-green foliage murmurs in the whispering groves, might the young strangers just catch on the wind the drift of exhaled words: *Je vais t'aimer toujours*. I will always love you.

But, oh, how we might so easily have lost one another at the criss-crossing of paths.